ASSAULT ON IDEOLOGY

APPLICATIONS OF POLITICAL THEORY

Series Editors: Harvey Mansfield, Harvard University, and Daniel J. Mahoney, Assumption College

This series encourages analysis of the applications of political theory to various domains of thought and action. Such analysis will include works on political thought and literature, statesmanship, American political thought, and contemporary political theory. The editors also anticipate and welcome examinations of the place of religion in public life and commentary on classic works of political philosophy.

ASSAULT ON IDEOLOGY

Second Edition

Aleksandr Solzhenitsyn's Political Thought

JAMES F. PONTUSO

LEXINGTON BOOKS
Lanham • Boulder • New York • Toronto • Oxford

LEXINGTON BOOKS

Published in the United States of America
by Lexington Books
An imprint of The Rowman & Littlefield Publishing Group, Inc.
4501 Forbes Boulevard, Suite 200, Lanham, Maryland 20706

PO Box 317
Oxford
OX2 9RU, UK

British Library Cataloguing in Publication Information Available

The previous edition of this book was cataloged by the Library of Congress as:

Pontuso, James F.
    Solzhenitsyn's political thought / by James F. Pontuso.
        p. cm.
    Includes bibliographical references.
    1. Solzhenitsyn, Aleksandr Isaevich, 1918–, —Political
and social views. I. Title.
PG3488.04 Z843 1990
891.73'44—dc20   90-34241

ISBN: 978-0-7391-0594-8

Printed in the United States of America
⊖™ The paper used in this publication meets the minimum requirements of American
National Standard for Information Sciences—Permanence of Paper for Printed Library
Materials, ANSI/NISO Z39.48–1992.

CONTENTS

FOREWORD

James Pontuso belongs to a small group of scholars who have discovered and then mined the political wisdom of Solzhenitsyn. This achievement is even more important because it helps overcome the prejudices and distortions that deform the majority of the accounts of Solzhenitsyn's political reflection. Solzhenitsyn is first and foremost an "artist" or "writer" but one who explores permanent truths about human nature and the human condition. It is above all in this sense that Solzhenitsyn is a political thinker. It was through the experience of human nature *in extremis* that Solzhenitsyn learned the truth about the human soul, most pointedly its prospects for self-knowledge and moral ascent through suffering in the camps amidst the more typical degradation of the human spirit brought about by modern totalitarianism. Nor is Solzhenitsyn an insular writer. Pontuso reveals Solzhenitsyn's intimate familiarity with the best political reflection of the West without ever reducing the great Russian writer to the category of "political philosopher."

Solzhenitsyn has understandably protested against the excessive politicization of his work and the tendency of some to read it as a vehicle for presenting a counter-ideology to the inhuman theory and practice of Communism. But Pontuso's work helps us understand that it is not necessary to choose between a reading of Solzhenitsyn as writer and a reading of him as political philosopher. Solzhenitsyn is a writer whose subjects are the human soul and the richness of God's creation. His concerns as a writer are thus inseparably aesthetic, ethical, and political. He does not share the romantic and postmodernist understanding of the writer as a "creator" of his own world. Rather, he unabashedly affirms the old-fashioned view of the writer as "a humble apprentice under God's heaven" who has a special "responsibility for all he writes and paints—and for all who apprehend it." The terrible totalitarian experiences of the twentieth century gave Solzhenitsyn his subject matter. He did not so much choose it as have it thrust upon him as a Russian born in the fateful year of 1918. But precisely the sense of ethical and political responsibility informing Solzhenitsyn's mission as a writer allows him to overcome the debilitating chasms between artist and thinker, and between moralist and aesthete, that dominates the modern articulation of the task of the writer. Solzhenitsyn is a political thinker because as a writer he wants to do justice to the richness of God's creation, including the political and social nature of man.

The Assault on Ideology is a revision of a book that Pontuso originally published in 1990. In updating it he has maintained its original focus on Solzhenitsyn's critique of communist totalitarianism. He rightly emphasizes the extraordinary role that Solzhenitsyn played in exposing the communist lie and undermining the most powerful tyranny in human history. His chapters on Solzhenitsyn's analyses of Lenin and Stalin confirm that terror and tyranny were coextensive with the establishment of the Soviet regime in October 1917. "Stalinism" is best understood as a development but not a perversion of the Marxism of the Soviet founder. In addition, Pontuso's lengthy chapter on Solzhenitsyn's explicit and implicit critique of Marxism is one of the highlights of the book and a model of how Marxist dogmatism can be effectively undermined by judging its theory by its practice.

The relatively unmodified character of this new edition allows the reader to experience once more the passions that raged around Solzhenitsyn's work in the 1970s and 1980s. Some lauded him as the prophet-witness who had exposed the real truth about Communism while others attacked him as a dangerous threat to international peace and a harbinger of a new McCarthyism in the West. His fevered critics, and not a few of his professed admirers, spent far too little time acquainting themselves with the rich reflection on human nature and political life found in Solzhenitsyn's writings. It became fashionable to hurl false and demeaning labels at Solzhenitsyn (e.g., Tsarist, agrarian, pan-Slavist, imperialist, even anti-Semite) and to dismiss him as a narrowly Russian thinker who had little or nothing to say about the universal experience of humankind. This misrepresentation of Solzhenitsyn led many to regard him as a courageous but already dated thinker and writer, one whose relevance would not survive the Soviet regime itself. Pontuso's book reveals the shallowness of these claims. His thoughtful examination of the "universal" and "classical" dimensions of Solzhenitsyn's work shows just how wrongheaded that common judgment really is. Solzhenitsyn is a great political thinker precisely because the political themes in his work are never merely confined to an analysis of the here and now, no matter how preoccupied Solzhenitsyn was with the fate of his nation and the world when confronted with the inhuman communist juggernaut. Solzhenitsyn's dissection of Marxist historicism, his analysis of the intellectual and political origins of the Gulag Archipelago, and his critique of the modern illusion that "man is the measure of all things" paradoxically serve no specifically political purpose other than a truthful rendering of Russian and Western history and of the universal human condition. The writer serves society by serving the truth and cannot help being the sworn enemy of a regime that denied the truth about the human soul by reducing man to a plaything of material forces, of an inexorable and soul-destroying Historical Process.

One of the strengths of Pontuso's excellent book is the way that it highlights and develops Solzhenitsyn's complex understanding of the human spirit. Pontuso rightly stresses that Solzhenitsyn wants to reawaken his readers to the spiritual side of human life, "including the spirited element in human life." Solzhenitsyn is no friend of Tolstoyan fatalism: human beings must defend their liberty and dignity against the assaults of tyrants and ideologues alike. Spirited resistance to evil is a powerful corrective to the moral relativism of the age and a salutary reminder that human beings must take responsibility for their individual and collective destinies. Pontuso illustrates how Solzhenitsyn judiciously balances the requirements of pride and self-restraint, defending self-limitation, repentance, as well as spirited resistance to evil as equally important requirements of decent moral and political life. These features of Solzhenitsyn's political thought are among the least appreciated aspects of his work and are crucial elements of his defense of political moderation.

This reader does not agree with everything Pontuso has to say (and the spirited author of this book would be disappointed if he did!). In my view, the author has a tendency to downplay the specifically Christian features of Solzhenitsyn's moral and political reflection. And he fails to place quite enough emphasis on the theme of self-government in Solzhenitsyn's political thought. A fuller account of Solzhenitsyn's vigorous endorsement in his most recent writings of "the democracy of small areas" would round out Pontuso's excellent presentation of Solzhenitsyn's political thought. But none of this is intended to depreciate Pontuso's considerable achievement. Writing at a time when commentary on Solzhenitsyn was hopelessly politicized, he recovered the high moral and political principles by which the Nobel Laureate's work ought to be judged. His book is a wise and insightful account of Solzhenitsyn's chronicle of the terrible evils unleashed by utopian ideology in the modern world.

Daniel J. Mahoney – Assumption College   July 2003

ACKNOWLEDGMENTS

I would like to thank most especially James W. Ceaser for his time, wise counsel, and encouragement. I could not have completed the book without him. Steven Rhoads offered valuable advice during the preparation of the manuscript. Inis Claude Jr. helped me think through many important issues during the early stages of writing. Carolyn Moscatel, Delba Winthrop, John Dunlop, Randall Strahan, Robert Strong, William Connelly, Clyde Lutz, Mark Rozell, Dante Germino, J. Patrick Jones, Keith Fitch, Cynthia H. Foote, Sheila-Katherine Zwiebel, and several anonymous readers offered excellent suggestions for revisions. Mary Carpenter at Rowman & Littlefield and Serena Leigh Krombach at Lexington Books encouraged me to work on a revised edition of this book. Rosalind Warfield-Brown edited this manuscript. Her help on this and many other projects is much appreciated. Thanks to my colleagues, Roger Barrus, John Eastby, and David Marion at Hampden-Sydney College for tolerating my eccentricities without so much as a complaint. Daniel Mahoney revived my interest in a topic that I had put aside. James R. DeViese Jr. and Jane Holland furnished invaluble technical assistance. The Earhart Foundation provided financial assistance for earlier revisions of the manuscript.

Sections of this book have been published previously in a somewhat revised form.

Parts of chapters 6 and 7 as: "Crisis of a World Split Apart: Solzhenitsyn on the West," *The Political Science Reviewer* 16 (Fall 1986): 185-236. Reprinted with permission.

Part of chapter 5 as: "Solzhenitsyn on Marx: The Problem of Love of One's Own," *Teaching Political Science: Politics in Perspective* 13 (Spring 1986): 108-19. Reprinted with permission of the Helen Dwight Reid Educational Foundation. Published by Heldref Publications, 4000 Albemarle St., N.W., Washington, D.C. 20016.

Chapter 2 as: "On Solzhenitsyn's Stalin," *Survey* 29 (Summer 1985): 46-69. Reprinted with permission.

INTRODUCTION

Aleksandr Solzhenitsyn is almost a forgotten man, a relic of the Cold War, a bit like some discarded chard of the Berlin Wall. Yet, he is also one of the most important writers of the twentieth century, and he has had more direct influence on the course of history than any other author since Jean Jacques Rousseau. When I was in college in the 1960s, Marxism was considered a viable, even worthy, successor to liberal democracy. Che Guevara and Mao Tse-tung were heroes to my fellow students. I recall one weekend seminar when the political union at my university discussed what the world would look like after the revolution. We all took it for granted that the overthrow of capitalism was inevitable.

It was at this critical moment after America's loss in Vietnam that Solzhenitsyn emerged as a towering moral force opposing a policy of appeasement toward an evil adversary. The publication of *The Gulag Archipelago*, beginning in the 1970s, sounded the death knell of Communism, for in it Solzhenitsyn shows with stunning clarity how Karl Marx's ideas had been the cause of Communism's inevitable descent into totalitarianism. Solzhenitsyn's pronouncements on East-West relations were so forceful that they dismayed and frightened many people in the West. He painted a particularly grim picture of the challenge facing Western civilization, arguing that Communism was a cancer that fed on the corpses of its victims while sapping strength from its adversaries in an effort to ensnare the entire world with its deadly doctrines. Meanwhile, he lamented the many people in the West, who, only half awake to the menace, were willing to sit idly by, content to amuse themselves with consumer goods, the bright and happy baubles of their materialistic culture.

Solzhenitsyn's rhetoric worked and rallied many to his cause. It is no coincidence that after his revelations about the Soviet Union came to light, the once-powerful Communist parties of Western Europe lost their rank and file. Intellectuals, especially in France, abandoned hope of radically reforming political life and moved on to literary criticism, and Western voters in Germany, France, Great Britain, and the United States elected the most fiercely anti-Communist leaders of the Cold War era. Georges Nivat, Solzhenitsyn's French biographer, recounts how "his unforgettable television appearance made him an intimate of the French public. He won us over with his ardor, his deftness, his knowing Gulag smile."[1]

Ronald Reagan, Pope John Paul II, and Mikhail Gorbachev are often credited with ending the Cold War. Solzhenitsyn, meanwhile, gets almost no recognition for his role in Communism's demise, either in the popular press or in intellectual circles. He has been called a religious fanatic, an anti-Semite, and a Russian nationalist blind to the merits of the West. Since the collapse of Communism, the world's most controversial writer has suffered another kind of ignominy: neglect. His writings have largely been ignored as Russia—along with the rest of the world—has plunged headlong into an exuberant materialism in order to reap the profits made available by the opening of global markets.

How are Solzhenitsyn's views relevant, now that the political system he so vigorously opposed has either vanished or—where it still exists—is considered a historical anachronism, soon to disappear?

First, it is important to establish an accurate historical record. During the Cold War, Solzhenitsyn's assessment of his homeland was suspect. Communist authorities denied his allegations, and people in West, although wary, thought them exaggerated. Solzhenitsyn's account of brutality and terror was considered by some Westerners to be the ebullition of a disgruntled ex-prisoner intent on getting even with his tormentors; it was believed to be no more crucial to understanding the Soviet Union or Communism than a convict's description of life in a Western penitentiary was needed to capture the essence of liberal democracy. After all, it was argued, Solzhenitsyn had been arrested during Joseph Stalin's reign, spent a number of years in forced-labor camps (the Gulag), suffered greatly during his imprisonment, and, upon his release, became a renowned dissident and a tenacious foe of the Soviet authorities. His readers naturally had to wonder whether his personal troubles had not biased his judgment. Was he so bitter that he reported rumor and innuendo as truth? Did he fabricate stories or take liberties with the facts in order to cast the worst possible light on his despised tormentor, the Soviet government?

Moreover, Solzhenitsyn is an artist, and artists often take liberties with facts in order to present their ideas with clarity and force. The reader of artistic works, especially historical novels of the type Solzhenitsyn writes, both gains and loses from the artist's technique. The accuracy of the historical record may be altered for dramatic effect, and a reader unaware of the change may be led astray. On the other hand, a great artist may be able to penetrate the jumble of facts to uncover the deeper meaning of events. Strictly speaking, the artist may have altered the details, but he has done so to convey the truth that he has apprehended from the mysterious tangle of day-to-day occurrences. Happily for the readers of Solzhenitsyn's *The Gulag Archipelago*, his most "historical" book and the source of his most thoroughgoing attack on Marxism, "there are no fictitious persons nor fictitious events." He claims that "it all took place just as it is here described."[2]

Solzhenitsyn's chronicle of events paints a dimmer picture of life under Communist rule than is found in more traditional histories of the Soviet Union. In particular, Solzhenitsyn offers higher estimates of the number of people imprisoned or executed by the Soviet government than those accepted by most Western commentators. Solzhenitsyn argues that prior to the collapse of the Communist regime, it was impossible to know Soviet history accurately since the traditional sources by which a historical record is established—eyewitness accounts, press reports, and public documents, such as laws, speeches, trial transcripts, and birth and death certificates—were systematically falsified to make conditions seem better than they were. Furthermore, virtually everything in the Soviet Union was kept secret. The press was made up of the very same group that controlled the government. Literature was suppressed, especially works of art critical of the state. Speech, both in public and in private, was monitored. The ubiquitous secret police were constantly on alert for any sign of opposition to the state. Those who let their differences with government policy be known were continually hounded; many were arrested.

The most egregious examples of Soviet brutality were difficult to document. There was an unwritten law of the Gulag that those who suffered the most did not live to tell their tales. For obvious reasons a government that proclaimed itself to be the greatest expression of human justice did not want stories of its cruelty to be aired in public; such stories must be where they could never be heard.[3] When eyewitnesses to the horrors of Communism emerged from its grip, their stories seemed too fantastic to be believed. Solzhenitsyn argues that, "Most people in the West receive either falsified news [about the Soviet Union] or none at all. Complete information is available only to the Westerners who have spent time in Soviet prisons—and not just fifteen days but fifteen years. But when such people arrive in the West, their testimony seems so wildly improbable that no one believes them."[4]

Solzhenitsyn depended for his history of Soviet repression on what he took away from the Gulag "on the skin of [his] back," on what he learned with his "eyes and ears," and on "reports, memoirs, and letters by 227 witnesses." Further materials were provided by certain Communist party officials who, "despite their intent and against their will," inadvertently aided Solzhenitsyn in re-creating events because they committed their deeds to writing. Finally, he relied on the books of "thirty-six Soviet writers, headed by Maxim Gorky."[5]

It fell to Solzhenitsyn to announce the truth because of a number of happenstance occurrences. He was wrongly incarcerated and he discovered while in prison that millions of others shared his fate. He managed to survive the ordeal which gave him a unique perspective on Marxist justice and made him grimly determined to report what he had seen. He was blessed with a good memory, attentive insight, superhuman stamina—he often wrote for two eight-hour stretches a day, sleeping only a few hours between sessions—and enormous artistic skill, all of which made it possible for him to chronicle what he had witnessed under Soviet rule. He had the good fortune to come to world prominence, and thus be protected by world opinion, during the brief thaw of the Nikita

Khrushchev era, an uncharacteristic period when government control over the arts was moderated.

Although Solzhenitsyn's familiarity with Soviet history is undeniable, he never surveyed the massive literature on that topic. Yet he maintained that his record was less distorted than other accounts because he actually lived in the Soviet Union and had been an inmate in the camps—the one place where Soviet citizens were truly free to speak their mind—and because, when he was released and became a prominent public figure, he refused to bend to the government's pressure. His reputation for implacability made it possible for him to gather information from people who might otherwise have remained silent.[6]

Solzhenitsyn has been proven correct. Secret police files made public since the collapse of Communism show that even the most apparently far-fetched anecdotes were true. As Solzhenitsyn maintained, the *central* fact of totalitarian Communism was atrocious cruelty.

Not only is Solzhenitsyn's history accurate but also his predictions—much-derided before the fall of Communism—have come true. Solzhenitsyn argued that Soviet Communism could not be reformed, but had to be overthrown. He declared that the Soviet Union's hostility to the West was a manifestation of its ideology, not of the national interests of Russia, as some "realist" experts on international affairs had insisted. He anticipated that Communism would disintegrate and that, when it did, nations freed from its ideological grip would cease supporting efforts to undermine the West. He foresaw that criminals nurtured in the Gulag would form an alliance with elements of the KGB to take control of Russia's economy. He predicted that it would take hundreds of years for Russia to recover from the unimaginable ecological, economic, and spiritual damage that Communism had inflicted on his homeland. At the time Solzhenitsyn wrote these warnings, Soviet experts in the West scoffed, but nobody is laughing at them now.[7]

Second, it is a truism—although not always an accurate one—that those who forget the past are destined to repeat it. Much time and effort has been expended in contemporary American culture recalling evil social movements and political doctrines of the past such as Nazism, racism, colonialism, and McCarthyism. Any number of important motion pictures have depicted the evils of Nazism, including *Sophie's Choice*, *Schindler's List*, *The Pianist*, and *Shoah*. One need only tune in to cable network's History Channel on almost any evening to view some aspect of Hitler's mad reign. By way of comparison, popular culture treatments of the evils of Communism are few. An internet search for "anti-Communism" yielded sites on McCarthyism and right-wing death squads infiltrating anti-Communist organizations. As Kenneth Llyod Billingsley has written, "The simple but startling truth is that the major conflict of our time, democracy versus Marxism-Leninist totalitarianism—what the *New York Times* recently called 'the holy war of the 20th century'—is almost entirely missing from American cinema."[8] Solzhenitsyn's work reminds us that as evil as Nazism was,

Communism lasted longer, dominated the lives of more people, and exterminated more victims.

Third, Solzhenitsyn' writings are still relevant because, despite his reputation as Communism's greatest critic, he also attempted to understand the attraction of Marxism. Why, after all, did Communism come to dominate more than half the world's population? Surely there must have been something in its principles that produced dedicated followers.

Fourth, the stark reality of life in the Gulag furnished Solzhenitsyn with a unique grasp of the experiential truth of moral precepts. Prisoners often had to decide whether to keep themselves alive by exploiting their fellow inmates or to risk death by adhering to moral strictures. "In those circumstances," he explained, "human nature becomes very much more visible."[9] Many had to make a choice between good and evil.

It is exactly those kinds of moral judgments—viewed by many in the West as old fashioned or naive—that Solzhenitsyn learned to admire. The conscious intent of his writing was to depict universal, timeless truths about the relationship between politics and human life. Even those who are otherwise critical of his ideas, such as Ronald Berman, saw that "Solzhenitsyn has insisted on making his ideas of culture and politics central to his work—in fact, they are the work itself. His work has a unique ability to portray the relation between the individual and the state."[10]

Solzhenitsyn argues that his kind of art is necessary to counteract the profound skepticism of the age. Relativism has become central to the modern understanding of the world. It has led many to question whether there are in fact universal and timeless truths of any kind. It has undermined belief in concepts such as truth and goodness. These ideas, if they are accepted at all, are seen as no more than social constructs or personal preferences. Of course, the reverse is also true: The concept of evil has also lost its importance as a restraint on human will. By proclaiming that we cannot know what is right, relativists have made it difficult for people to resist what is evil. Although proponents of the theory of relativism have rarely committed crimes against humanity themselves, their doctrine has established a principle by which all acts, no matter how dastardly, can be excused as matters of individual or societal prerogative.[11]

Solzhenitsyn claims that relativism has not, as yet, been able to shake the human attachment to Beauty. The beauty of art, he explains, "prevails even over a resisting heart." His hope is that although "the overly straight sprouts of Truth and Goodness have been crushed, put down, or not permitted to grow . . . perhaps the whimsical, unpredictable, and ever surprising spheres of Beauty will force their way through and soar up to that very spot, thereby fulfilling the task of all three."[12]

At first glance there seems to be little beauty recorded on the pages of Solzhenitsyn's books. Rather, he describes an almost unbearable procession of gratuitous suffering, so much so that it takes a certain amount of fortitude to read his books to the end. How can stories about cruelty and injustice be beautiful? At first, the answer is not easy to perceive, but for all the misery he chronicles, Solzhenitsyn's writings are not a harbinger of despair. Those who survived the ordeal of life under Communist rule, those who withstood the trial by fire, sometimes emerged with an inspiring independence of spirit and command over their lives. Although he writes of a great social illness, his heroes point the way to recovery.

Fifth, Solzhenitsyn elaborates the connection between Marx's ideas and totalitarian Communism. He shows, against the prevailing opinion in nearly all of academia, that the inhuman system established in the Soviet Union was created not because Russians had somehow misapplied Marx's principles but rather because Soviet leaders followed Marx's suggestions, almost to the letter, and with horrific results.

Finally, although Solzhenitsyn's interpretation of the politics of the East was controversial, it paled in comparison to the storm of protest touched off by his remarks on the West. Even his mostly sympathetic biographer noted: "Where Solzhenitsyn seemed to have the power and talent to measure up to his Russian mission, in the West he appeared to be overreaching himself, and among those not swayed by his charm, authority, and charisma, a sense of disillusionment began to be perceptible."[13]

The usual charge leveled against Solzhenitsyn's views of the West is that his Russian nationalism made it impossible for him to grasp the concept of an open, pluralistic society. Neither his former life in the Soviet Union nor his reclusive existence at his home in Vermont prepared him for the vitality and freedom of democratic societies. Some commentators thought him confused and perhaps even irresponsible for attacking the Western way of life. At the very least, many agreed, Solzhenitsyn was guilty of ingratitude, for it was pressure from the West that kept him out of a Soviet prison in the early 1970s, and it was the freedom of the West, which he derided, that made it possible for him to express his creative insights.[14]

Critics of Solzhenitsyn have been most puzzled by his finding fault with both East and West. His critics maintained that there were only two models of political organization: pluralistic societies, which give their citizens the freedom to decide how to live, and authoritarian regimes—be they of the left or the right—which attempt to mold people into predetermined patterns. By berating the West, his critics charged, Solzhenitsyn placed himself in the same camp as the hated enemies in his homeland.

However, Solzhenitsyn's views on the West are neither inconsistent nor unappreciative. Quite the contrary, his principles derive from a deep understanding of the philosophic roots of Western culture. Moreover, Solzhenitsyn's criticism is not meant to undermine the resolve of the West, but rather to restore its highest principles and aspirations. It is exactly because Solzhenitsyn admires what is noble in Western life that he has spent so much effort trying to warn the West about the dangers it faces. It is also important to note that Solzhenitsyn sees an intimate connection between the doctrines of Marx and the philosophic underpinning of Western liberalism. Both doctrines, he says, grew out of a desire to satisfy the needs of the body at the expense of the needs of the soul. Communism was a vain and ultimately merciless effort to fulfill the Enlightenment dream of conquering and exploiting nature in order to establish a perfectly rational and just society on earth.

Perhaps the source of the confusion about Solzhenitsyn's thought is that his principles cannot be traced to the contemporary East, the contemporary West, or even to Russian nationalism, as is so often claimed. Rather, his views have been informed by an often-neglected tenet of Western thought which holds that human beings are capable of deciding right from wrong, noble from base, and just from unjust. It is our capacity to reason that makes such judgments possible. For example, we need not accept every form of expression, no matter how degrading, in order to protect our liberty. Instead, we can use our freedom wisely by putting laws into effect that—while not endeavoring to dictate every aspect of our lives—point us in the direction of what is proper and fitting for members of a civilized society. Nor need the task of providing for our material well-being necessarily result in an unending pursuit of wealth. Perhaps the clearest message of Solzhenitsyn's work is that the quest for freedom and security, although they are important goals in life, must be put to the service of some higher, spiritual end if life is to have meaning and importance.

One last point—this book was written, as the title *Assault on Ideology* implies, to clarify Solzhenitsyn's criticism of Marxist doctrine. Therefore, most of the book focuses on tracing the causes of the horrific events that took place in the Soviet Union, beginning with Stalin's megalomania back through the cruel precedents laid down by Vladimir Lenin to the ideology established by Marx, and ultimately to the philosophic movement begun during the Enlightenment. I have only touched on the kind of government that Solzhenitsyn favors. I have not included Solzhenitsyn's views of how Russia should be governed now that Communism has collapsed. Readers interested in the post-Communist ideas of Solzhenitsyn should consult Daniel J. Mahoney's *Solzhenitsyn: Ascent from Ideology*. Although my book was written prior to Mahoney's, they compliment each other. In a sense they constitute a before-and-after-the-collapse-of-Communism analysis of Solzhenitsyn's principles.

Notes

1. Lawrence A. Uzzell, "Solzhenitsyn the Centrist," *National Review*, 28 May 1990, 29.

2. Aleksandr Solzhenitsyn, *The Gulag Archipelago*, trans. Thomas P. Whitney (New York: Harper and Row, 1973), vi (hereafter cited as *Gulag I*).

3. Aleksandr Solzhenitsyn, "Communism at the End of the Brezhnev Era," trans.

Alexis Klimoff, *National Review*, 21 January 1983, 34. See Also, Michael Scammell, *Solzhenitsyn: A Biography* (New York: Norton, 1984), 15; John Muggeridge, "Review of *Solzhenitsyn: A Biography* by Michael Scammell," *American Spectator*, 8 August 1985, 31; John Dunlop, Richard Haugh, and Michael Nicholson, eds. *Solzhenitsyn in Exile: Critical Essays and Documentary Materials* (Stanford, Calif.: Hoover Institution Press, 1985), 3-142.

4. Aleksandr Solzhenitsyn, "The Artist as Witness," trans. Michael Glenny, *Times Literary Supplement*, 23 May 1975, 558, 561.

5. *Gulag I*, xi, xii.

6. Aleksandr Solzhenitsyn, *Invisible Allies*, trans. Alexis Klimoff and Michael Nicholson (Washington, D.C.: Counterpoint, 1995).

7. See Jerry Hough, *Soviet Leadership in Transition* (Washington, D.C.: Brookings, 1980); Alex Inkeles and Raymond Bauer, *The Soviet Citizen* (Cambridge, Mass.: Harvard University Press, 1959); Chalmers Johnson, *Change in Communist Systems* (Stanford, Calif.: Stanford University Press, 1970); Isaac Deutscher, *The Unfinished Revolution: Russia, 1917-1967* (Oxford: Oxford University Press, 1975); Frederich Fleron, ed., *Communist Studies and the Social Sciences* (Chicago: Rand McNally, 1969). For some of the controversy surrounding Solzhenitsyn's views, see Scammell, *Solzhenitsyn*, 931-49.

8. Kenneth Lloyd Billingsley, "Hollywood's Missing Movies: Why American Films Have Ignored Life under Communism," *Society* 32 (June 2000), 26.

9. Aleksandr Solzhenitsyn, interview by David Aikman, *Time*, 24 July 1989, 60.

10. Ronald Berman, "Through Western Eyes," in *Solzhenitsyn at Harvard: The Address, Twelve Early Responses, and Six Later Reflections*, ed. Ronald Berman (Washington, D.C.: Ethics and Public Policy Center, 1980), 75.

11. On the inability of the Left to pronounce anything evil see Christopher Hitchens "So Long, Fellow Travelers," *Washington Post*, 20 October 2002, B1, B3.

12. Aleksandr Solzhenitsyn, "The Nobel Lecture on Literature," in *East and West*, trans. Alexis Klimoff (New York: Harper & Row, 1908) 7-8 (hereafter cited as *East*). For Solzhenitsyn's remarks on the inability of many in the West to make judgments concerning "good and evil," see Aleksandr Solzhenitsyn, *Warning to the West*, trans. Harris Coulter, Nataly Martin, and Alexis Klimoff (New York: Farrar, Straus, & Giroux, 1976), 46 (hereafter cited as *Warning*).

13. Scammell, *Solzhenitsyn*, 916.

14. Scammell, *Solzhenitsyn*, 969-73. See also Charles Trueheart, "Solzhenitsyn and His Message of Silence," *Washington Post*, 24 November 1987, D1, D4.

CHAPTER 1

A CHRONICLE OF TERROR

SCATTERED INCIDENTS

During the harvest season of 1931, six collective farmers in a place called Tsar-skoye Selo in the Soviet Union spent the day mowing hay. After completing their work for the collective, they went back to the fields and mowed a second time along the stubs to get a little feed for their own cows. Under the Soviet law of that time the six were arrested, tried, and convicted of banditry—stealing from the state. The sentence for such a crime was death and all six were shot. Commenting on the incident Solzhenitsyn writes, "Even if Stalin had killed no others, I believe he deserved to be drawn and quartered just for the lives of those six Tsarskoye Selo peasants!"[1]

If only that were all; perhaps, if the Soviet Union had committed only this one act of cruelty it might have justly assumed the mantle of progressive leadership for mankind, a role that, given its Marxist principles, it claimed for seventy years. Regrettably, Solzhenitsyn tells us, this incident was not unique in Soviet history. It was but one example of inhumanity among countless others—a mere snowflake in a blizzard of terror.

The extent of the terror can be seen in its sheer magnitude. Using the analysis of former University of Leningrad professor of statistics I. A. Kurganov, Solzhenitsyn estimates that sixty-six million people were killed at the hands of the Soviet state. No government, not even the widely accepted archetype of evil, Nazi Germany, has so much brutality to answer for.[2]

Numbers, of course, cannot tell the whole story. They can never convey the personal anguish of those who suffered or the arbitrariness of the state's violence. Solzhenitsyn's art brings to life the human tragedy of political terror; it puts flesh on the skeletons in the Soviet Union's past. The recounting of particular incidents is, for Solzhenitsyn, more than a simple narrative of evil. These unjust occurrences have formed his principles; they stand as his evidence—as the facts behind his accusation—against the Soviet state and against all Communist governments. What follows is Solzhenitsyn's description of life under the heavy hand of Soviet rule.

At the height of the party purges in 1937 a district party conference met in Moscow. Presiding was the newly appointed secretary for the district party, replacing one recently arrested. At the meeting's conclusion the customary tribute to Comrade Stalin was offered. All jumped to their feet to hail the Great Leader with "stormy applause, rising to an ovation." But after ten minutes the clapping had not ceased. Although their hands were aching, no one wanted to be the first to stop. Finally, one party member summoned his nerve, stopped clapping, and sat down; relieved, the rest quickly followed. That night the man was arrested on some trumped-up charges and was given a ten-year sentence. During his final interrogation he was reminded: "Don't ever be the first to stop applauding!" Solzhenitsyn comments, "Now that's what Darwin's natural selection is. And that's also how to grind people down with stupidity."[3]

A tailor stuck his needle into a newspaper so that it would not get lost. It happened to pierce the eye of a picture of a high party official. A customer happened to observe the "offense." The tailor received a ten-year sentence for terrorism.[4]

Finding no other paper available, a saleswoman scribbled down a note on a piece of newspaper. Some of the writing ended up on a photograph of Stalin. She was given ten years.[5]

A tractor driver used a pamphlet about candidates for the Supreme Soviet to fill the hole in the sole of his shoe. When the person responsible for the pamphlets noticed one missing, she found out who had it. The man was given ten years for counterrevolutionary activity.[6]

An old night watchman was sent to retrieve a bust of Stalin, but he found the statue too heavy to carry. Finally, he figured out that if he slung his belt around the bust's neck, he could barely manage to transport the load through his village. It was an open-and-shut case: ten years for terrorism.[7]

A person who Solzhenitsyn met in the camps named Maksimov was sentenced to eight years for praising German equipment. His criminal act arose from a speech he had been asked to give to rally the troops for a winter offensive against the German invaders. Maksimov said, "We have to drive him out, the bastard, while the storms are raging, while he has no felt boots, even though we ourselves have ordinary shoes on now and then. But in the spring it's going to be worse because of his equipment."[8]

In 1950 some schoolchildren wrote and circulated a letter which read, "Listen workers! Are we really living the kind of life for which our grandfathers, fathers, and brothers fought? We work—and get only a pitiful pittance in return, and they even cut down on that too. Read this and think about your life."[9] Since anyone over twelve years old could be tried as an adult, they were all given ten-year sentences.

In 1941 many of those who stayed in Moscow and armed themselves to resist the Nazi onslaught were arrested once the danger had passed. For their courage they were denounced as enemy sympathizers who had waited for the Germans to arrive. Their accusers were none other than the party and government officials who had fled in panic.[10]

During and after World War II any Soviet soldiers captured by the Germans were considered spies against their homeland. Upon their liberation they were moved from the harsh life of Nazi concentration camps to the somewhat harsher life of Soviet forced-labor camps.[11]

All of these incidents occurred during the Stalinist era, a time well known for its cruelty and injustices. Yet Solzhenitsyn takes great pains to point out that although the terror reached its zenith under Stalin, the dictator did not institute the machinery of state-sponsored violence, nor did his death bring an end to political oppression.

For example, in 1922 Tanya Khodkevich was arrested because she wrote these lines to her children, "You can pray freely. But just so long as God alone can hear." The Soviet tribunal before which she was tried acknowledged her right to self-expression; after all, the revolution had liberated people. Nonetheless, it sentenced her to ten years hard labor for sharing the verses with her children. Evidently, the judge's rationale was that one could voice one's deeply held religious beliefs, but not so that anyone could hear—especially one's children.[12]

In the same year the Metropolitan of the Russian Orthodox Church was tried as an enemy of the state. There was nothing unusual in this, given the sentiment of the party, as presented at the trial by People's Commissariat of Justice Pyotr Krasikov who explained, "The whole church" is "a subversive organization. Properly speaking, the entire church ought to be put in prison." The proceedings were not a model of judicial impartiality. The defense attorney was continually threatened with arrest for pointing out: "There are no proofs of guilt. There are no facts. There is not even an indictment."

Despite what seemed to be convincing arguments in his favor, the church leader was convicted. The defense attorney escaped imprisonment only by allowing his gold watch to be expropriated. A witness for the defense was not so lucky. Professor Yegorov was summarily arrested after giving evidence supporting the Metropolitan. Yegorov was well aware of Soviet jurisprudence and had packed a bag.[13]

From the beginning of the revolution in 1918 and for most of Lenin's rule, members of the Cheka, the original name for the Soviet security police, shot more than one thousand people per month. These officially documented executions did not include those nameless thousands who, with Lenin's approval, were sunk on barges.[14]

In 1962, when Khrushchev was in power, the entire town of Novocherkassk rose up in a general strike to protest simultaneous, but unrelated, economic directives that lowered piecework rates for factory workers at the same time they increased food prices, resulting in a 30 percent drop in the workers' real buying power. According to Solzhenitsyn, soldiers fired on protesters demonstrating in front of party headquarters until "puddles of blood . . . formed in the depressions of the pavements."[15] But the people of Novocherkassk would not surrender. In the evening they demanded to meet with Anastas Mikoyan, a member of the Soviet Central Committee who had arrived on the scene to hear their grievances. Finally, a group of workers were granted an audience and it was decided that the soldiers responsible for the shootings would be punished and that the local party organization would be investigated.

The next day Mikoyan announced on the radio that peace had been restored and that the agent provocateurs and enemies of the state who had begun the disruption and fired into the crowd were now safely in custody. In reality, authorities had arrested all the workers who had met with the local party committee. The dead and wounded simply disappeared and their families were deported to Siberia. Until the publication of the *Gulag Archipelago*, these events were not reported in the Soviet or Western media.[16]

These incidents have been presented to give the flavor of Solzhenitsyn's life and times. Such tales fill volumes, but even then they tell only part of the story. What of those who were too frightened to tell their secrets? What of those who want to put the suffering behind them and forget what happened? What of those who suffered the worst? The dead can tell no tales. To fully understand the terror of living in the Soviet Union one must understand the Soviet legal system. Solzhenitsyn's account of life under the socialist penal law provides an insight into how arbitrary the Soviet regime was.[17]

SOVIET LAW

Solzhenitsyn's research led him to believe that during the Russian Revolution the Cheka (later to be known by it various acronyms MGB, NKVD, KGB) had almost unlimited authority to combat enemies of the newly established socialist state. In many ways it was a unique institution, since it combined the powers of investigation, arrest, interrogation, trial, and execution of sentence. It is not surprising that a harsh and uncompromising force was necessary to secure order and to ensure a Bolshevik victory during the turbulence of the revolution and the violence of the civil war. Certainly Lenin did not hesitate to call for such measures to insure his takeover. Solzhenitsyn quotes the following letter that Lenin wrote to the head of the Cheka:

> I am sending you an outline . . . of the Criminal Code. . . . The basic concept
> . . . is . . . openly to set forth . . . the motivation . . . and the justification for
> terror, its necessity, its limits. The court must not exclude terror. It would be
> self-deception or deceit to promise this, and in order to . . . legalize it . . . it is
> necessary to formulate it as broadly as possible, for only revolutionary right-
> eousness and revolutionary conscience will provide the conditions for apply-
> ing it more or less broadly in practice.[18]

As is the case in many violent upheavals, Bolshevik terror did not cease once the revolution had succeeded. Quite the contrary, Solzhenitsyn argues, once the revolution had been won and the civil war put down, the Cheka was ordered to intensify its suppression of the bourgeoisie. Repression was not employed to quell civil unrest; rather, it grew out of an ideological commitment to overturn the class structure of society. For Marxist revolutionaries, the middle class, which is normally the most law-abiding group, was the enemy. Lenin announced that a common, unifying purpose of the new revolutionary order was "to purge the Russian land of all kinds of harmful insects." The "insects" were, of course, those born to the wrong families, that is, "class enemies." This group included "workers malingering at their work" and "saboteurs who call themselves intellectuals."[19]

Lenin's newly established government seemed intent on breaking the will of its own citizens—if need be, by destroying millions of them. Wave after wave were arrested and punished under various pretexts. No summary account could begin to tell of the countless numbers of innocent people who were terrorized simply for their association with outlawed groups. There were "wreckers," workers accused of sabotaging the Soviet economy, "centers," people who belonged to any organization not sponsored by the Communist party, and "counterrevolutionaries," anyone whom the party did not consider loyal. Those singled out were "all scientific circles, all university circles, all artistic, literary . . . and engineering circles." Millions of other people were imprisoned or shot on random inexplicable charges. Solzhenitsyn explains that, "executions were carried out . . . on the basis of lists—in other words, free people were simply arrested and executed immediately." Since the Cheka always conducted its business in absolute secrecy, it is impossible to know what prompted it to go after one person while leaving another alone.[20]

In addition to people who one day discovered that a group to which they belonged had suddenly become illegal or those who expressed any doubt whatsoever about the infallibility of Soviet rule, Solzhenitsyn reports that many people were arrested merely because they had been denounced by a neighbor, relative, or coworker. The practice was universally accepted by the police ("the Organs" as they called themselves) as sufficient grounds for arrest and, usually, conviction. In reality, Solzhenitsyn explains, informing on others to the Organs, an act invariably carried out in secret, often was done for personal gain, to obtain the position of a higher-up, or as a way of keeping oneself out of trouble. The arrested were rarely confronted by their accusers. They were simply picked up by the Organs and tortured into confessing to some fabricated crimes. Often they were made to implicate others in their "plot," as the circle of those under suspicion and then arrested widened.

What is most surprising about the practices of what the Soviets called socialist justice, according to Solzhenitsyn—who bases his claim on extensive conversations with his fellow prisoners during his incarceration and after his release—was that almost all of those arrested were innocent, not only of any crime, but of any political activity whatsoever. Despite the severity of Communist rule, few people actively contemplated its overthrow, and even fewer took steps to effect it. Various members of the ruling group undoubtedly had different opinions, of course, but punishment for such dissension would account for only hundreds—at most thousands—of the millions put in camps or shot for no apparent reason.[21]

To say that people were apprehended for no reason may seem an exaggerated statement. Solzhenitsyn presents the following examples. One woman went into NKVD headquarters to ask what to do with the unweaned infant of a neighbor who had just been taken into custody. She waited with the child for two hours, whereupon she was thrown into a cell and later given a sentence. Solzhenitsyn presumes that the NKVD had not met its quota and needed a body. In another case in point, a judge was arrested after a court proceeding in which he opposed the sentence proposed by the state prosecutor. One fellow ran afoul of the law when he claimed that highways in the United States were paved. Some engineers were jailed as wreckers—a term employed to place for the failing economy on random citizens—who espoused an "anti-Soviet" theory concerning the physical properties of metals.[22]

Along with the usual humiliation of arrest, prisoners faced grueling interrogations at the hands of the Organs. Most perplexing about the ordeal was that the interrogators usually were not trying to uncover the truth. The actual purpose of interrogation, Solzhenitsyn explains, was to wrench a confession from the accused to justify an anonymous accusation. Prisoners were also coaxed into implicating others so that the Organs could fabricate new cases, thereby justifying their own power and privilege.

How were confessions obtained? Solzhenitsyn describes a variety of ingenious methods ranging from persuasion ("You are going to get a prison term anyway, so why not make it easy on yourself?") to screaming threats, confusing prisoners with night interrogations, playing on family affections, tickling, extinguishing burning cigarettes on the skin, employing bright lights or loud noises, beatings, stuffing the accused into boxes, throwing them into latrine pits, forcing prisoners to stand still or kneel or sit on backless benches for days, denying them sleep, food, and water, leaving them in cells infested with lice or insects, squeezing off their fingernails, bridling them by binding their hands and feet together behind their backs, or breaking their backs.[23]

Solzhenitsyn calls interrogations the malevolence of the Middle Ages magnified by science. Many of the bravest people did not survive the ordeal because they refused to implicate friends or family. By refusing to submit, such people gained nothing in this life, except perhaps a sense of maintaining their personal integrity. They perished alone, their strength of character unacknowledged, except as a minor annoyance to their interrogators, their gallantry unrewarded by the honor it deserved. Solzhenitsyn explains that interrogations constituted the first great divider of souls. As the weak and the average yielded, they were more likely to be spared, while the best people were singled out for destruction by their acts of resistance. Yet he does not condemn those who broke. Faced with the well-fed energy of the Organs, it is little wonder that most could not withstand the secret police's onslaught. Those who have never found themselves in an utterly hopeless situation, he reminds his readers, should not cast stones at those who have.[24]

Since in most cases interrogation resulted in a confession, the outcome of the trials was predetermined. Yet there were other reasons why hapless people standing before socialist judges had little chance of a fair hearing, Solzhenitsyn explains. First, most courts were closed and their proceedings kept secret; thus, they could be conducted in any manner the state saw fit. Second, there was no separation between the investigative and the judicial organs of government (or generally between the executive and the judicial departments). Nicholai Krylenko, chief prosecutor for the Soviet Union before his own downfall at the hands of Stalin, explained that the All-Russian Central Executive Committee "pardons and punishes at its own discretion without any limitation whatever," which, he concluded, "shows the superiority of our system over the false theory of separation of powers." Yakov Sverdlov, the committee's chairman, added, "It is very good that the legislative and executive powers are not divided by a thick wall as they are in the West. All problems can be decided quickly." For example, Solzhenitsyn explains that a judge could change a ruling—over the telephone if need be, and invariably to give a tougher sentence—six months to ten years after the original decision had been handed down.[25]

Third, socialist law was not fixed. It could be changed from case to case according to the circumstances. Solzhenitsyn again quotes Krylenko:

> The purpose of judicial proceedings was not to discover the truth or to insure that justice be done, but to further the political aims of the government. Hence, Krylenko commented that Soviet tribunals were "at one and the same time both the creator of the law . . . and a political weapon."[26]

The political weapon of socialist justice could be effective only if a new sort of guilt or innocence were introduced into the courtroom. Krylenko reasoned:

> "A tribunal is an organ of the class struggle of the workers directed against their enemies [and must act] from the point of view of the interests of the revolution . . . having in mind the most desirable results for the masses. . . . No matter what the individual qualities [the defendant], only one method of evaluating him is to be applied: evaluation from the point of view of class expediency."[27]

Solzhenitsyn points out that defendants who found themselves to be "inexpedient" had virtually no chance of proving their innocence. Again he quotes Krylenko, who explained that if "'this expediency should require that the avenging sword should fall on the head of the defendants, then no . . . verbal arguments can help.'" Guilt could even be applied to the offenses that a person *might* commit. As Krylenko put it, "'We protect ourselves not only against the past but also against the future.'"[28] Solzhenitsyn traces the oppressive nature of socialist justice to Marx, who argued that as history changes, so do notions of right and wrong, and of just and unjust. The concept of justice may recur, but its content varies according to how the ruling group defines it. Marx held that the only unvarying truth in history is that change does occur and that it will eventually bring the socialist era into being. Whatever aids in that endeavor is just; whatever hinders it is unjust. Marxism provides an excuse for doing whatever one wants and calling it lawful.[29]

Fourth, even when there were statutes protecting those on trial or in prison, no one paid attention to them. Solzhenitsyn tells of many instances in which both captive and captor were surprised when confronted with an actual Soviet statute.[30]

Finally, the law was all-inclusive and it covered every possible human activity, even thought. "In truth," Solzhenitsyn writes, "there is no step, thought, action, or lack of action under heaven which could not be punished by the heavy hand" of Soviet justice.[31]

The absolute character of Soviet law originated in Article 58 of the Criminal Code. Drafted by Lenin as a way of making any form of opposition illegal, the code was adopted in 1926. Once the draft had hardened into law, citizens could be imprisoned under the sweeping provisions of Article 58 for

> Anti-Soviet Agitation, Counter-Revolutionary Activity, Counter-Revolutionary Trotskyite Activity, Suspicion of Espionage, Contacts Leading to Suspicion of Espionage, Counter-Revolutionary Thought, Dissemination of Anti-Soviet Sentiments, Socially Dangerous Element, Criminal Activity [unspecified], Member of a Family (of a person convicted under one of the foregoing categories).

Solzhenitsyn comments, "Hand me St. Augustine and in a trice I can find room in that article for him too."[32]

As if the parameters of Article 58 were not broad enough, the authorities insisted on giving its provisions the widest possible interpretation. For example, Solzhenitsyn points out that people did not have to actually commit a crime to be prosecuted; they had only to *intend* to commit an offense. As Krylenko said, whether the deed "was carried out or not has no essential significance." The effect of the law was to make intent identical to action, an absurdity which caused Solzhenitsyn to remark, "Whether a man whispered to his wife in bed that it would be a good thing to overthrow the Soviet government or whether he engaged in propaganda during an election or threw a bomb, it was all one and the same! And the punishment was identical!!!"[33]

LIFE ON THE INSIDE

It should be clear that most people who stood before Soviet courts ended up in prison. Solzhenitsyn distinguishes those in prison according to their offenses. There were politicals, who usually had been convicted under one of the provisions of Article 58, and thieves, incarcerated for the crimes punished by every society—murder, theft, robbery, and so forth. Sentences for thieves varied according to the crime, as they did for politicals during the early years of the revolution. However, by the mid-1920s sentences for politicals were increased and made a standard length, eight to ten years (usually ten) of forced labor. When the death penalty was abolished after World War II, the standard sentence was set at twenty-five years.[34]

Of the number who received "the supreme measure," as a shot in the back of the head was called, only rumor survives. Solzhenitsyn estimates that between 1 and 1.7 million were executed. He reports that the NKVD men who were swept into prison in the downfall of state security chief Nicholai Yezhov boasted that a half million people had been killed in 1937-1938 alone.[35]

After being sentenced, the vast majority of prisoners were sent to toil in what the party called "corrective labor camps" and what Solzhenitsyn calls, in a play on words, "destructive labor camps." He argues that since Marx contended that man is constituted by labor, it is little wonder that the state turned to labor as a way of disposing of its outcasts. The rationale was to reform—or to reforge, in Soviet parlance—the wayward through physical labor. As the party tightened its control over the population, the forced-labor camps, the Gulag, quickly grew. Solzhenitsyn estimates that at their peak, the camps held perhaps one-fifth of the Soviet population. The entire nation was affected, since virtually everyone had family or friends serving a sentence. Vast islands of prisoners cropped up in even the harshest and remotest regions of the Soviet Union, until, as Solzhenitsyn suggests, the inhabitants of the Gulag, united by the cruelty of their overlords, became a nation of slaves within their own country.[36]

Great convoys of prisoners lumbered among the many camps, delivering the convicted to serve their sentences. Prisoners were often packed hundreds to a railroad car so that they were unable to move, or even to relieve themselves. Without proper food, ventilation, or sanitation, many did not survive the ordeal. One former prisoner described the transit sites, where prisoners were assigned to labor camps, as follows:

> People were stuck there for several months at a time. The bed bugs infested the board bunks like locusts. Half a mug of water a day; there wasn't any more!—no one to haul it. There was a whole compound of Koreans, and they all died from dysentery, every last one of them. They took a hundred corpses out of the compound every morning. They were building a morgue, so they hitched the zeks to the carts and hauled the stone that way. Today you do the hauling and tomorrow they haul you there yourself. And in the autumn the typhus arrived. And we did the same thing; we didn't hand over the corpses till they stank—and took the extra rations. No medication whatever. We crawled to the fences and begged: "Give us medicine." And the guards fired a volley from the watchtowers. Then they assembled those with typhus in separate barracks. Some didn't make it there, and only a few came back. The bunks there had two stories. And anyone on an upper who was sick and running a fever wasn't able to clamber down to go to the toilet—and so it would all pour down on the people underneath. There were fifteen hundred sick there. And all the orderlies were thieves. They'd pull out the gold teeth from the corpses. And not only from the corpses.[37]

When the rigorous journey was at its end, zeks, the name given to Soviet prisoners, reached the forced-labor camps. A major topic of Solzhenitsyn's work is an account of the nature of these camps and a recollection of their history. He relates the story of the first camp on Soloveysky Island in the White Sea and explains how that experiment spread, cancer-like, until its evil encompassed the entire nation. In fact, he maintains that the Gulag was, and continued to be for seventy years, an integral part of the Soviet system.[38]

Conditions in the camps, he reports, were unbelievably harsh. Only those jobs that no one else would perform were given to the zeks. They were expected to labor at the most physically exhausting tasks without the necessary means of survival. Their daily ration of food consisted of soup or gruel and fourteen ounces of wet black bread. Even this meager portion could be cut if zeks did not complete their work quota. They were rarely issued proper clothes even in the most inclement weather. Some zeks were even forced to work in the bitter cold of Siberia wearing the same attire in which they had been arrested the previous summer. Veterans of the camps never gave up their heavy coats and winter boots, even on the hottest days. They knew that clothing which wore out or was lost would probably not be replaced and that Russian winters without such apparel were lethal.

Zeks lived in cold, insect-infested barracks cramped together for security reasons. They labored without proper construction equipment. But of course this was the point. Since the nation could not afford to build factories to produce labor-saving devices, it turned to labor-intensive methods to build the economy. Zeks were made to dig vast canals through frozen tundra using only picks and shovels. The life of the zeks, Solzhenitsyn says,

> Consists of work, work, work; of starvation, cold, and cunning. This work, for those who are unable to push others out of the way and set themselves up in a soft spot, is that self-same general work which raises socialism up out of the earth, and drives us down into the earth.[39]

In order to build socialism in the Soviet Union, zeks mined gold in regions above the Arctic Circle (the bitter cold froze most of them to death), toiled in copper mines (the dust was lethal within a year), cut and hauled timber by hand out of the vast Russian forest, and labored at any miserable and dangerous jobs that the authorities threw at them. Marx may have reasoned that labor had made the species human, but Solzhenitsyn concludes that the labor which zeks were made to perform made most of them corpses.

Zeks had to contend not only with backbreaking labor and the harsh environment but also with man-made cruelty. First, explains Solzhenitsyn, they were organized into work brigades. Ostensibly, the brigades were a way of demonstrating socialist worker solidarity. In reality, they were a means of coercion, since the entire brigade was given a work quota, which, if not attained, resulted in the group receiving short rations. Such a practice created enormous social pressure on every individual to meet the quota.[40]

Second, the work norms were set so inhumanly high that the extra rations awarded if the goal was met did not compensate the worker for the energy expended: a method intended to drive the always-hungry prisoners to toil by dangling food in front of them. The goal was to extract the maximum amount of labor at the minimum cost except in human lives. Solzhenitsyn explains:

> Those who increase work norms in industry can still deceive themselves into thinking that such are the successes of the technology of production. But those who increase the norms of physical labor are executioners par excellence! They cannot seriously believe that under socialism the human being is twice as big and twice as muscular. They are the ones . . . who should be tried! They are the ones who should be sent out to fulfill those work norms![41]

Under such conditions people were reduced to the lowest level of humanity, acting purely on the basis of their hunger. Solzhenitsyn states:

> Your mind is absorbed in vain calculations which for the present cut you off from the heavens—and tomorrow are worth nothing. You *hate* labor—it is your principal enemy. You hate companions—rivals in life and death. You are reduced to a frazzle by intense envy and alarm lest somewhere behind your back others are right now dividing up that bread which could be yours, that somewhere on the other side of the wall a tiny potato is being ladled out of the pot which could have ended up in your bowl.[42]

Third, the guards were given complete power over prisoners. They could and sometimes did shoot zeks for fun or for something as capricious as when an individual chanced to step out of a marching line. Guards were never punished for their actions. Beatings and torture were common. Already dehumanized by their training, guards looked on the lines of pitiful prisoners shuffling before them as diseased animals. All this was planned, reasons Solzhenitsyn. The goal was to leave zeks with no wills of their own and to make their every action, no matter how minute, dependent on the guards. Racked by hunger and terrorized by their wardens, zeks had little choice but to obey.[43]

Fourth, informers (stool pigeons, Solzhenitsyn calls them) were everywhere. Every action, lack of action, or conversation that might even vaguely present a threat to the authorities was reported to them by informers. Zeks' lives were made all the more abject by the danger they faced for the slightest whisper of a complaint. For every moment of their existence, they had to be watchful that someone was not informing on them. As for the stool pigeons, their lives were only slightly less miserable; they received extra rations for their secret reports.[44]

Fifth, trustees, who performed the easiest and most desirable jobs in the camps, stole from their fellow prisoners. For example, Solzhenitsyn explains that zeks assigned to kitchen duty ate food allotted for the whole camp. Since there was rarely enough food to go around and since a short ration meant certain death for those working at hard labor, the good fortune of the trustees rested on the corpses of their campmates.

Trustees got their favored positions by performing some service for the guards. Stool pigeons traded information, women exchanged sex, and thieves bartered anything they could pillage from the packages sent by families of hapless politicals.[45]

Finally, political prisoners were victimized by the thieves. Bands of thieves, united by their criminal code, continually badgered and bullied the unorganized politicals, frightening them into handing over whatever meager articles they possessed. Both in and out of prison, thieves preyed upon innocent and law-abiding people, whose virtue and honesty they disdained as gullible foolishness. The thieves' code consisted of little more than debauchery and the satisfaction of immediate physical desires, which reduced them, Solzhenitsyn comments, to the level of beasts. Many of these hardened criminals seemed to have no moral compass whatever and to have passed a threshold of evil beyond which redemption becomes all but impossible. Solzhenitsyn calls them people without souls.[46]

The thieves came to play a special role in the camps, one that, Solzhenitsyn argues, reveals something important about the character of Marxism. It is true, of course, that common criminals were a social nuisance and had to be incarcerated, but it is also true that a life of misconduct was often excused and sometimes even fostered by the Soviet authorities. After all, the Progressive Doctrine, as Solzhenitsyn ironically calls Marxism-Leninism, claimed that human beings are not responsible for their actions. Instead, economic conditions are the cause of aberrant behavior. Thus, criminality did not indicate a lack of character on the thieves' part, but showed, once again, the corrupting influence of bourgeois society. Once the levers of oppressive capitalist society were removed, Marxism maintained, crime would vanish. In fact, the thieves were considered social allies of the revolution, since they too were enemies of private property. Stalin, who once robbed banks, fondly characterized the thieves' behavior as redistribution of wealth, an additional form of class struggle.

Given the ideological tolerance toward thieves, Solzhenitsyn argues, it is little wonder that prison authorities formed an alliance with them to crush political prisoners, considered to be the true enemies of the revolution. With the concurrence of the guards, thieves terrorized politicals, keeping them divided and distraught, and, not incidentally, lessening the possibility of resistance against the established order. Thieves were allowed to become informal power brokers within the camps. They held the best jobs and used their positions to further the interests of their band (a sort of criminal patronage system).

In the topsy-turvy world of the Gulag, real criminals were thought of more highly than the honest, upright people who had been interned for some fabricated offense or for being from the wrong social class. Solzhenitsyn maintains that this inversion of the normal order of society was symptomatic of Marxist egalitarianism. Thieves were accepted by the party because they were part of the lower class. Their alliance with the progressive forces of history depended on the condition of their being lower. But, Solzhenitsyn wonders, was their place in the social hierarchy not the result of their own behavior? Did not their creed preclude any thought of the future in their perpetual quest for instant gratification? Did not this lack of what once was called virtue make it impossible for them to rise in social rank, as honest, hardworking people might? Solzhenitsyn contends that by honoring the lower elements of society, Marxism actually rewarded profligacy and vice at the same time it punished virtue.

Solzhenitsyn goes on to make an even more insidious comparison between thievery and Marxism. Both, he says, depend on a kind of redistribution. There is, however, little nobility in this urge to expropriate. It is spurred by envy. What is envy but a passion turned against the talent, industriousness, and success of others?[47]

According to Solzhenitsyn the Progressive Doctrine misunderstood the intransigence of the thieves, and as a result, a strange thing occurred. Thieves were not reformed by their experience in the collective labor camps; rather, their hardened credo became the prevailing ethos of the Gulag. The guards learned from the rapacity of the thieves to use their position to take all they could. And what else could politicals do but adopt many of the principles of this egocentric way of life merely as a means of survival?

An even more shameful result of the leveling of humanity, Solzhenitsyn insists, is that the criminal creed spread outward from the camps, ultimately engulfing the whole of Soviet society. After all, the thieves' sentences were comparatively light, and on more than one occasion Stalin saw fit to issue them a blanket pardon. Hardened criminals were turned loose to prey on an unsuspecting populace. But when they were caught again, their punishments were just as slack. And there for all to see was an example of how crime paid. If a society coddles and even praises its criminals while millions of innocent people are imprisoned, then the lesson learned is the one taught by the thieves. Solzhenitsyn saw that the morality of the Gulag had become the dominant cultural norm of Soviet society, and he foresaw that if Communism fell, Gulag ethics would come to dictate most social interactions. Little wonder that Russia has had such difficulty implementing free-market economics, civic responsibility, and the rule of law in the post-Communist era.[48]

Both nature and man seemed to conspire against the political zeks. Forced into slavery by the masters of a new age, stripped of all human dignity and personal initiative, they found their lives almost unendurable. Critically harsh conditions forced them to face the deepest dilemma of their lives. Should they gain a little something for themselves by informing on their fellow inmates, or by selling out to become whores of the guards, or by stealing food intended for the mouths of others? In the Gulag the choice was starkly clear: survival or conscience. Solzhenitsyn writes, "Survive! At any price! This is a great fork of camp life. From this point the roads go to the right and to the left. One of them will rise and the other will descend. If you go to the right—you lose your life, and if you go to the left—you lose your conscience."[49]

The majority, of course, chose to save their own skins. Yet not all did. Many people of strong character and high morals silently carried their virtue with them to the grave. Some even survived the Gulag without compromising and in the process gained a spiritual strength unimaginable in the outside world. The courage of those who failed to be corrupted by the camps raises another question concerning Marxist principles. Solzhenitsyn doubts that people's social environment is fully responsible for forming their characters. Life in the camps, he says, shows that Marx was wrong. Human beings can act independently of the economic structure, even if it is an economy of slave labor. "In camp," Solzhenitsyn writes, "existence did not determine consciousness, but just the opposite: consciousness and steadfast faith in the human essence decided whether you became an animal or remained a human being."[50]

Solzhenitsyn estimates that perhaps one-fifth, or even as few as one-eighth, of the camp veterans ever lived to see release. Yet even the end of jail term did not bring a return to normal life. Many of those who were not given another jail term were cast, in perpetuity, into internal exile, some in the very region where they had served as prisoners. Treated as pariahs, they often could find work only in the brigades that they had so recently left. They led marginal lives until the Khrushchev period, when the majority of Stalin's slaves were allowed to return home.[51]

Even when they returned to the mainstream of Soviet life, zeks were rarely free from the memory of the camps. For most, the experience had shattered their health and broken their spirit. Not only did they have to contend with all the psychological problems associated with a long and bitter captivity but they were confronted with a culture now permeated with the camp ethos. Solzhenitsyn explains:

> Everything of the most infectious nature in the Archipelago—in human relations, morals, views, and language—in compliance with the universal law of osmosis in plant and animal tissue . . . dispersed through the entire country. While the government attempted . . . to re-educate the prisoners through slogans . . . the prisoners more swiftly re-educated the entire country. . . . The thieves' philosophy, which initially had conquered the Archipelago, easily swept further and captured the All-Union ideological market, a wasteland without a stronger ideology. The camp tenacity, its cruelty in human relations, its insensitivity over the heart, its hostility to any kind of conscientious work—all this . . . made a deep impression on all freedom.[52]

LIFE ON THE OUTSIDE

What sort of life did the Soviet Union provide for those lucky enough to remain free from the Gulag? To begin with, Solzhenitsyn maintains, even on the outside the long arm of the Gulag reached out and touched every Soviet citizen. Since nearly everyone had a friend or relative on the inside, all realized that they too could disappear into the camps; and fear hung like a pall over Soviet society.[53]

The Gulag was not the only form of terror that the party inflicted on the Russian people. Solzhenitsyn points out that, among other crimes, it also:

1. Dispersed the Constituent Assembly.
2. Capitulated to the Germans in World War I.
3. Introduced punishment and execution without trial.
4. Crushed workers' strikes.

5. Plundered the countryside to such an extent that peasants revolted in an uprising that was crushed in the bloodiest manner possible.
6. Destroyed the Church.
7. Pioneered one of the first uses of concentration camps.
8. Introduced the use of hostages—the Organs seized not fugitives, but rather members of their families or simply someone at random, and threatened to shoot them if the fugitives did not turn themselves in.
9. Deceived workers by false decrees on such things as land ownership and freedom of the press.
10. Exterminated all other parties
11. Carried out genocide of the peasantry—fifteen million peasants were shipped off to their deaths; reintroduced a kind of serfdom, the so-called internal passport system; and created a famine, causing six million persons to die in the Ukraine between 1932 and 1933.[54]

To round the picture out, he explains that the Soviet government stifled Russian culture, suppressed Russian literature, engaged in a senseless military buildup that impoverished the nation, and created the most elaborate secret police force in history, the primary aim of which was to spy on its own people.[55]

Solzhenitsyn argues that it is difficult to imagine a system of government which could have a more devastating effect on its people. He explains the elements of Soviet rule that gave the regime its totalitarian character.

1. People were in constant fear. Everyone knew of the midnight arrests, the disappearances of neighbors or fellow workers; they had heard of the executions and seen reports of the show trials. Some were so frightened that they were actually relieved to be arrested. They all understood that the wrong word or gesture could send them into the abyss.

Yet arrest was not the only threat. There were also "purges, inspections, the completion of security questionnaires . . . dismissal from work, deprivation of residence permit, expulsion or exile."[56]

2. Average Soviet citizens were in a position of servitude. Their fate was in the hands of the authorities who held the power of life and death over them. There was not even a place to complain. The least criticism could be taken as disloyalty and could result in a term in the camps. Nor was there a place to run. The internal passport system insured that people stayed where they were, where they could be watched.

3. Society was permeated with secrecy and mistrust. Secret denunciations were universally accepted by the Organs as grounds for arrest and conviction. People rarely came face to face with their accusers. Everyone was suspect and on guard. Such an atmosphere made candor impossible. Open and sincere conversations were rare.

4. The population was ignorant of what was going on around it. Not only did the party keep almost everything secret but also fear made even the simplest communication between people difficult. Solzhenitsyn explains:

Hiding things from each other, and not trusting each other, we ourselves helped implement that absolute secrecy, absolute misinforma-
tion, among us which was the cause of causes of everything that took
place—including both millions of arrests and the mass approval of
them.[57]

5. Squealing (as Solzhenitsyn calls informing) was developed to an extraordinary extent. Solzhenitsyn speculates that perhaps one in four or five city
dwellers in the Soviet Union were recruited by the secret police. He speculates
that an important reason for enlisting so many people—even though most of
their information was of little consequence—was to establish the impression that
the Organs were everywhere, always watchful.

6. Betrayal became a way of life. People became so terrified that they did
nothing when neighbors and friends mysteriously disappeared. As if struck by a
plague, people avoided the families of the arrested. Not a finger was lifted in
protest because to do so could bring a prison term of one's own. Betrayal was so
widespread that public denunciations came into vogue. It was not uncommon to
hear in some public meeting or read in some Soviet newspaper, "I, the under-
signed, from such and such a date, renounce my father and mother as enemies of
the people."[58]

7. People became corrupt. Success came to those who, imitating party officials, used any means to achieve their goals. Soviet citizens came to believe that
advancement depended less on ability and achievement than on brutality and
cunning. Denunciation of one's superiors became a particularly attractive
method of moving up the ladder of success.

8. The lie became a form of existence. Arrest, upheaval, brutality, shortages,
inefficiency, and starvation were the way of life in the Soviet Union, but one
could never speak of these things. Rather, one had to applaud the leadership's
every deed and every word. When something went wrong the party blamed it on
some malevolent conspiracy, instigated by the West and intent on destroying
socialism. A surrealistic atmosphere gripped the nation. Normal people had to
contend daily with reportage of the type taken from *Pravda*, 28 May 1938:

> Heightening our revolutionary vigilance, we will help our glorious intelligence
> service, headed by the true Leninist, the Stalinist People's Commissar Nikolai
> Ivanovich Yezhov, to purge our higher educational institutions as well as our
> country of the remnants of the Trotskyite-Bukharinite and other counterrevolu-
> tionary trash.[59]

Solzhenitsyn insists that the lie was not merely a mischief; rather, it permeated the ways people spoke and even thought. He states:

> There exists a collection of ready-made phrases, of labels, a selection of ready-
> made lies. . . . And not one single speech . . . nor one single book . . . can exist
> without the use of these primary clichés. In the most scientific of texts it is re-
> quired that someone's false authority or false priority be up held somewhere,

and someone be cursed for telling the truth; without this lie even an academic work cannot see the light of day.[60]

9. The whole system rewarded cruelty. It spread downward. The brutal were rewarded with advancement; the more reticent were passed over, replaced, or even purged. How could it be otherwise? Class warfare was praised and mercilessness instilled, while pity, kindness, and mercy were ridiculed. Given the pervasive ethic of class hatred, it is little wonder that many lost sight of the difference between good and evil.

10. Soviet citizens adopted a slave psychology. Most feared loss of their jobs, their families, their freedom, and, of course, their lives. They knew there was always something more that the state could take from them, something to make their lives more miserable. And what could they do? The state totally controlled the media. It spewed a constant barrage of propaganda, aimed at instilling the ideas of socialist superiority while casting Western nations as warmongers on the verge of attacking the peace-loving Soviet Union. So total was the state's grip on the flow of information that even history could be changed—and was, any number of times, to accommodate shifts in the leadership. No news of the armed peasant uprisings ever appeared in *Izvestia* nor was the truth of the workers' strikes ever printed in *Pravda*.[61]

Public opinion could not counteract the state's high-handed measures. Any opposition that might have formed—for instance, in churches, among workers, or in non-Communist parties—was eradicated. For any who did speak out, arrest was sure and swift. A perverse natural selection occurred in which the brave perished and the weak survived. Furthermore, Russians did not have a strong tradition of involvement in national government, although Solzhenitsyn maintains that there was a history of participation at the local level. As in any society, most people were naturally lawful and did what they were told. Even after arrest, people's most common response was to believe that it was all a mistake that would be straightened out in the morning. What experience the Russian people did have in public affairs was embodied in their cultural tradition. But to the Progressive Doctrine a national culture was not progressive; thus Russia's rich traditions were systematically destroyed, to be replaced by sterile party jargon. In fact, Solzhenitsyn complains, the attack on the indigenous culture was so complete that the Russian language itself degenerated.[62]

Despite all the extenuating circumstances—the terrible strength of the Progressive Doctrine and its incalculable brutality—one should not suppose that Solzhenitsyn excuses the Russian people for having become slaves. Quite the contrary, he accuses them of a loss of "civil valor." Expressing his own frustration at having been part of the mob carried into servitude, he writes:

> We didn't love freedom enough. And even more—we had no awareness of the real situation. We spent ourselves in one unrestrained outburst in 1917, and then we hurried to submit. We submitted with pleasure! We purely and simply deserved everything that happened afterward.[63]

Notes

1. *Gulag I*, 437.

2. These figures are much disputed, of course. Roy Medvedev holds that no more than twenty-five to twenty-six million perished, while Robert Conquest projects about thirty million. Even with the KGB files now open to scholars, the truth may never be established because few official records exit. Any of the numbers listed above stagger the imagination and lead one to wonder whether this is not a unique phenomenon in human history. Yet Solzhenitsyn contends that China may have committed even greater atrocities, given its greater population. *East*, 106; *Warning*, 10. Roy Medvedev, *Let History Judge*, trans. Colleen Taylor (London: Macmillan, 1971), 38; Robert Conquest, *The Great Terror* (New York: Macmillan, 1968), 200-11.

3. *Gulag I*, 69-70.

4. Ibid.

5. Ibid.

6. Aleksandr Solzhenitsyn, *The Gulag Archipelago II*, trans. Thomas P. Whitney (New York: Harper & Row, 1975), 293 (hereafter cited as *Gulag II*).

7. Ibid.

8. Ibid., 294.

9. Ibid., 316.

10. *Gulag I*, 200. Perhaps these accusations fell on sympathetic ears. Stalin had left the city himself.

11. Ibid., 247.

12. *Gulag I*, 37.

13. Ibid., 351.

14. Ibid., 435.

15. Aleksandr Solzhenitsyn, *The Gulag Archipelago III*, trans. Harry Willetts (New York: Harper & Row, 1976), 511 (hereafter cited as *Gulag III*).

16. Solzhenitsyn comments concerning the deaths of 2 June 1962: "Rather fewer than before the Winter Palace, yet all Russia was outraged by January 9 and observed its anniversary yearly. When shall we begin commemorating June 2?" (*Gulag III*, 510n; see also 511-14).

17. Socialist is used here and throughout as the Soviets and Solzhenitsyn use it—a term interchangeable with Communism and one denoting that regime founded by the Russian Revolution.

18. *Gulag I*, 353; see also 28.

19. Ibid., 27; see also 34.

20. Ibid., 31; see also 24-91.

21. *Gulag II*, 393.

22. *Gulag I*, 11, 378; *Warning*, 32-33.

23. *Gulag I*, 103-16.

24. Ibid., 101-5, 133.

25. Ibid., 307; see also 287, 298-311, 431.

26. Ibid., 307-8.

27. Ibid., 308. See also Stephen Carter, *The Politics of Solzhenitsyn* (New York: Holmes & Meier, 1977), 37.

28. *Gulag I*, 308-9. Solzhenitsyn comments that, "people lived and breathed and suddenly found out their existence was inexpedient" *Gulag I*, 309.

29. Solzhenitsyn quotes lines from Faust: "The whole world changes and everything moves forward, And why should I be afraid to break my word?" *Gulag I*, 290.

30. *Gulag II*, 147; *Gulag III*, 496; Nerzhin, the leading character of the novel *The First Circle*, loves to make prison guards live by the letter of the law. See Aleksandr Solzhenitsyn, *The First Circle*, trans. Thomas P. Whitney (New York: Harper & Row, 1968), 147.

31. *Gulag I*, 60.

32. Ibid., 284. 354.

33. Ibid., 364.

34. One prisoner noted concerning his sentence, "It is strange. I was condemned for lack of faith in the victory of socialism in our country. But, can Kalinin [president of the Soviet Union] himself believe in it if he thinks camps will still be needed in our country twenty years from now?" *Gulag I*, 455.

35. Ibid., 438.

36. It is somewhat mystifying, as Solzhenitsyn points out, how people arrested for their bourgeois social origins could be reforged. Is not consciousness determined by class origin? Even labor cannot change one's parents. See *Gulag II*, 13, 67, 86, 103, 502-3.

37. *Gulag I*, 536.

38. *Gulag II*, 14.

39. Ibid., 198; see also 155-56, 209.

40. Ibid., 78, 158; Carter, *Politics of Solzhenitsyn*, 37-38.

41. Ibid., 201.

42. Ibid., 620, Solzhenitsyn's emphasis.

43. *Gulag I*, 468.

44. *Gulag II*, 355-59.

45. Ibid., 159.

46. See ibid., 428 where Solzhenitsyn explains the thieves' code: "1. I want to live and enjoy myself; and f— the rest! 2. Whoever is strongest is right! 3. If they aren't (beat)ing you, then don't ask for it. (In other words: as long as they're beating up someone else, don't stick up for the ones being beaten. Wait your turn)." See also Meyer Galler, *Soviet Prison Camp Speech: A Survivor's Glossary Supplement* (Madison: University of Wisconsin Press, 1972).

47. Solzhenitsyn calls Stalin *pakhan*, or ringleader of a band of thieves. *Gulag I*, 134; see also 502, 506-7, and *Gulag II*, 44, 440.

48. *Gulag II*, 307, 428. Some of the thieves, in contradiction to the progressive principle that human beings are products of their environment, were born after the Bolshevik Revolution. For Solzhenitsyn's impressions on the lawlessness of the post-Communist era see David Remnick, "The Exile Returns," *The New Yorker*, 14 February 1994, 64-83; and David Remnick, "Deep in the Woods" *The New Yorker*, 6 August 2001, 32-40.

49. Ibid., 602-3; see also Carter, *Politics of Solzhenitsyn*, 37.

50. *Gulag II*, 626; see also 603-5.

51. *Gulag III*, 445. Solzhenitsyn surmises that the heirs of Stalin also had their slaves.

52. *Gulag II*, 564-65.

53. *Gulag I*, 43 in. See also Carter, *Politics of Solzhenitsyn*, 16, where he wonders if there was any place in the Soviet Union that could be considered the outside. He notes:

as Solzhenitsyn points out, practically no one in the prison camps is either guilty of a crime or any sort of threat to society. This is contrary to any theories of reasonably wide currency about the justification of punishment or imprisonment. . . . In fact, in such a situation, one can make no distinction between those in prison and the rest of society. Hence, prison and normal society seem in this sense to have no dividing lines between them, although of course prison life does have some appalling restrictions which are not directly encountered elsewhere.

54. *Warning*, 14-17. See also *Gulag III*, 363, where Solzhenitsyn explains, "No Genghis Khan ever destroyed so many peasants as our glorious Organs, under the leadership of the Party."

55. *Warning*, 12.

56. *Gulag II*, 633; see also *Gulag I*, 17.

57. *Gulag II*, 635.

58. Ibid., 640.

59. Quoted in ibid., 646.

60. Ibid., 646-47.

61. Ibid., 632-55; *Gulag I*, 106, 335; *First Circle*, 138, 636; *Warning*, 82; Aleksandr Solzhenitsyn, Mikhail Agursky, A. B., Evgeny Barabanov, Vadim Borisov, F. Korsakov, and Igor Shafarevich, *From under the Rubble*, trans. A. M. Brock, Milada Haigh, Marita Sapiets, Hilary Sternberg, and Harry Willetts under the direction of Michael Scammell (Boston: Little, Brown, 1975), 2, 7 (hereafter cited as *Rubble*); Aleksandr Solzhenitsyn, *The Oak and the Calf*, trans. Harry Willetts (New York: Harper & Row), 171 (hereafter cited as *Oak*); Carter, *Politics of Solzhenitsyn*, 55.

62. *Gulag I*, 11-12, 35-37, 188, 262; *Gulag II*, 304, 382n, 393-94; *Gulag III*, 92-93; Aleksandr Solzhenitsyn, *Lenin in Zurich*, trans. Harry Willetts (New York: Farrar, Straus, & Giroux, 1976), 215 (hereafter cited as *Zurich*).

63. *Gulag I*, 13n. Solzhenitsyn explains his idea of civil valor as follows:

And how we burned in the camps later, thinking: What would things have been like if every Security operative, when he went out at night to an arrest, had been uncertain whether he would return alive and had to say good-bye to his family? Or if, during periods of mass arrests, as for example in Leningrad, when they arrested a quarter of the entire city, people had not simply sat there in their Lairs, paling with terror at every bang of the downstairs door and at every step on the staircase, but had understood they had nothing left to lose and had boldly set up in the downstairs hail an ambush of half a dozen people with axes, hammers, poles, or whatever else was at hand? After all, you know ahead of time that those were out at night for no good purpose. and you could be sure ahead of time that you'd be cracking the skull of a cutthroat. Or what about the Black Maria sitting out there on the street with one lonely chauffeur—what if it had been driven off or its tires spiked? The Organs would quickly have suffered a shortage of officers and transport and, notwithstanding all Stalin's thirst, the cursed machine would have ground to a halt!

CHAPTER 2

SOLZHENITSYN'S STALIN

Solzhenitsyn's indictment of the reign of terror in the Soviet Union raises some obvious questions: How could such awful things happen? Why were millions of innocent people rounded up, convicted of fictitious crimes, summarily executed, or imprisoned in labor camps to be worked to death? Can all suffering be explained by the fact that the Bolshevik Revolution fell prey to a "cult of personality"—a Soviet euphemism, one suspects, for madman? Was such behavior necessary, as others argued, to prepare the Soviet Union for war? Was it, as the philosopher Maurice Merleau-Ponty postulated—but later retracted—the price of rapid industrialization?[1] Perhaps there is an even deeper meaning to it all. If Marx's determinism is correct, History may have demanded that the gruesome game be played out.

To determine the causes of the Soviet terror, it is appropriate to begin with the most obvious target—Stalin.

SOME EXPLANATIONS OF THE TERROR

It is ironic, Solzhenitsyn muses, that the man whose name was revered by half the population of the world as the Great Leader of Socialism should now be blamed for leading the Progressive Movement down the false path of tyranny. Yet today the former Great Leader of Progressive Mankind is the scapegoat on whose head those who defend Marxism place many of the evils of the movement.

At one time, of course, adherents of the Progressive Movement defended Stalin's every action, even his excesses, with a variety of rationalizations—some serious, some frivolous. Solzhenitsyn's appraisal of those explanations and his own account of Stalin's motives provide a fuller understanding of the roots of the Soviet Terror.[2]

First, Merleau-Ponty, among others, has argued that because all the great world powers stood against Communism, the Soviet Union had to be more intolerant of divergent opinions than were its enemies, the states in the West. Faced with a continual threat to its political life, the Soviet government had no alternative but to enforce strict discipline. In short, foreign policy considerations were the source of the Great Terror.

Solzhenitsyn's analysis of the Stalinist era dismantles this argument. A government does not make loyal subjects of its people by terrorizing them, he contends. The opposite is likely to occur, and did, at the outbreak of World War II. Many Soviet citizens, especially in the Ukraine, welcomed the German invaders as liberators. These hapless citizens, unable to accept the mindless propaganda fed to them by their government, simply could not believe that those who had been the most advanced people in Europe had suddenly become barbarians. Not until the Nazi SS began to spread its own terror, Solzhenitsyn reports, did the Russian people decide that their own devil was better than a foreign one.[3]

Stalin might have believed he could terrorize people into becoming active participants in "defense of socialism," as his measures were called by the party. That policy can be summarized as the idea that one should hurt one's friends so that they will hurt one's enemies. All governments do this to a certain extent; they compel people to serve in the military and forbid them to desert. Yet the Soviet rulers went far beyond this limited form of compulsion. A rational person could have expected that the policy of terror would make its victims resentful. Is it not reasonable to assume that a citizen might look upon a foreign invader as a friend when his own government has become his worst enemy?

Still, Solzhenitsyn's reasoning about Stalin's motivation may not be conclusive: Stalin might actually have believed that starving people to death, torturing them, and sending them to death camps would engender a type of esprit de corps. Solzhenitsyn believes that Stalin was a tyrant, mad with his own power. More important for Solzhenitsyn, as we shall see, Stalin dedicated himself to a policy of terror as a result of his adherence to Marxist ideology. In any case, Stalin's behavior is difficult to explain in terms of Soviet "encirclement" by threatening foreign nations.

A second thesis in defense of Stalin is that he behaved as he did because he was preparing the nation for war. The prescience of the Great Friend of the Soldiers led him to rid the nation of its soft elements while assigning the strong to key positions.[4] Solzhenitsyn, who can lay a certain claim to being a military historian, given the research he undertook for *August 1914*, argues against this idea. Stalin was totally unprepared for Hitler's attack and for the war that followed; Stalin was fooled by Hitler.[5] Solzhenitsyn claims that in order to demonstrate to Hitler its peaceful aims, Stalin's government "did everything it could to lose the war: destroyed lines of fortification; dismantled tanks and artillery; removed effective generals; and forbade armies to resist."[6] He even accuses Stalin of treason. He explains:

> Treason does not necessarily involve selling out for money. It can include ignorance and carelessness in preparations for war, confusion and cowardice at its very start, the meaningless sacrifice of armies and corps solely for the sake of saving one's own marshal's uniform. Indeed, what more bitter treason is there on the part of a Supreme Commander in Chief?[7]

There is a third explanation for the terror: Stalin's hand was forced by real differences within the party's leadership and by the threat that elements hostile to socialism would seize on any weakness to overthrow the government. In order to maintain stability, this theory goes, Stalin had to keep the warring factions in check. Hence, the terror was necessary to save the regime and, through it, socialism.

The Soviet government probably could not have survived without the use of terror, Solzhenitsyn agrees, but he argues that there is little reason to believe that differences within the party existed or that an organized opposition stood in the wings, ready to seize power. Even taking into account Sergei Kirov's murder and the party purges that followed, the overwhelming majority of those arrested before 1937 had little or nothing to do with politics. Most were ordinary people trying to cope with their daily lives. Casting them as a political opposition, hungry for power, twists the facts. History has been misrepresented, Solzhenitsyn maintains, because the party members who lived through the ordeal were people of letters who could write about their suffering. They encouraged the myth that the terror included only party members, and that they alone took the brunt of Stalin's excesses. Although a far greater number of ordinary people suffered few of them wrote about it.

Solzhenitsyn points out that there were few real differences within the party. Communist leaders, except for Trotsky, applauded everything Stalin did, right up to the time they were thrown into the Gulag themselves. He writes:

> the majority of those in power, up to the very moment of their own arrest, were pitiless in arresting others, obediently destroying their peers in accordance with those same instructions and handed over to retribution any friend or comrade-in-arms of yesterday. And all the big Bolsheviks, who now wear martyrs' halos, managed to be the executioners of other Bolsheviks (not even taking into account how all of them in the first place had been the executioners of non-Communists).[8]

There were some minor divergences of opinion on specific policies, such as the pace of industrialization. There was competition in the party scramble for advancement and power. Yet Solzhenitsyn maintains that on all important matters, the party was remarkably united. All agreed that industrialization had to advance, and that the position of the party had to be unchallenged. No cries of indignation were heard from loyal Communists when other parties were eliminated, when civil liberties were ignored, or when the kulaks (successful peasant farmers) were exterminated.

To make his point, Solzhenitsyn describes the attitudes of party members who found themselves in the Gulag. Almost to a person, they separated themselves from the other prisoners whom they considered, in accordance with the propaganda, enemies of socialism. Generally, they displayed the same contempt and haughty indifference toward the camp community as they had toward the

general population before their incarceration. They accepted without question
the necessity of the Gulag; they objected only to their own arrest. Under conditions that might have shaken the faith of Abraham, they refused to disavow their
earthly saint, Stalin.[9] A few may have shown independence of spirit, but not
many.[10] The true cost of party discipline was the loss of individual points of
view. All their beliefs, everything they had worked for, rested on loyalty to the
party. Where else could they turn for guidance but to the party? The party demanded that they grovel.[11]

The only exception to the Communists' obsequiousness toward Stalin in the
camps was the Trotskyites. They staged a long and difficult hunger strike for
better conditions for political prisoners, especially themselves. Solzhenitsyn
writes of them:

> They conducted a regular underground struggle in the late twenties, deploying
> all their experience as former revolutionaries, except that the GPU arrayed
> against them was not as stupid as the Tsarist Okhrana [internal police]. I do not
> know whether they were prepared for the total annihilation which Stalin had al-
> lotted them, or whether they still thought that it would all end with jokes and
> reconciliations. In any case, they were heroic people.[12]

The Trotskyites failed to bring about better conditions in the Gulag. In truth,
Solzhenitsyn concludes, they had little chance of succeeding against the formidable adversaries they confronted. If they did not jump every time the Great
Leader lifted his finger, the rest of the party did, and in the end, that is why they
were defeated.

But where were all the great revolutionaries who had so staunchly defied
the tsar's jails? Many Communists who had served jail sentences under the old
regime were unprepared for the brutality of the new order. Solzhenitsyn argues
that very few socialists had been tortured by the tsar's police. The revolutionaries were rarely abused by the tsar's prison guards because many of them had
turned against the government. If those engaged in hunger strikes or in some
form of passive resistance to the monarchy were convicted the sentence was an
added three months in prison. The same offense under Communist rule brought
immediate execution. In fact, the number of people who were given the death
penalty under the tsar was minuscule compared to the number shot after the
revolution. Hard labor in tsarist prisons was almost a pleasure outing compared
to life in the Gulag. Prisoners could write manuscripts if they so desired. Lenin
published two of his most important books while in prison and exile. Even
though he refused to do manual labor, he was not punished. Solzhenitsyn, who
had no choice but to toil as a bricklayer and was denied writing implements, had
to memorize thousands of lines of poetry to keep the stories of the Gulag alive
so he could later commit them to paper.

There can be little doubt, Solzhenitsyn claims, that the conditions of the
prisoners under the tsars were far superior to those under what Marxists believed
to be the historically more advanced stage of Communism. First, he explains,

although Russia was not a democracy before 1917, its rulers were influenced by public opinion. For the most part, people were allowed to speak their minds and, to a lesser extent, to write freely. These freedoms had an enormous effect on what the government could do and could not do. Second, the tsars of Russia, autocrats though they were, did not consider their power to be unlimited. They were restrained by a Christian moral code passed down to them for generations. They were prohibited from doing what Marxist ethics allowed. God knows, they probably would have loved to shoot a few revolutionaries, but their moral compunctions acted as a brake on their ruthlessness.

Solzhenitsyn tells the story of Tsar Alexander II putting himself in prison for a few hours in order to experience what those he had sentenced were suffering. Three hours is not much, but can anyone suppose that Stalin—or Lenin, for that matter—ever tried to feel such empathy for his fellows, for his political enemies?[13]

When Communists were released from prison and rehabilitated, they did not protest the brutal treatment that their fellow citizens continued to endure, nor did they object to the insane policies that had led to so many being imprisoned. They went right back to their old jobs and carried them out with the same ruthless vigor as before, all the while extolling the virtues of the Best Friend of the Prison Guards.

Another theory about the Stalinist era maintains that it was merely a throwback to earlier times. Russian culture and history, the argument goes, have conspired to make Russians easy fodder for tyrants. Prestigious scholars such as Richard Pipes and Robert C. Tucker have concluded that Stalinism was a betrayal of Marxism-Leninism and a reversion to tsarism.[14]

Partly in response to the theses of Pipes and Tucker and partly in response to other American scholars and statesmen such as George Kennan, Averell Harriman, and Henry Kissinger, Solzhenitsyn presented his position in an essay in *Foreign Affairs* entitled "How Misconceptions about Russia Are a Threat to America." He argues that any comparison between Stalin and even the worst tsars is misleading. "What model," he asks, "could Stalin have seen in the former tsarist Russia?" He continues:

camps there were none; the very concept was unknown. Long stays in prison were very few in number, and hence political prisoners—with the exception of terrorist extremists, but including all Bolsheviks—were sent off to exile, where they were well fed and cared for at the expense of the state, where no one forced them to work, and whence any one who wished could flee abroad without difficulty. . . . The number . . . of prisoners . . . [was] less than one ten-thousand [that] of [the] Gulag. All criminal investigations were conducted in strict compliance with established law, all trials were open and defendants were legally represented. The total number of secret police operatives . . . was less than presently [early 1970s] available to the KGB of the Ryazan district alone. . . . In the army there was no secret intelligence . . . whatsoever . . . since Nicholas II considered [such] activity an insult to his army. To this we may add the absence of special border troops and fortified frontiers, and the complete freedom to emigrate.[15]

Solzhenitsyn maintains that before the Bolshevik Revolution, although Russia was not as advanced as most Western European nations, it nonetheless had begun an evolution to modernity. He notes Russia could boast of

a flourishing manufacturing industry, rapid growth, and a flexible, decentralized economy; its inhabitants were not constrained in their choice of economic activities . . . the material well-being of peasants was at a level that has never been reached under the Soviet regime. Newspapers were free from preliminary political censorship . . . there was complete cultural freedom, the intelligentsia was not restricted in its activity, religion and philosophical views of every shade were tolerated, and institutions of higher education enjoyed inviolable autonomy.[16]

Most historians believe that pre-1917 Russia was a backward, barbaric nation that could be modernized only through revolution. Solzhenitsyn claims that this image was carried to the West by émigrés who were themselves revolutionaries and whose agenda was to undermine support for the tsar. Their aim was to convince the West, which was undergoing its own social revolution, that the old regime was intolerably cruel and had to be overthrown. They were successful, Solzhenitsyn notes, for the aversion they produced against the tsar has rarely been matched in academic circles by a similar indignation against subsequent Soviet rulers.[17]

No, Stalin was not a throwback to old Russia. He was no modern-day tsar so imbued with Russia's defective national character that he instinctively oppressed his own people.[18] The European left fabricated the concept of a flawed Russian national character, Solzhenitsyn claims, as a means of salvaging something of their socialist ideals once the truth about Stalin became known. Stalin had little connection to the past or to Russia's national heritage—except during World War II, when his people's love of country saved him from military defeat. Solzhenitsyn explains:

Only by some evil figment of the imagination could Stalin be called a "Russian nationalist"—this of the man who exterminated fifteen million of the best Russian peasants, who broke the back of the Russian peasantry, and thereby Russia herself, and who sacrificed the lives of more than thirty million people in the Second World War, which he waged without regard for less profligate means of warfare, without grudging the lives of the people.[19]

PORTRAIT OF STALIN

One view of Stalin that Solzhenitsyn does accept is that, at least in part, the Georgian was a tyrant in the traditional sense of the term, a man who ruled on the basis of his own passions and interests. In his novel *The First Circle*, Solzhenitsyn crafts a stunning sketch of Stalin as dictator. Although Solzhenitsyn's vision of Stalin derives from speculation rather than personal knowledge,[20] Stephen Allaback notes: "There is probably no portrait of the dictator which is especially superior to this one."[21] Solzhenitsyn uses the device of an internal monologue to present the ruler's ideas and motivations. The reader is given to believe that he is privy to Stalin's innermost thoughts and feelings.[22] In fact, Allaback objects that such a method "rarely works with historical personages." It is as if "Stalin is squatting in Solzhenitsyn's hand."[23] Yet it is a testament to Solzhenitsyn's artistry that the method is insightful; it is the most thoughtful examination of the motivations of a tyrant since Xenophon's *Heiro*. The reader should be warned, however, that Solzhenitsyn's depiction of Stalin is fictional. The importance of the characterization rests more on how it reveals the impulses of a dictator than it does on the historical accuracy of the facts.

In Solzhenitsyn's creation, Stalin is presented as a man who has not entered public life exclusively for altruistic reasons. He has used his position to satisfy his desire for female companionship, good wine, and good food, his greatest pleasure.[24] At least he once loved these things before old age overtook him and robbed him of the pleasure of their charms. Along with physical decline, boredom has crept into his life, creating a deep languor known only to those whose every wish is immediately fulfilled.[25]

Stalin trusts only those subordinates who, like him, are self-seeking. He does "not understand the motives . . . of people committed to staying poor, like Bukharin." He even allows Soviet soldiers to plunder Germany at the war's end, a decision based on "what he himself would have felt had he been a soldier."[26]

Whether Stalin's physical appetites ever actually waned can only be surmised. Yet Solzhenitsyn's portrayal is meant to convey a subtle warning to all pleasure seekers of this world. He instructs them, as did Epicurus—whose ideas figure prominently in *The First Circle*—that delights of the body are fleeting at best, and that even people who have the fullest opportunity to satisfy their every desire may find enjoyment slipping from their grasp and their lives empty of meaning.

If Stalin of the *First Circle* has lost some of his sensual desires, his love of praise has certainly not diminished. He enjoys the fact that his name, "filled the world's newspapers, was uttered by thousands of announcers in hundreds of languages, cried out by speakers at the beginning and end of speeches, sung by the tender young voices of Pioneers, and proclaimed by bishops."[27]

But what is the meaning of the cult of personality? Solzhenitsyn suggests that, as with most people who harbor great political ambition, Stalin wants to be remembered for his deeds. He hopes his biography, which, he is comforted to know, is selling in the millions, will perpetuate his achievements.

The elemental, honest words of this book acted on the human heart with serene inevitability. His strategic genius. His wise foresight. His powerful will. His iron will. From 1918 on he had for all practical purposes become Lenin's deputy. (Yes, yes, that was the way it had been.) The Commander of the Revolution found at the front a rout, confusion; Stalin's instructions were the basis for Frunze's plan of operations. (True, true.) It was our great good fortune that in the difficult days of the Great War of the Fatherland we were led by a wise and experienced leader— the Great Stalin. (Indeed, the people were fortunate.) All know the crushing might of Stalin's logic, the crystal clarity of his mind. (Without false modesty, it was all true.) His love of the people. His sensitivity to others. His surprising modesty. (Modesty—yes, that was very true).

He is also proud of his literary achievement, since he knows "his every word straightway belonged to history."[28]

True, the Greatest of Greats had attained many honors in his life, but he wondered whether he should not aspire to one more. After all, "there was nothing bad with the word 'emperor.' It simply meant 'commander,' 'chief.'"[29]

However, a price must be paid for his great accomplishments: He is estranged from ordinary human companionship. When one reaches his level, who is left as an equal? He worries that "there was no one to ask advice from; he alone on earth was a true philosopher. If only someone like Kant were still alive, or Spinoza, even though he was bourgeois. . . . Should he phone Beria? But Beria didn't understand anything at all."[30]

The problem confronting Stalin in his quest to be respected, loved, and even glorified is that the adulation is false. Indeed, he terrorizes people in order to obtain it. His desire for honor derives not from the noble sentiment of magnanimity but from the stronger passion of envy;[31] a fact over which Abakumov muses before entering his chief's office:

> But he knew his Boss. One must never work full force for Stalin, never go all out. He did not tolerate the flat failure to carry out his orders, but he hated thoroughly successful performance because he saw in it a diminution of his own uniqueness. No one but himself must be able to do anything flawlessly. So even when he seemed to be straining in harness, Abakumov was pulling at half-strength—and so was everyone else. Just as King Midas turned everything to gold, Stalin turned everything to mediocrity.[32]

Stalin is especially mindful of all the bearded men who had laughed at him in the hectic year of 1917. None of them would ever mock him again. They could no longer say anything to diminish his glory. Even Lenin's writings had to reflect this. They had been changed, twice. He ordered the founder's works rewritten that Stalin's role in the revolution would be more significant.[33]

Solzhenitsyn's derisive account of the cult of personality makes the serious point that Stalin is caught in a trap of his own making. His insecurity forces him to crave the praise of others. Yet those same anxieties make him fearful of what people might say if they were free to speak their minds. He demands that others tell him what he wants to hear, yet there remains in his mind a nagging doubt; all the cheers ring hollow. Perhaps even the dim recognition has arisen that the respect he so deeply covets can be given only by free people, but is readily feigned by slaves. Underneath the bizarre histrionics that all but deified Stalin during his career, Solzhenitsyn perceives a man desperately trying to gain in quantity what he could never achieve in quality.[34]

An even more dangerous passion that Stalin exhibits in Solzhenitsyn's portrait is not a wholly ignoble one. Like many ambitious people, Stalin wants the world to dance to his tune, but not simply because he loves to wield power. The world, after all, is a very untidy place. People disagree with one another on just about everything. They are always at cross purposes, and often their squabbles become violent and cruel. Stalin's experience has taught him that "the people themselves swarmed with shortcomings."[35] He wants to cure humanity of its maladies, a feat he can accomplish only by making everyone follow a single lead. In this endeavor Stalin can legitimately claim that he has been more successful than any other person in history. Solzhenitsyn writes, "There had been many other remarkable edicts. However, he still found one weak spot in the whole architectonic system, and gradually an important new edict was ripening in his mind. He had everything nailed down for good, all motion stopped, all outlets plugged, all 200 million knew their place—only the collective farm youths were escaping."[36] Of course, he has even greater aspiration: "How would that sound, Emperor of the Planet? Emperor of the Earth!"

Yet, even for the Best Friend of Communist Leaders, things never worked out quite correctly. There "were always people who interfered"—for example, Tito, who "was apparently a British spy." "When one had been removed, someone else always turned up to take his place."[37]

What makes Stalin's grandiose designs particularly vile is the overlay of ideology. Tyrants of old believed that they could bring their countries to heel, but none had so many zealous followers who believed it with them. They were intoxicated by their own self-importance, but in reality they stood alone. They did not have a philosophy of History that vindicated their every act. Marxist ideology compounds the natural megalomania of tyrants by providing a "scientific" justification for all they do.

Solzhenitsyn's glimpse into Stalin's life presents two other traits usually associated with tyrannical rule: cruelty and cunning. From an exchange between Stalin and Abakumov in *The First Circle*, the reader learns that

> Stalin was terrifying because one mistake in his presence could be that one mistake in life which would set off an explosion, irreversible in effect. Stalin was terrifying because he did not listen to excuses, made no accusations; his yellow tiger eyes simply brightened balefully, his lower lids closed up a bit—and there, inside him, sentence had been passed, and the condemned man didn't know: he left in peace, was arrested that night, and shot by morning.
>
> The silence and that squint of the lower lids were the worst of all. If Stalin threw something heavy or sharp at you, if he stamped on your foot, spat on you, or blew a burning coal from his pipe in your face, that anger was not the ultimate anger, that anger passed. If Stalin was crude and cursed, even using the worst profanity, Abakumov rejoiced: it meant that the Boss still hoped to straighten him out and go on working with him.[38]

Furthermore, Stalin's cruelty has spread downward, engulfing the entire society. Just as one real Stalin rules the nation, many little Stalins govern its parts.[39]

A tyrant is not in power long if he lacks cunning. Stalin shrewdly destroyed all those who might have challenged his supremacy. They were "choked, shot, ground into manure in the camps, poisoned, burned, killed in automobile accidents or by their own hands."[40]

Solzhenitsyn reports as a fact in *The Gulag Archipelago* that a key element of Stalin's success was his ability to manipulate people. "Therein lay his dark and special talent, his main psychological bent and his life's achievement: to see people's weaknesses on the lowest plane of being."[41] He maneuvered the members of the Politburo into signing the death warrants of their fallen colleagues. They all knew they were sending innocent people to their graves, but they went along out of fear. As, one by one, their own turns came, they had no grounds for defense. They could not plead innocence. Those who defend lawlessness, after all, should not be surprised when lawlessness overwhelms them.[42]

Solzhenitsyn's Stalin seems to have learned Niccolò Machiavelli's lesson. Stalin knows the "ancient key to popularity: first to encourage the executioners and then, in good time, to repudiate their immoderate zeal. He had done this many times and always successfully."[43]

No picture of a tyrant is complete without an examination of the driving force of his life: fear. Stalin's fear borders on paranoia. It began in 1937, at "the twentieth anniversary of the Revolution, when there was so much reinterpretation of history." Solzhenitsyn writes:

> He had decided to look over the museum exhibits to be sure they hadn't got something wrong. In one of the halls . . . he had seen as he entered two large portraits high on the opposite wall. The faces of Zhelyabov and Perovskaya were open, fearless, and they cried out to all who entered: "Kill the tyrant!"
>
> Stalin, struck by their twin stares as by two shots, drew back, wheezed, coughed. His finger shook, pointing at the portraits. They were removed immediately. . . . From that very day, Stalin had ordered shelters and apartments to be built for him in various places. He lost his taste for dense city surroundings, and settled in this house in the suburbs, this low-ceilinged night office near the duty room of his personal guard. And the more people's lives he took, the more he was oppressed by constant terror for his own.[44]

Only the secret police discovery of plots can quell Stalin's foreboding. No effort is spared in unearthing "terrorism" aimed at "his priceless person." But what if no conspiracies exist? The secret police must show its vigilance; thus it fabricates intrigues. The dissatisfied must be arrested and the unhappy controlled. But since knowledge of so much unrest strikes greater fear into the tyrant's heart, malcontents must be thwarted before their plans "reach the stage of actual preparation." Abakumov reassures his chief, "We catch them at the moment of inception, of intention."[45] In the deadly game Abakumov plays with the Boss, he must convince the aging despot that his apprehensions are not merely cowardice (yes, conspiracies do exist), without frightening him completely (we work tirelessly to expose them). But no head of state security can ever accomplish such a feat.

Solzhenitsyn's scathing attack on Stalin's tyrannical life concludes with a not-so-subtle warning to would-be tyrants. Their lives could become as miserable as did Stalin's just before his death: "Growing old like a dog. An old age without friends. An old age without love. An old age without faith. An old age without desire."[46]

STALIN AND MARXISM-LENINISM

Solzhenitsyn accepts the fact that Stalin's peculiar personality played a part in the terror, but he rejects the idea that the "cult of personality" was the sole, or even the most important, reason why Stalin acted as he did. After all, Stalin justified his massive upheaval of society as the price of rapid industrialization.

The clearest expression of the rapid industrialization doctrine is found in Arthur Koestler's novel *Darkness at Noon*. Koestler argues that Russia before the revolution was a backward, almost feudal society. The people, primitive in their folkways, were ill-prepared for the industrial age. In order to modernize such a country, the fabric of society had to be ripped apart and rewoven anew. Not only did the economy have to be overhauled but the psychological makeup of the people had to be transformed. Peasants, the vast majority of the population, needed to learn the routines of the technological era.

Proponents of this view argue that such massive change entails hardship. Measured against the suffering of, say, the English peasants of the seventeenth century, who were forced off their land and into factories by market capitalism, the Russian peasants fared no worse. The real difference had to do with time. What took a century in Great Britain was accomplished during the first Five-Year Plan in the Soviet Union. In any case, the argument concludes, Russian society, including the peasantry, was better off, materially and otherwise, after the transformation.[47]

Solzhenitsyn accepts that the goal of industrialization motivated Stalin, but he maintains that the Soviet leader could have pursued this policy in a far more humane manner. Instead, Stalin promoted the ideologically correct—but totally inefficient—method of forced collectivization. To accomplish his ends, the kulaks had to be destroyed. Party propaganda painted them as rich, fat peasants who had more land than they could use and who exploited others into cultivating it. They were "bloodsuckers" on the socialist community, and it was the duty of the Great Leader to eliminate them.[48]

Is there not another way of looking at these people? It is impossible to see them as industrious, skilled farmers, who, when given the opportunity to improve themselves, did just that? If some gained a measure of success greater than others, that did not necessarily make them mercenary, it meant only that they were good at what they did. Once again, the practical effect of Marxist equality was to punish the virtue of hard work and to reward the unproductive and the unprepared.[49]

Those peasants not forced into the camps were made to join the kolkhoz, communal farms. The "community" of the kolkhoz was not built on the traditional communal life of the village. Instead, people were more or less thrown together, their former lives wrenched from them. In the name of progress, they were given internal passports that made it all but impossible for them to leave their place of work. When, in the dark days before socialism, people were tied to the land, the political and economic system was called serfdom. Living on a kolkhoz was probably less attractive than traditional serfdom, since conditions were not ameliorated by a rich local and religious culture, extending back for generations. At least there was one noticeable improvement: Serfdom had a new name.[50]

Industrialization was not solely the burden of the peasants, of course. The entire society was made to bear its weight. Solzhenitsyn does not offer the typical explanation of how industrialization was accomplished—the party seized excess capital from the population and used it to underwrite industrial projects. Rather, he argues that the real contribution of the population was its sweat—or in this case blood—equity. Could Russia have developed into a modern industrial economy at the pace the party demanded without the use of forced labor? From a certain perspective, the camps were an ideal solution to an almost intractable problem. They could provide a ready source of labor with little cost and an absolute minimum outlay of resources, in economic terms with few opportunity costs. Work was obtained by a method learned from the Eskimos: A fish on a pole dangled before a running dog team. Continually driven by hunger, the zeks were compelled to labor for their meager ration of food.[51]

But camps had a more insidious purpose, Solzhenitsyn reports. Dirty, distasteful, and backbreaking labor could be extracted from workers without the enormous additional expense of providing them with a social infrastructure. He explains:

> The reason why the camps proved economically profitable had been foreseen as far back as Thomas More, the great-grandfather of socialism, in his Utopia. The labor of the zeks was needed for degrading and particularly heavy work, which no one under socialism would perform. For work in remote and primitive localities where it would not be possible to construct housing, schools, hospitals, and stores for many years to come. For work with pick and spade—in the flowering of the twentieth century. For erection of the great construction projects of socialism, when economic means for them did not yet exist.[52]

Gulag economics did have its costs, however. Solzhenitsyn appraises the price tag of the Belomar (White Sea) Canal at a quarter of a million lives. A pet project of Stalin, the canal was built mostly by hand, in such haste that it was too shallow to transport any but the lightest ships. In effect, a quarter million prisoner-laborers' lives were sacrificed for nothing.[53]

But the zeks built useful things.[54] Indeed, they succeeded in building a socialist economy, or at least they were instrumental in industrializing Russia for their Communist masters. In doing so, Solzhenitsyn insists, they demonstrated that the camps were the main prop of the regime.[55] After all, if rapid industrialization was necessary to fulfill the principles of the party, and the slave labor of the Gulag built the greater part of that industry, what other conclusion is possible?

Granting, as Solzhenitsyn does, that the terror was successful in bringing modernization, one is led to raise further questions: Why was modernization needed at all? More precisely, why was industrialization so dear to Stalin that it had to be accomplished immediately? The answer to this question, Solzhenitsyn suggests, cannot be found by looking solely at Stalin's personal motives of self-aggrandizement. Rather, the answer lies in the ideology that put so much stress on economic development.

In almost all the policies he adopted, Stalin was guided by the ideas of Marxism-Leninism. His actions rarely deviated from tenets of that doctrine. Solzhenitsyn states,

> We must justifiably wonder whether "Stalinism" is in fact a distinctive phenomenon. Did it ever exist: Stalin himself never tried to establish any distinctive doctrine . . . nor any distinctive political system of his own. All Stalin's present-day admirers . . . insist that he was a faithful Leninist and never in any matter of consequence diverged from Lenin.[56]

There was one important point of departure that Stalin made from the Progressive Doctrine. As Solzhenitsyn's portrait makes clear, Stalin was a tyrant and, seeking personal aggrandizement, he raised his own importance by lowering that of the party. Solzhenitsyn explains:

> Stalin did perhaps manifestly depart from Lenin in one respect (though he was only following the general law of revolutions): in the ruthless treatment of his own party, which began in 1924 and rose to a climax in 1935. Can this be the decisive difference, the distinguishing mark which tells our present-day progressive historians that "Stalinism" belongs in the exclusive list of anti-human ideologies, whereas its maternal ideology does not?[57]

Despite this one difference Solzhenitsyn concludes that a

> close study of modern history shows that there never was any such thing as Stalinism (either as a doctrine, or as a path of national life, or as a state system), and official circles in our country, as well as the Chinese [Maoist] leaders, have every right to insist on this. Stalin was a very consistent and faithful—if also very untalented—heir to the spirit of Lenin's teaching.[58]

Finally, Solzhenitsyn maintains, no serious adherent of the Progressive Doctrine can subscribe to the idea that "Stalinism" was an independent variable that prompted historical change or that all the faults of the Soviet government can be traced to the cult of personality. There are two reasons for this. First, if Stalin is to blame for the terror, then it must be admitted that human volition directs history. To grant that a single individual, even a dictator, has free choice undermines the principle of historical necessity, the core of Marx's argument. Second, if Stalin engineered modernization in the Soviet Union, then it was he, and not the law of economic development, who is responsible for the movement of history. In either case, Marx's theory of history is wrong, and socialism is neither inevitable nor, for that matter, choice worthy.

If a serious Marxist adopts the concept of "Stalinism," Solzhenitsyn reasons, he is logically driven to give up the theoretical underpinnings of Marxism. Yet the alternative is surely no more attractive. To embrace Marx's historical determinism, one is compelled to admit that History's plan was at work in all the evil deeds, all the suffering, and all the terror. It was all necessary and happened just the way it was supposed to in order to bring about a higher stage of economic development."[59]

We can sum up Solzhenitsyn's position as follows: He blames some of the terror on the peculiar personality of Stalin and on the wily Georgian's quest for personal aggrandizement. Yet, as we shall see in what follows, Stalin gained justification for his actions from the historical precedents set down during the reign of Lenin. And, in the most important respect, Stalin was led to behave as he did because he was a follower of the principles of Marx.

Notes

1. Maurice Merleau-Ponty, *Humanism and Terror*, trans. John O'Neill (Boston: Beacon Press, 1969), 1-24, 70.

2. *Gulag II*, 330.

3. *Gulag I*, 237-76; *Gulag III*, 22-28.

4. Stalin's nicknames abound. Besides *pakham*—translated as plow man in *The First Circle*—Solzhenitsyn gives Stalin many titles, but not so many as were accorded him during his life. Solzhenitsyn's list includes: Leader of Nations, Father of Western and Eastern People, Father of Peoples, Best Friend of Communications Workers, Greatest Genius of Geniuses, Great Generalissimo, Most Brilliant Strategist of All Times and People, Best Friend of Counter-Intelligence Operatives, Most Humane Statesman, and so forth. It is obvious that Solzhenitsyn wants his readers to recall just how far the idolization of Stalin had gone.

5. *First Circle*, 122.

6. *Gulag I*, 240.

7. Ibid., 253n. After the invasion and after most of European Russia had been conquered, Stalin recovered and pursued the war vigorously, Solzhenitsyn acknowledges.

8. Ibid., 129. See also Stephen Carter, *Politics of Solzhenitsyn*, 26, 31. Carter states: "Solzhenitsyn makes the point that those who defend illegality, even if their reasoning is based on impeccable Marxist principles, cannot expect legal principles themselves. . . . [Since] justice and legality are indivisible, those who participate in injustice have no claim on justice themselves."

9. *Gulag II*, 322-52. Again one must raise the question of whether Stalin believed there to be serious splits within the party. Solzhenitsyn insists that there was no objective evidence of resistance to Stalin. Any opposition that might have existed was in Stalin's imagination. As we shall see, Solzhenitsyn's depiction of Stalin endeavors to show that Stalin was paranoid.

10. Solzhenitsyn's memoirs are not kind to Communists imprisoned in the camps. Many broke immediately. They humbled themselves before their interrogators, admitted to crimes they had not committed, and implicated friends and associates in their fictitious crimes. In the camps they became stoolies, and, in trustee jobs, they stole food from the rations of others. See *Gulag I*, 129-32, 201; *Gulag II*, 346, 351.

11. Solzhenitsyn takes the same position as Arthur Koestler in *Darkness at Noon*, trans. Daphne Hardy (New York: Bantam, 1966); see *Gulag I*, 409. See also *Gulag I*, 405-9, 412, 418, 477.

12. *Gulag II*, 317-18.

13. *Gulag I*, 6, 106, 116, 131-33, 145, 190n, 191, 226, 242, 352, 409, 432-35, 440, 460, 462, 465-67, 500; *Gulag II*, 203-4, 222-23, 317, 339n; *Gulag III*, 36, 62, 77, 80-82, 110, 329, 384, 397, 514, 635; *Oak*, 1-2; *Zurich*, 73.

14. Richard Pipes, *Russia under the Old Regime* (New York: Charles Scribner's Sons, 1974); Robert C. Tucker, "Stalin, the Last Bolshevik," *New York Times*, 21 December 1979, 35.

15. Aleksandr Solzhenitsyn, "How Misconceptions about Russia Are a Threat to America," *Foreign Affairs* 8 (Spring 1980): 797-834; reprinted as *The Mortal Danger*, trans. Michael Nicholson and Alexis Klimoff (New York: Harper & Row, 1980), 14-15 (hereafter cited as *Mortal*).

16. Ibid., 15-16. See also James Y. Simms, "The Crisis in Russian Agriculture at the End of the Nineteenth Century: A Different View," *Slavic Review* 36 (September 1977): 377-93.

17. *Mortal*, 16. Two well-researched works on this topic seem to bear out Solzhenitsyn's own research: W. Bruce Lincoln, *Passage through Armageddon: The Russians in War, 1914-1918* (New York: Simon & Schuster, 1987); Mikhail Heller and Aleksandr Nekrich, *Utopia in Power: The History of the Soviet Union from 1917 to the Present* (New York: Summit, 1987).

18. He was Georgian.

19. *Mortal*, 14. Solzhenitsyn's own connection to Russian nationalism has been an important topic of controversy among his critics. Some suggest that he is a Slavophile. See the essay by Ronald Berman, "Through Western Eyes," in Berman, *Solzhenitsyn at Harvard*. Berman seems to argue that Solzhenitsyn's defense of the old regime is, in reality, a call for a return to tsarism, or rather, to a Russian theocracy. In other words, Solzhenitsyn has no standard of judgment other than that supplied him by Russian tradition.

One could remark that love of one's country—its people and culture—was not always perceived as an ignoble sentiment. In any case, Solzhenitsyn never once calls for a return to the old regime or for the founding of a theocracy. He merely compares the tsarist government to the one that came after it. If the facts prove life to have been superior before the revolution, that does not make Solzhenitsyn a Slavophile. Solzhenitsyn is well aware of the defects of autocracy. See *August 1914*; *Gulag III*, 15. He even says that old Russia experienced "Asiatic Slavery." *Gulag II*, 152, 154. Yet he is still able to judge one government superior, the other inferior, one generally good, the other mostly bad. The ability to make such decisions is not rooted in an attachment to Mother Russia, but rests on the human capacity to make rational valuations based on a careful examination of the empirical evidence.

20. *Oak*, 78. In order to distinguish Solzhenitsyn's fictional account from the facts of Stalin's rule as Solzhenitsyn represents them, the present tense is used in this section when referring to Solzhenitsyn's portrait of Stalin in *The First Circle*.

21. Stephen Allaback, *Aleksandr Solzhenitsyn* (New York: Taplinger Publishing, 1978), 86.

22. Andrej Kodjak, *Aleksandr Solzhenitsyn* (Boston: G. K. Hall, 1978), 8.

23. Allaback, *Aleksandr Solzhenitsyn*, 86.

24. *First Circle*, 100, 122. Xenophon's *Heiro*, or *On Tyranny*, explains the desires of tyrants in much the same way.

25. Ibid., 102. On his birthday, "the works of thousands upon thousands of master craftsmen, the finest gifts of the earth stood, lay, and hung before him. But there, too, he felt that same indifference, that same fading interest. He quickly became bored."

26. Ibid., 121, 118.

27. Ibid., 99.

28. Ibid., 100, 120.

29. Ibid., 130.

30. Ibid., 112.

31. Aristotle, *Nichmachean Ethics*, trans. J. A. K. Thompson (Middlesex, England: Penguin Books, 1955), book 2, chapter 3.

32. *First Circle*, 123.

33. Ibid., 104, 106.

34. Ibid., 102.

35. Ibid., 103.

36. Ibid., 109.

37. Ibid., 107, 104.

38. Ibid., 117.

39. *Gulag III*, 431.

40. *First Circle*, 113.

41. *Gulag I*, 412.

42. *Gulag II*, 332; see also Carter, *Politics of Solzhenitsyn*, 26, 31.

43. *First Circle*, 129.

44. Ibid., 124-25.

45. Ibid., 126.

46. Ibid., 134.

47. Koestler, *Darkness at Noon*. See also Barrington Moore, *The Social Origins of Dictatorship and Democracy* (Boston: Beacon Press, 1966).

48. *Gulag III*, 353.

49. Ibid., 350-68.

50. Solzhenitsyn makes a great deal of the destruction of the peasant way of life, its language, its customs, and, most peculiar of all, its animals. For example, he points out that the party was "pitiless to horses. . . because horses were a kulaks' animal and also destined to die." By eliminating the farmers' means of production, the party was successful in changing the way farmers lived. For one thing, they became dependent on industrialization, particularly as it applied to tractor factories.

Not only were horses killed, but dogs were also singled out for extermination. They were rounded up, hauled off, or shot on the spot, Solzhenitsyn explains, as a means of attacking the individuality of their masters. Dogs, unlike Stalin, never lose sight of a most ancient verity of social life: one should help one's friends and hurt one's enemies. No matter how much propaganda the party broadcast over the radio or printed in the newspapers, dogs could not be convinced that their masters had become enemies of the people, to be dragged off in the middle of the night by strangers. Because dogs were beyond the control of the state, they had to be eliminated.

Solzhenitsyn implies that the party's loathing for these pets originated in Marxist principles. The Progressive Doctrine states that man becomes human through labor. His relationship to nature is instrumental and exploitive. If all life is bound up in productive forces, surely animals are too. They are useful or harmful according to whether they are necessary to a certain historical epoch.

If one makes an animal a pet, however, one quickly learns, mostly from the animal, that although our species may be the superior in intelligence, we are only one of its parts—the so-called chain of being. Friendship between man and beast teaches us that our relationship with nature need not always be exploitive, but may be communal. Perhaps this is reading too much into it, but Solzhenitsyn's point seems to be that Marx had it wrong from the start. *Gulag II*, 429-30n.

Marx writes, "Where a relationship does exist, it exists for me. The animal has no 'relationship' with anything, no relations at all. Its relations to others do not exist as relations. Consciousness is thus from the very beginning a social product and will remain so long as men exist." Lloyd Easton and Kurt Guddat, eds. and trans., *Writings of the Young Marx on Philosophy and History* (Garden City, N.Y.: Doubleday, 1976), 422 (hereafter cited as *Writings of the Young Marx*); see also 293, 308. For a good discussion of the issue, see Oliver Clement, The *Spirit of Solzhenitsyn*, trans. Sarah Fawcett and Paul Burns (London: Search Press Ltd., 1976), 104-5.

51. *Gulag II*, 78.

52. Ibid., 578-79.

53. Ibid., 102.

54. Ibid., 591-93 for a partial list.

55. Ibid., 122, 198, 577-78; *Gulag III*, 394, 493, 505.

56. *Rubble*, 8-9. Solzhenitsyn comments: "Was not the land given to the peasants during the revolution only to be taken into state ownership soon afterward? . . . Were not the factories promised to the workers, but brought under central administration in a matter of weeks? When did the trade unions begin to serve not the masses but the state? . . . What of the concentration camps (1918-1921)? . . . None of this was Stalin . . . [and even rapid industrialization] . . . was not his invention." *Gulag I*, 613n.

57. *Rubble*, 9-10. Whether Lenin changed the ideas of Marx will be considered in the next chapter.

58. Ibid., 10. Of his dawning personal awareness that Stalin alone was not the cause of the Soviet Union's problems, Solzhenitsyn explains, "In my pre-prison and prison years I, too, had long ago come to the conclusion that Stalin had set the course of the Soviet state. But then Stalin died quietly—and did the ship of state change course very noticeably? [A]ll followed the beaten path exactly as it had been signposted, step by step." Solzhenitsyn recognizes elsewhere that the government did change after Stalin's demise. *Gulag III*, 445.

59. Aleksandr Solzhenitsyn, "Solzhenitsyn Speaks Out," trans. Albert and Tanya Schmidt, *National Review* 27 (6 June 1975): 606.

CHAPTER 3

SOLZHENITSYN'S LENIN

According to Solzhenitsyn the causes of the terror cannot be adequately grasped by examining its excesses; a full understanding is possible only by studying its roots, by looking at the contribution of Vladimir Lenin.

LENIN'S RISE TO POWER

Lenin is often portrayed as the long-suffering revolutionary whose prescience, determination, and tactical genius allowed him to consolidate the disparate elements of the Russian Revolution into a spectacular Bolshevik victory. Solzhenitsyn does not fully share this view of his former hero. In fact, his controversial depiction of the great revolutionary differs markedly from almost every other. He claims that the true history of Lenin has been "carefully concealed" and that actual events "have received little attention."[1] Solzhenitsyn's characterization rests on "forty years" of "working on the image of Lenin." Over those years, he "gathered every grain of information . . . every detail" of Lenin's life so as "to recreate him alive, as he was."[2]

To begin, according to Solzhenitsyn, Lenin was not long-suffering. He lived the petit bourgeois existence of an émigré. He did not work, except to labor for the revolution. He lived on the good graces of his family and on contributions given to the party, often from guilt-ridden industrialists. Even his arrest and exile were not terribly onerous. His sentence was light—mere exile.[3] He was not forced to work, and, with his mother's help, he was able to "afford a balanced diet." The solitude made it possible for him to write two political tracts.[4]

Lenin was also not particularly prescient. Solzhenitsyn maintains that Lenin was surprised when World War I broke out and even more astonished when a rebellion began in his own country.[5]

No one can doubt Lenin's persistence, or the fact that he was a good tactician.[6] Solzhenitsyn even claims to have imitated his onetime idol during his own struggles with Soviet authorities.[7] Yet, the author of *Lenin in Zurich* does not subscribe to the theory that Lenin's influence was crucial in initiating the revolution. On the eve of the war in 1914, Solzhenitsyn claims, Lenin was fighting indecisive battles against Swiss socialists for leadership of the international socialist movement. At times, Solzhenitsyn writes, "fewer than a score, mostly those who evaded the draft" came to Lenin's meetings. Lenin's organization in Switzerland consisted of eight people. Once Lenin called a meeting to which no one at all showed up. Between 1905 and the outbreak of World War I while Lenin was living in Zurich, revolutionary fervor cooled in Russia. After 1905 his party had "shriveled to nothing." The workers had "swarmed into legal bodies." Trade unions "sapped the underground of its vitality."[8]

Given his inability to shape world events from his home in Switzerland, it is little wonder that Lenin greeted World War I with such enthusiasm. Publicly he paid lip service to the socialist line opposing all wars, but in reality he knew that a major conflict presented socialists with a remarkable opportunity to advance their cause. His agenda was to convert the war into a civil war.[9]

When one thinks of the Russian Revolution, the usual image that comes to mind is of Lenin and the Bolsheviks being swept into power in the wake of a popular uprising. In reality, Solzhenitsyn argues, the revolution began without any positive ideals or goals. It was not initiated *for* anything, but *against* Russia's catastrophic losses during the war. Millions of Russian soldiers died needlessly, he asserts, because "Nicholas II prolonged senseless war with Wilhelm instead of saving his country by concluding a separate peace."[10]

Despite the terrible strain on his nation, the tsar felt honor bound to uphold his commitment to Russia's allies. Solzhenitsyn explains:

> Nicholas II, in fact, lost his throne because he was too loyal to England and France, too loyal to that senseless war of which Russia had not the slightest need; he allowed himself to be drawn into that atmosphere of militarist madness which reigned in liberal circles at the time. And these liberal circles were anxious to get their Western allies out of trouble at the expense of the lives of Russian peasants—they were afraid of getting a low rating from the Allies.[11]

The tsar's momentous decision to pursue the war might not have been so costly, Solzhenitsyn reasons, if Russia had been better prepared for conflict. But during the years of relative peace prior to World War I, the officer corps had become heavy with careerists who used their bureaucratic skills to gain promotion, but who understood little about leading men into battle. Unlike their German counterparts, Russia's military leaders had not studied the latest tactics and strategies of warfare. When conflict came, they were consistently outmaneuvered.

Along with the ineptitude of its military leadership, Solzhenitsyn argues that Russia's technological backwardness contributed to its defeat. The reader of *August 1914*, Solzhenitsyn's account of General Alexander Samsonov's disastrous rout at the hands of the Germans—a cataclysm from which Russia never recovered—is tempted to say that the tsar's forces had lost the war before the first shot was fired. They lost because Nicholas would not, or—given the plight of the economy—could not compete in the European arms race.[12] When his troops engaged in modern warfare without modern equipment, they were slaughtered. To end the useless massacre, they rebelled, and in doing so, initiated an even worse calamity.[13] Comparing Solzhenitsyn's *August 1914* to General N. M. Golovin's *The Russian Campaign of 1914*, Dorothy Atkins sums up Russia's weaknesses in its first decisive engagement as follows:

> Both authors stress the blunder made by the Russian military command at the conference table with France before the war: Acceptance of a commitment to begin an offensive on the 15th day of mobilization. Both criticize the decision to conduct offensive operations simultaneously on two fronts. Both convey a dismal impression of military leadership where seniority and favoritism stifled talent and initiative. Both complain of general unpreparedness, of technical inadequacies that compounded problems of transport, communication and supply. Both point to the difficulties faced . . . by [commanders] compelled to carry out plans they disapproved with staffs they had not chosen.[14]

A second widely accepted reason for the Bolshevik rise to power was the aid given to its leaders by the German high command. Solzhenitsyn maintains that this assistance was far more extensive than Lenin's renowned train ride through Germany under the wary eye of the German army. Solzhenitsyn argues that the Bolsheviks were supported financially and given indirect access to the Germans by the shadowy figure Alexander Parvus (an alias for Alexander Helphand). With Leon Trotsky, Parvus had taken a leading role in the 1905 revolt in Russia.[15] By 1914, he had become an enormously wealthy German citizen and an agent of the German high command. True, Lenin resisted Parvus's more outlandish schemes, partly out of "socialist honor" and partly because he feared the forceful Parvus might emerge as the leader of the revolution.[16] Yet, as Solzhenitsyn documents, on the theory that an enemy of my enemy is my friend, the Germans sent aid to Russian radicals and, thanks to Parvus, much of the subsidy found its way into Bolshevik hands.[17]

A less immediate, although perhaps more significant, reason the Bolsheviks so easily gained power, Solzhenitsyn reasons, was that the old regime had lost its credibility. The tsar had fallen into disfavor after a revolt in 1905 had been put down by a massacre at St. Petersburg, and he had never regained the broad approval he had once enjoyed. As his personal popularity slipped, so did the legitimacy of his government. "The youth of well-to-do families" took to disobeying the laws, Solzhenitsyn explains, and "began to consider a prison term an honor."[18] Few of those engaged in revolutionary activities were ever caught, and even fewer actually went to prison. The most common punishment was internal exile, from which revolutionaries easily escaped to Europe or even back to their own homes. With the sanctions behind the laws lost, or at least seriously undermined, confidence in the regime slipped even lower.

For Solzhenitsyn, Tsar Nicholas was far less an oppressor than popular history has made him out to be. Usually he is depicted as a ruthless, authoritarian monarch so intent on keeping power that he employed any means, even the dreaded secret police, to achieve his ends. Solzhenitsyn claims that this distorted picture of the Russian autocrat was carried to the West by intellectuals, who, although they were fleeing Bolshevik violence, had a score to settle with the tsar. Rather than being ruthless, Solzhenitsyn concludes, the tsar's government, for the most part, was merely inept.[19]

The decline of the Orthodox Church further eroded public confidence in the old regime. The church provided a justification for the social order and a spiritual basis on which the inequalities within Russian society could be accepted. Its message lifted believers beyond the cares of improving their lot in this life. Its teachings made them more concerned with salvation of their souls than with bodily needs. People dedicated to such ideals are notoriously bad revolutionaries. However, "on the eve of the revolution," Solzhenitsyn writes, "the Church . . . was utterly decrepit and demoralized."[20] With their religious faith shaken, many Russians turned to politics and revolution, believing that social transformation would change their lives for the better.

While the spiritual basis of tsarism withered, its intellectual support disappeared. In his essay on the relationship between the intelligentsia (both prerevolutionary and postrevolutionary) and society, translated as the "Smatterers," Solzhenitsyn contends that almost the entire educated class deliberately set out to undermine the stability of their society before the revolution. He defends this thesis by characterizing the intelligentsia using a witticism of G. Fedotov: They were a group of people "united by the idealism of their aims and the unsoundness of their ideals." In a more serious vein he cites Vladimir I. Dal, the author of a Russian dictionary and Solzhenitsyn's authority on many terms, who defined the intelligentsia as "the educated, intellectually developed part of the population." But Dal added, "We have no word [for] moral education," which "educates both mind and heart."[21]

Although the old intelligentsia embodied many virtues, according to Solzhenitsyn, it was led to "revolutionary humanism" by its belief in the possibility of the "immediate reform" of society.[22] It disdained moderation and fanatically sought to remake the world according to abstract notions of egalitarian justice. Leftist ideas became particularly popular among the intelligentsia because in them was found the hope of becoming part of "the Great Natural Order," a quest necessitated by the intelligentsia's all but obligatory atheism.[23] Indeed, leftist principles and atheism were closely allied. Christianity, which had traditionally provided an explanation of the purpose of life, encouraged people to concentrate not on social reform but on their own personal salvation. Christian ideas were anathema to the left because they led people to accept the edicts of any government, no matter how backward, as long as it allowed them to practice their beliefs. Reacting to this supine passivity, the left abandoned religion entirely; for them social reform became the purpose of human existence.

In their rush to transform the world, Solzhenitsyn explains, Russian intellectuals lost sight of the limits of political reform. With little or no knowledge of Russian history or tradition, they deified the people, blaming all their faults on the state and proclaiming that under a new order their sorrows would vanish. With virtually no experience in public affairs, intellectuals insisted that abstract notions of right could be applied directly to society, replacing age-old customs and institutions. Perhaps most important, intellectuals allowed their "love of egalitarian justice, the social good and material well-being of the people" to paralyze its "love and interest in the truth."[24] It is ironic, comments Solzhenitsyn, that the intellectual class should throw themselves into a movement whose collective nature denied their individual creativity. In doing so, he asks, were not intellectuals relinquishing the very thing that gave their lives meaning?[25]

Solzhenitsyn even criticizes the great novelist Leo Tolstoy's later writings, which certainly were not irreligious, for helping to bring about the revolution. Although Tolstoy's ideas about the merits of the simple life, nonresistance to evil, and the universal brotherhood of mankind were never put into practice in Russian life, Solzhenitsyn argues that they molded more than one generation's notions of ethics and politics.

Stated briefly, Tolstoy's belief was that human beings do not and cannot control history, and that love of fellow human beings is people's best hope for salvation. The two propositions are connected, for if one cannot control history, one need not worry about the consequences of his actions. There is no reason to be prudent since events will run their course no matter what. Thus one has a right and an obligation to obey the commandment to love his neighbor and not take violent actions against other human beings, even to resist their evil deeds.[26]

However, if, as Solzhenitsyn suggests, human beings *can* influence the course of history, then the love commandment is politically foolish. It results in the acquiescence of moral people, who embrace nonviolence, to the dominance of evil people. Allowing evil to have its way surely cannot be the goal of moral principles. Hence, prudent opposition to evil must not be abandoned.[27]

Solzhenitsyn acknowledges that Tolstoy's views were noble in theory. But in practice they encouraged people to accept fate, which may have encouraged some in prominent military circles not to prepare adequately for war. Tolstoy's teachings also created unrealistic expectations for the possibility of social reform, bordering on perfectionism and self-interested appropriation of pacifist ideals to avoid military service, that is, cowardice.[28] Clearly, Solzhenitsyn concludes, it is imprudent to propose ideas that could bring about defeat in war, with all the dire consequences that it entails. It is also unwise to promote moral practices that can easily be used as a justification for saving one's own skin.[29]

The most expansive reason Solzhenitsyn offers for the downfall of tsarism is that history seems to be moving toward greater and greater forms of equality and away from associations resting on a complex social hierarchy. The autocracy and class structures of the old regime depended for their stability on beliefs about an individual's relationship to society and the place of the human race in the whole of the created universe. For various reasons (some of which will be discussed later) those beliefs had been largely discredited by 1917 to be replaced by a burning passion for equality. The institutions of tsarism, born of an aristocratic age and being no match for the new egalitarian principles, were easily swept aside. Indeed, Solzhenitsyn wonders whether any social structure, except one supported by force, could have withstood the desire for equality. All social institutions, not just those of feudal Russia, depend on some form of hierarchy; thus, all have come under attack because of their inequities. Certainly Lenin was aware of the temper of his times; he always attacked his political adversaries from the left.[30]

These claims about the rise of the yearning for equality seem, at first glance, to contradict Solzhenitsyn's argument about the possibility that the human race controls history. After all, how much choice can there be if history is rushing ever onward in the direction of greater forms of equality? On this point, Solzhenitsyn's views are similar to those of Alexis de Tocqueville and unlike those of Marx.[31] For both Solzhenitsyn and Tocqueville the movement of history toward social equality is inexorable. Yet for both, the real issue is what form that equality will take in the future. Will people be free and equal or will they become equally slaves? Will equality provide the opportunity for human excellence to develop, or will it smother talent and ambition, reducing humanity to its lowest common level? In spite of the movement of history (one is tempted to say, because of the movement of history) mankind is faced with a choice. Depending on what decision is made, both Solzhenitsyn and Tocqueville make clear, either liberty or servitude will prevail.[32]

For Solzhenitsyn, one of the most important reasons the Bolsheviks were able to seize power was the ineffectiveness of all the moderate political parties. These parties were controlled by liberal intelligentsia who had succeeded in shaking the old order enough to make it collapse but were unprepared to govern effectively when given the chance. The intelligentsia's ideals were impractical, their reforms unworkable, and, most important, their notions about how to rule naive. He writes of their inexperience:

> The intelligentsia proved incapable of taking action, quailed, and was lost in confusion; its party leaders readily abdicated the power and leadership which had seemed so desirable from a distance; and power, like a ball of fire, was tossed from hand to hand until it came into hands which caught it and were sufficiently hardened to withstand its white heat (they also, incidentally, belonged to the intelligentsia, but a special part of it). The intelligentsia had succeeded in rocking Russia with a cosmic explosion, but was unable to handle the debris.[33]

Solzhenitsyn is especially caustic in blaming Russian liberals for their indecisiveness during the provisional government. They were far better at criticizing than ruling.[34] He complains:

> These were the same liberal statesmen who, for years, went on protesting that they were worthy to represent Russia, that they were wonderfully clever, that they knew everything there was to know about how to guide Russia, and that, of course, they were far superior to the Tsarist ministers. In fact, they turned out to be a collection of spineless mediocrities, who let things slide rapidly into Bolshevism.[35]

He further argues that there never truly was an "October Revolution" in which liberals let "power slip from their hands." Rather, "they were never able to seize power in the first place" because the February Revolution "was going nowhere except into anarchy" and "fell unaided." Russian liberals could not maintain their ascendant position either because they did not understand or because they would not undertake the harsh necessities of political life.[36]

In the face of this attack on liberal principles, one could point out that liberals have a healthy aversion to wielding power. They believe in limited government and the protection of citizen rights. Had the provisional government of the liberals been serious about consolidating its position and bringing order to the vast Russian empire then in a virtual state of chaos, it would have had to employ stern measures—measures more violent than those formerly used by the tsar. Despite the dire consequences of inaction, liberals simply drew back from making that choice.

Moreover, the critic of Solzhenitsyn might say that if Russian liberals were mediocre, it is because those who hold liberal principles are wary of high ambition. Exemplary character and democratic government, not to mention party politics, are rarely compatible. The types of people who might be capable of achieving great goals are often excluded from high office in democratic societies. After the overthrow of the tsar, there was one person who might have led Russia from tumult to stability and to the establishment of a stable democratic government. But Prime Minister Pytor Stolypin was tragically assassinated before his reforms could take root, and there was no one of his caliber able to take his place.[37]

By comparison, the United States has been fortunate. After all, historians might be writing today about the mediocrity and weakness of American politicians (if any such country by that name existed) had not America's two greatest leaders, George Washington and Abraham Lincoln, held power, by happy coincidences, during its two greatest crises. As leader of the Continental Army, Washington could easily have abused his power and authority. Lincoln was elected president by the fewest popular votes of any chief executive in American history.

Solzhenitsyn maintains that liberals should not have overthrown the tsar if they were unprepared to take the sometimes agonizing steps needed to govern. A period of slow but steady accommodation would have been superior to a chaotic upheaval.[38]

In the end, leadership passed to people who were not reticent to use power. Solzhenitsyn contends that Lenin and the Bolsheviks succeeded because they were more ruthless than all their opponents. They defended their use of terror as a legitimate means of securing compliance with their orders. Lenin is said by Solzhenitsyn to have based his actions on the bloody Jacobin dictum: "Man has a right to wrest from his fellow man not only superfluous possessions but bare necessities. So as not to perish himself, he has a right to cut his neighbor's throat and devour his still quivering body." Lenin also learned from the Paris Commune that compromise with other parties and classes was impossible. Only by "shooting hostile classes wholesale" could the proletarian victory be gained.[39] Even after power had been secured, Lenin insisted that the party "must not exclude terror" as a tool for maintaining its position.[40]

Solzhenitsyn goes so far as to claim that the Bolsheviks' only claim to rule was their willingness to use greater force than their adversaries. They had virtually no popular support. Only a few elements of the intelligentsia embraced them. In his continuing effort to revise the historical interpretation of Russian history, Solzhenitsyn argues,

> The whole February Revolution was the work of two capital cities; the entire peasant country, the entire active army, only learned with bewilderment about the revolution after it happened . . . the Civil War is quite incorrectly assumed to have been between Reds and Whites, whereas, in reality, the most important thing was the popular opposition to the Reds in the years 1918 to 1922—a war in which, according to modern reckoning, 12 million people were lost.[41]

After considering Solzhenitsyn's account, one wonders who fought for the Reds. But whether this controversial interpretation is valid, it is certainly beyond doubt that the Bolsheviks had little compunction about seizing and holding power.

Solzhenitsyn gives one last explanation for the Bolshevik rise to preeminence: luck. Fate seemed to have favored them in a number of cases—too many for Solzhenitsyn. He mentions, for example, the battle of Sivash Bay, where winds caused the shallow water to recede, giving the Bolshevik army the open attack route that was key to its triumph in the engagement. The outcome of this battle is acknowledged to have affected decisively the course of the civil war.[42]

PORTRAIT OF LENIN

Solzhenitsyn portrays Lenin as a man of great strengths but even greater weaknesses. Lenin's strengths included a passionate commitment, bordering on an obsession. In *Lenin in Zurich,* Solzhenitsyn's fictitious account of one period in Lenin's life, from which much of what follows in this section is derived, the leading Bolshevik is pictured as becoming "ill" if "a single . . . hour" was wasted away from his work. "Everything . . . in his life—food, drink, clothes, house and home—had not been for him; indeed, he had wanted nothing of all this except as a means of keeping himself going for the sake of the cause." Even when luxuries were readily available, Lenin had a "deep antipathy" toward them. For him "there had to be discipline" in everything, especially if one wanted to "build up" the "powerful drive" necessary to inspire a revolution.[43]

It was to Lenin's credit, Solzhenitsyn concedes, that he could convey his sense of urgency to others. He "open-heartedly lavished all his fervor" on his comrades "so that each one felt himself to be the most important person in the world." In order to further socialist aims, he treated "every youngster as his equal, with perfect seriousness," and never begrudged "the effort spent on conversation with the young, wearing them down with questions, questions, questions, until he could slip a noose on them." [44]

Not only did Lenin have a great ability to *enlist* others in his cause, Solzhenitsyn notes, but he had an even greater ability to *use* others for his cause. For instance, he was financially supported by his family, particularly his wife and mother. The former provided him with a stable and orderly home life, so that all his energy could be spent on his work, and the latter "helped him out of family funds." Often he persuaded his friends to do his bidding for him. They carried on the bitter factional struggles that took place at almost every socialist meeting, allowing Lenin to remain above party infighting. Despite his well-publicized differences with other socialists, he persuaded them to provide him with financial support. He was not ashamed to seek the help of the capitalist arm of oppression, the police, when he felt threatened. He was not averse to enjoying the civilized and comfortable libraries of Switzerland, despite considering that country a "lackey's republic" and an "imperialist state." He even accepted money from capitalists bestowed "in a fit of businessman benevolence." [45]

One knack that Lenin used with great success, Solzhenitsyn explains, was his ability to play on the sympathies and antipathies of liberals. He is described as having turned a "youth-day" antiwar rally into a pro-socialist march, and as having engineered an anti-tsarist campaign, trading on the liberal press's animosity toward autocracy. Not only did he plan for Russia to be "shaken by destructive propaganda" from within, he also wished it to be "besieged by a hostile world press." He mounted an attack on the old regime in socialist newspapers throughout Europe, foreseeing that the "excitement of Tsar baiting" would "spread to the liberals . . . the dominant section of the press throughout the world," and might even "win public opinion in the United States." [46]

Solzhenitsyn admires Lenin's tactics, especially his sense of when to act, when to seize the crucial moment between "no longer" and "not yet." [47] Lenin was also famous for splitting the party and splitting it again until he was left with a dedicated and disciplined group willing to employ any means necessary to achieve victory.

While Lenin's strategy of creating a small, strongly motivated party was undoubtedly an asset in the scramble to gain power, Solzhenitsyn contends that it must be considered a weakness from the perspective of Marxist egalitarian principles. Indeed, Solzhenitsyn portrays Lenin as an elitist who "was careful to assert his superiority" in both his private and professional life. Despite claiming the universality of rights, for example, Lenin never treated his "womenfolk" as peers, expecting them instead to sit "quietly in their seats" and "not to fidget" too much. He considered himself superior to all his socialist colleagues and considered some of them so foolish that "equality" with them "was unthinkable." [48]

Although Lenin worked feverishly to bring about a revolution on their behalf, he never put much trust in the masses. Solzhenitsyn claims that he considered them, especially the peasants, "ignorant rabble," who could be made to understand ideas only through the use of slogans and propaganda. Lenin was always aware of the need to translate his positions into "Marxist vernacular."[49]

According to Solzhenitsyn, Lenin also had serious reservations about majority rule. He preferred to undermine any moderate position taken within his coalition by holding up strict socialist ideals. He always attacked from the left, which, ironically, led him to favor a resolute minority over a placid majority. This was especially true in times of social upheaval, when, he realized, a tiny group of provocateurs could halt the normal workings of society, and even a single shrill voice could precipitate a riot.

Solzhenitsyn maintains that one of Lenin's more obvious faults was his love of personal success. He is depicted as longing for the revolution partly from an ideological commitment and partly out of the hope that he would lead the movement. His soaring ambition blinded him to the effects of his own self-interest. For example, even as the party took care of his needs and provided him with an occasional extravagance, Solzhenitsyn describes him as rationalizing his delight in personal gratification. Lenin believed that a "professional revolutionary should be relieved of the need to worry about his livelihood." He even considered his good health a weapon of the revolutionary struggle and insisted that "party funds be used for its maintenance" and for "excellent doctors." When the party expropriated some funds (the Tiflis affair) in 1908, he was not averse to buying concert tickets, having a holiday in Nice, traveling, taking cabs, living in a hotel, or renting a Paris apartment for a thousand francs.[50]

These minor exceptions do not change the fact that, for the most part, the leader of the Bolshevik Revolution lived austerely, limiting his material comfort in order to further his cause. But did he deny himself out of a true commitment to socialist ideals, or was his moderation part of a public image essential to becoming the leader of the socialist movement? Stated differently, did Lenin's quest for high honor and renown turn him away from petty concerns for material well-being? Solzhenitsyn implies that ambition was at least as important as ideological purity in taming Lenin's avarice.[51]

By raising the issue of Lenin's personal pleasures, Solzhenitsyn prompts his readers to consider whether others could attain Lenin's level of asceticism. After all, not everyone is Lenin. How can those less devoted to the cause of social transformation and less driven to deny the pleasures that tempted even Lenin hope to live up to his rigorous standards of self-denial? If they cannot (and Lenin's theory of a conspiratorial party seems to concede that fact), then do not the principles of a socialist revolution, which demand subordination of one's own interests and desires to the interests and desires of all humanity, run counter to the desires and aspirations of the majority of mankind? Does such a movement not ask more than most people are willing to sacrifice? Does it not violate some common elements of human nature itself?[52]

Lenin's zeal for his movement also led him to disavow other important aspects of life. Solzhenitsyn suggests that he mistook the laws of revolutionary struggle for the laws of life in general, causing him to miss certain experiences that might have broadened his awareness and given depth to his understanding.

For example, he is depicted as having no true friends. From time to time people were close to him but, as situations changed, so too did those relationships. He made alliances to further his aims, but as each crisis passed, so did his comrades. Solzhenitsyn writes that, an "hour" after leaving associates, "they were already receding, and he would soon clean forget who they were and why he had needed them." With the possible exception of his lover, Inessa Armand, "all men and women Lenin had ever met in his life he had valued only if, and as long as, they were useful to the cause."[53]

In fact, Lenin consciously chose to cut himself off from humanity. A bitter experience with G. V. Plekhanov early in his career, and interminable factional squabbles thereafter, had taught him never to "believe anyone" and never to "let sentiment tinge his dealings with others." He developed a siege mentality, saw enemies at every turn, and took offense at the smallest slight. He made decisions about people solely on the basis of their party loyalty, so much so, in fact, that he was a poor judge of character. He had full confidence in Roman Malinovsky, who professed ideological orthodoxy, but who, it turned out later in a much celebrated incident, was an agent of the tsar's secret police.[54]

Solzhenitsyn claims that Lenin was not a generous person. In seeming contradiction to the ideal—from each according to his ability—Solzhenitsyn depicts Lenin excluding a particularly famished émigré from his dinner table, scolding his wife for feeding the destitute fellow breakfast, and instructing her to give the man nothing so he would stop coming to their house.[55]

Lenin's disdain for others extended to his scholarship. It upset him to talk to anyone who strenuously opposed his views, and therefore he mostly avoided the divergent Russian émigré community in Switzerland. His conversations with others were not open and free discussions in which partners exchange ideas in order to deepen their own understanding but resembled instead "a teacher confronting his class: the whole class may disagree, but the teacher is right just the same." Because of his isolation, Solzhenitsyn claims, Lenin had no one on whom to test his ideas. He fabricated his own reality, regardless of the facts confronting him. When writing, "he had all his findings clearly in mind long before he had" finished a work. At times, "his foresight . . . became so acute that he knew remarkably early, before he sat down to write, what his conclusions would be."[56]

One cannot help but be struck by the irony of Solzhenitsyn's portrayal of Lenin: The great revolutionary leader of a movement dedicated to the community of the human species led astray by his separation from other people. The real tragedy for Solzhenitsyn was that Lenin failed to perceive or comprehend crucial aspects of everyday life because he so fully committed himself to the abstract, theoretical dogma of Marx. For example, at one point Lenin is shown planning the reform of Swiss society. Although his general goal was to achieve equality of condition, he seemed to construct specific proposals for change out of thin air. Lenin made arbitrary decisions about how much land each family would be allowed to own, how much tax each person would be assessed, and who would be given citizenship. The deadly serious point behind Solzhenitsyn's sarcastic characterization is that Lenin became ruler of one of the largest nations on earth without any previous practical experience in public affairs. Is it any wonder that chaos ensued?[57]

The intellectual amaurosis that afflicted Lenin because of his dedication to Marxism manifested itself in a variety of other ways. Solzhenitsyn explains, for instance, that "all opposition exasperated" Lenin, especially on theoretical questions, "where it implied a claim to his leadership." He spent much of his adult life engaged in factional strife in order to assert his supremacy, thinking it naive "that all Marxists stood for the same things, and could work in harmony."[58] One can only wonder why these fervent differences of opinion did not suggest something to Lenin. How could Marx's prophecy that the state would wither away come true if even dedicated socialists could not agree among themselves? Socialists held fairly similar beliefs and, except on questions of leadership, had similar interests. But what of those differences of opinion that arise when interests clash? How could all be united in a Communist society without some sort of referee—that is, a state—to ameliorate the naturally divergent sentiments so common to social life? For Solzhenitsyn, Lenin gave no hint of how he would solve these political problems because he was oblivious to the questions.

It is well documented in Lenin's own writing that his adherence to Marxist theory led him to make false predictions. As Solzhenitsyn points out, Lenin's *Imperialism: The Highest Stage of Capitalism* contends that revolutions would begin only in advanced industrial nations. Even Switzerland, a country renowned for its political stability and social harmony, Lenin believed ripe for civil strife.[59]

Solzhenitsyn forces his readers to face an even more important difficulty. Why should Lenin have favored a revolution in Switzerland at all? Why did he wish to overturn a popularly elected government in which citizens fully participated and under which they enjoyed almost complete civic freedom? It is not as if the Swiss had to make a choice between hunger and freedom, as is often the case in developing nations today. Switzerland was a land of plenty; everyone had enough to eat—too much for Lenin's tastes. Luxuries were available to all, although admittedly in varying degrees. Even property, which Lenin wanted to confiscate, was held by the vast majority of Swiss. Furthermore, despite its traditional requirement that a citizen militia be maintained, Switzerland followed the openly avowed socialist line, denouncing World War I and refusing to enter it. Why would Lenin wish to transform Swiss culture and mores when it was exactly those long-standing practices that had allowed the Swiss to prosper?[60]

At one point in Solzhenitsyn's portrait, Lenin is depicted telling a Swiss member of his socialist group in Zurich that he should "educate himself." Despite his socialist leanings, the fellow just could not grasp the need for a revolution in his homeland. But what was Lenin really asking? Should his comrade have immersed himself in Marxist literature and thus be led to dismiss the virtues of Switzerland? In a sense, Lenin's "education" had led him to deny the evidence of his own senses. So intent was he on creating a perfect world fashioned after an as yet unseen ideal, that he was incapable of recognizing even the most decent society right before his eyes. Lenin saw politics in global terms, it is true; hence, a worldwide revolution was necessary to sweep away the evils of capitalism. Yet this very dedication to universal upheaval, Solzhenitsyn claims, hindered Lenin from appreciating the particular, namely, Switzerland. Solzhenitsyn makes the point masterfully, writing of Lenin:

> He rolled along, a short stocky figure, scarcely troubling to avoid those in his path. There, close by, was the city library. He could go there, but he had journals and books for today's work on call at the cantonal. He hurried fast as he could along the loathsome bourgeois embankment, where the smell of delicatessen and pastry wafted from doorways to tickle jaded appetites, where shopkeepers had performed miracles of ingenuity to offer their customers a twenty-first version of sausage and a hundred and first variety of patisserie. Windows full of chocolates, smokers' supplies, dinner services, clocks, antiques flashed by. . . . It was difficult on this smart embankment to imagine a mob with axes and firebrands someday smashing all the plate glass to smithereens. But—it must be done![61]

Lenin also failed to acknowledge the fairness of bourgeois society. Many of his socialist comrades entered business and became rich, ostensibly to aid the cause. Despite this evidence, Lenin refused to acknowledge the justice inherent in equality of opportunity. But, if even socialists could become successful, was not the road open to all?

Solzhenitsyn presents Lenin as having been so wrapped up in the revolutionary struggle that he overlooked important experiences in his personal life that might have led him to question his ideals. This was particularly true of his relationship with Inessa Armand. To a dedicated Marxist, Solzhenitsyn explains applying Marx's ideas literally, human interactions are supposed to be governed by economics and by the laws of class analysis. But Lenin's feelings for his mistress fell outside the net of Marxian causality. It seems that Eros, one of the most potent human motivations, has little or nothing to do with the productive forces of society.[62]

For Solzhenitsyn, one of Lenin's most grievous faults was his hatred of his own country. Lenin was jubilant when war broke out. He considered war a gift of history since dislocation and misery, endemic to armed conflict, were the breeding ground of rebellion. He needed his people to suffer, for their torment was his road to success. Only by experiencing the agony of war would they come to see the wisdom of his principles.

Lenin wanted Russia to lose the war. He knew that defeat would disgrace those in power and sound the death knell of tsarism. Given his stand, he was, in all but name, a German sympathizer. Solzhenitsyn describes Lenin's admiration for German efficiency and weapons, while he despised Russian perseverance in the face of hideous losses in defense of the nation. Lenin is depicted as having followed the war closely, heartened by fresh news of Russian catastrophes and frustrated by the steadfast endurance of the Russian peasants.[63]

Lenin would just as soon have had Russians turn their bayonets against their fellow countrymen if such acts would have aided the socialist cause. Solzhenitsyn makes his readers ponder the costs of such a policy. What of all those who suffered and died so that the Bolsheviks would triumph? Were they not part of that humanity that Lenin's doctrine was so intent on saving?[64]

It is true that committed socialists could not be patriots; they had to be "anti-patriots," their loyalties beyond the borders of any one nation encompassing all mankind. In Solzhenitsyn's view, however, Lenin's internationalism was little more than a manifestation of his loathing for his homeland, its people, and its culture. He is said to have considered Russia a "slovenly, slapdash, eternally drunk country"; his only tie to his homeland was his interest in ruling it.[65] Much like the Russian aristocracy he despised, Lenin found his native tongue inferior and used it only as a necessary expedient.

Solzhenitsyn makes his readers reexamine the high ideals of socialist internationalism. For these ideals to succeed, the long-standing ties that bind a nation together had to be torn asunder. One is obliged to ask whether such ideals do not violate an ancient rule of political life. Lenin, at least, was driven to hurt his countrymen, those who would normally be considered his friends, and to help his nation's foes in war, those who, in the traditional view, would have been his enemies.

For Solzhenitsyn, who considers nations "the wealth of mankind" that harbor "a unique facet of God's design," the disappearance of nations "would impoverish us not less than if all men should become alike."[66]

LENIN'S IDEAS IN ACTION

What happened when Lenin was able to put his ideas into practice? The first thing he discovered was that people's behavior did not match his theory. When people's shortcomings became evident, Lenin was faced with a choice. He could either abandon his abstractions or force the recalcitrant into conforming to his ideals. Except for a time during the N.E.P. (New Economic Policy), Solzhenitsyn maintains that Lenin chose the latter course of action; his commitment to Marxism gave him tyrannical impulses.[67]

Indeed, according to Solzhenitsyn, Lenin's success at seizing and holding power rested on a lesson he had learned from the Paris Commune. Lenin reasoned that the French workers' revolt of 1871 had failed because progressive forces had not destroyed their enemies en masse. To win future revolutions, he concluded, the proletariat could not compromise or bargain; it had to annihilate its opponents.

Lenin justified and supported the use of terror to secure the victory of socialism. Terror is the random use of violence, undertaken as a means of frightening a population into compliance. Therefore, it should not seem at all strange that Solzhenitsyn holds Lenin accountable for the bizarre and merciless events chronicled in chapter 1.[68] It is true, no doubt, that Stalin put his particularly vicious imprint on the scale of the terror—he arrested one hundred to find two who might be suspicious—but the use of terror was the same as Lenin's in principle. It was Lenin who instituted the arbitrary use of violence against his own people that set an example for Stalin to follow.[69]

Furthermore, after he came to power, "Lenin never dropped violence and terror as fundamental methods of his program." It was he, not Stalin, who appropriated land from the peasants in 1922; who deceived the workers by not letting them manage the factories; who used the military to subdue peasant uprisings; who destroyed the nobility, the clergy, and the merchant classes; who forced trade unions to become tools of the state; who set the Soviet Union on the road to collectivization and superindustrialization; and who instituted a system of government without the rule of law.[70]

Lenin was also responsible for creating an atmosphere of hatred and intolerance in his country. It was Lenin who called the nonproletariat "insects" to be crushed. A prime example of this attitude is evident, according to Solzhenitsyn, in Lenin's dealings with the intelligentsia. In a letter to Maxim Gorky, who was attempting to intercede for some of his imprisoned friends, Lenin expressed his thoughts about the intelligentsia. "In actual fact they are not [the nation's] brains, but shit." Elsewhere, he explained that the "pious" educated classes were "slovenly" and that they had never been true allies of the workers' cause.[71]

Inevitably, Solzhenitsyn explains, Lenin's subordinates adopted his attitudes. Because he was a dictator, his attitudes became public policy. For example, in 1920 a group of the intelligentsia who attempted to steer a middle ground between the various schools of thought within Russian society was brought to trial in the case of the Tactical Center. These people, among them Tolstoy's daughter, were not charged with forming an opposition—joining any independent organization was held to be a serious offense and a challenge to the party's total control—but rather with having undertaken to familiarize themselves with one another's views (they were talking to each other). Nikolai Krylenko, chief Soviet prosecutor, argued during the trial that "even if the defendants . . . did not lift a finger" in opposition to the government, "nevertheless . . . even a conversation over teacups as to the kind of system that should replace the Soviet system . . . is counterrevolutionary. . . . [Not] only is any kind of action against [the Soviet state] a crime . . . but the fact of inaction is also."[72]

The intent behind the Bolsheviks' attack on the intelligentsia is clear, Solzhenitsyn claims. It was not that intellectuals actually took part in activities opposed to the party; quite the contrary, most supported its goals. They were persecuted merely because their independence of mind made them a *potential* source of resistance. As Krylenko made clear, "this social group" speculated about things other than the workers' state, and thus it had "outlived its time." Members of the Tactical Center received three-year sentences, subsequently, the term for being a Russian humanist was increased.

Although Krylenko is quoted here, clearly Lenin knew and approved of what was going on. He was not one to sit idly by while important matters were being decided. Later, when Stalin all but extinguished the prerevolutionary intelligentsia, was he doing any more than carrying out Lenin's plans for the disposal of "social refuse"?[73] Lenin rid his society of "social refuse" by establishing the forced-labor camps, first at the Solovetsky Islands and then throughout the country. So began the Gulag Archipelago with its millions of tragic stories, of which Solzhenitsyn professes to have uncovered only a fragment.

Again the same question forces itself to the surface: Why did Lenin do it? Again Solzhenitsyn insists that the question can be answered only by going deeper. "The whole trouble," he writes, "lies at the roots of [Marxist] doctrine; this doctrine could not bear other fruits than those it actually bore."[74]

Solzhenitsyn's assertion obviously raises serious issues. After all, it cannot be denied that Lenin changed Marx's teaching. The revolution was supposed to take place in an advanced industrial nation and not in a relatively backward almost feudal society such as Russia. As Marx foresaw it, the actual revolt would be a mass uprising in which impoverished workers, the vast majority of the human race, would expropriate the riches of the few remaining overbloated capitalists. One need not read very far in Lenin's writings to discover that he rejected a mass movement in favor of a disciplined and conspiratorial group that would act as the vanguard of the proletariat.

Solzhenitsyn does not disagree with this view. He acknowledges that the revolution occurred "too soon" to accord with Marx's analysis, and that extraordinary measures were needed to modernize Russia's economy. He concedes that Lenin made a unique contribution to Marxist doctrine. He explains:

> Lenin did indeed develop Marxism, but primarily along the lines of ideological intolerance. If you read Lenin, you will be astonished at how much hatred there was in him for the least deviation, whenever some view differed from his even by a hair's breadth. Lenin also developed Marxism in the direction of inhumanity.[75]

If Lenin changed Marxism, how can Marxist doctrine be blamed for Lenin's political activities? Solzhenitsyn maintains that it was not that Lenin went astray by changing Marx's principles; rather, it was adherence to those precepts that made Lenin's intolerance, callousness, and elitism inevitable. In other words, Solzhenitsyn argues that Marx's philosophy is such a misrepresentation of the realities of human life that those under its influence are propelled into making tragic errors. If, as he argues, Communism developed exactly as should have been expected, given its premises, then Marx can be held responsible for the deeds of both Lenin and Stalin.

CONCLUSION

To sum up, Solzhenitsyn claims that the Bolshevik rise to power was far from a popular uprising. It was partly the result of weaknesses within the ruling class whose way of life had been undermined by the "progressive" ideas of the Enlightenment. The Bolshevik success also resulted from its leaders' willingness to employ violence as a means of securing power. Indeed, they were willing to do almost anything, even cede a vast stretch of Russian territory to the enemy, in order to prevail.

Solzhenitsyn argues that the ruthlessness of the Bolsheviks in acquiring power set the tone for the way they governed once they were in command. They were heartless in pursuing their policies; they showed little sympathy for the Russian people and their way of life; and they set in motion a lawless system of government, which, while it never rivaled Stalin's in the extent of its horrors, did not differ from Stalin's in its basic principles.

In placing blame for the genesis of this brutal regime, once again Solzhenitsyn finds more than one culprit. Lenin was partly the cause. His single-minded pursuit of success and his narrow partisan perspective helped set the tone for the tyrannical government that the Bolsheviks established. Yet there was also an element in the ferocity of Bolshevik rule that Solzhenitsyn blames on Marx's ideas. This controversial assertion can be considered only after we have reached a fuller understanding of Solzhenitsyn's treatment of Marx.

Notes

1. *Zurich*, 270.

2. *Warning*, 113. Whether Solzhenitsyn is accurate about Lenin is a matter of debate. To judge the matter fairly one would have to re-create Solzhenitsyn's research, attempting to find not only Lenin's personality but his place within the long tradition of revolutionary activities in Russia. That task is beyond the scope of this book. Various views of Lenin can be found in *Zurich*, 269-70; Adam Ulam, *Lenin and the Bolsheviks* (New York: Fontana, 1966); B. Wolfe, *Three Who Made a Revolution* (New York: Pelican, 1966); R. Payne, *The Life and Death of Lenin* (New York: Pan, 1964). See also Vladimir I. Lenin, *Collected Works*, 45 vols. (London: Lawrence & Wisehart, 1960). Carter makes the same criticism as he did of Solzhenitsyn's Stalin: it is as if the author was inside Lenin's head and knew his thoughts. Carter, *Politics of Solzhenitsyn*, 110. See Solzhenitsyn's remarks on his characterization of Lenin in Dunlop, *Solzhenitsyn in Exile*, 329-40. See also Scammell, *Solzhenitsyn*, 944-45.

3. Lenin's mother, who provided him money until her death, received a government pension from the benefits of her deceased husband. *Gulag III*, 89. See also *Gulag III*, 79-85, 89-91.

4. *Zurich*, 73; *Gulag III*, 81-83.

5. *Warning*, 114. In January 1917 Lenin stated that he doubted whether he would "live to see the decisive battles of the upcoming revolution." Quoted in Edward H. Carr, *The Bolshevik Revolution: 1917-1923* (New York: Macmillan, 1951), 69.

6. *Zurich*, 55.

7. *Oak*, 140.

8. *Zurich*, 21, 47, 198, 250.

9. Ibid., 37.

10. *Mortal*, 16.

11. *East*, 150.

12. Solzhenitsyn has been accused of opposing modern science, a charge that he denied. *Mortal*, 64. He does seem to worry, however, that the discoveries of science are

invariably turned into the weapons of war. As long as separate nations remain, each state will have a compelling interest in converting knowledge into the means of destruction. See, for example, Solzhenitsyn's remarks on how a "disarmed" Russia still might have to arm itself against its enemies. *East*, 113; see also *Warning*, 120-21. On the whole, Solzhenitsyn seems sympathetic to premodern scientists who, fearing mankind's capacity for brutality and greed, refused to make their discoveries public. *Rubble*, 15.

13. Mary McCarthy views as a "debatable proposition" the assertion that the Russian defeat could "'cause' Stalin." "The Tolstoy Connection," in John Dunlop, Richard Haugh, and Alexis Klimoff, eds., *Aleksandr Solzhenitsyn: Critical Essays and Documentary Materials* (Belmont, Mass.: Nordland, 1975), 336. But a cause can be necessary without being sufficient. According to Solzhenitsyn the Stalinist era need not have occurred as the result of losing the war, but it could not have happened had that defeat never taken place.

14. Dorothy Atkins, *"August 1914*: Historical Novel or Novel History," in Dunlop, *Critical Essays*, 411.

15. *Zurich*, 285-87.

16. *Zurich*, 267-68, in which Solzhenitsyn quotes the following dispatch:

(Count Brockdorff-Rantzau, German ambassador in Copenhagen, to the Ministry of Foreign Affairs. Top secret) We must now definitely try to create the utmost chaos in Russia. To this end we must avoid any discernible interference in the course of the Russian revolution. But we must secretly do all we can to aggravate the contradictions between moderate and extreme parties, since we are extremely interested in the victory of the latter, for another upheaval will then be inevitable, and will shake the Russian state to its foundations. . . . Support by us of the extreme elements is preferable, because in this way the work is done more thoroughly.

See also, Scammell, *Solzhenitsyn*, 942.

17. *Gulag I*, 458.

18. *Gulag III*, 79-97; *Mortal*, 14-15; *Rubble*, 237-39.

19. *Rubble*, 238.

20. Ibid., v-viii, 238.

21. Ibid., 235.

22. Ibid., 236. See ibid., 230-31, in which Solzhenitsyn outlines the qualities of the old intelligentsia including:

A universal search for an integral world view, a thirst for faith (albeit secular), and an urge to subordinate one's life to this faith. . . . Social compunction, a sense of guilt with regard to the people. . . . Moral judgments and moral considerations occupy an exceptional position in the soul of the Russian intellectual: all thought of himself is egoism; his personal interests and very existence must be unconditionally subordinated to service to society; puritanism, personal asceticism, total selflessness, even abhorrence and fear of personal wealth as a burden and a temptation. . . . A fanatical willingness to sacrifice oneself—even an active quest for such sacrifice; although this path is trodden by only a handful of individuals, it is nevertheless the obligatory and only worthy ideal aspired to by all.

23. *Gulag III*, 91.

24. See *Rubble*, 230-31, in which Solzhenitsyn describes the faults of the old intelligentsia:

Clannishness, unnatural disengagement from the general life of the nation. . . . Intense opposition to the state as a matter of principle. . . . Individual moral cowardice in the face of "public opinion," mental mediocrity. . . . Love of egalitarian justice, the social good and the material well-being of the people, which paralyzed its love of and interest in the truth; "the temptation of the Grand Inquisitor": let the truth perish if people will be the happier for it . . . ideological intolerance of any other . . . Fanaticism that made the intelligentsia deaf to the voice of life. Daydreaming, a naïve idealism, an inadequate sense of reality. . . . A strenuous, unanimous atheism which uncritically accepted the competence of science to decide even matters of religion . . . of course negatively; dogmatic idolatry of man and mankind . . . and even hostility to autonomous spiritual claims.

Delba Winthrop comments that the intelligentsia misunderstood "what political philosophy is and how it relates to politics and to man's place in the whole." Delba Winthrop, "Solzhenitsyn: Emerging from under the Rubble," a paper delivered at the American Political Science Association Annual Meeting, New York, September 1978, 6.

25. Winthrop argues that Russian intellectuals went astray because they lost sight of the fact that intellectual pursuits have a value all their own and cannot have as their aim material well-being or fame, Winthrop, "Emerging," 7.

26. Tolstoy's love commandment was more in line with Kant's categorical imperative than with the traditional Christian doctrine of love they neighbor.

27. Kathryn Feuer, ed. *Solzhenitsyn: A Collection of Critical Essays* (Englewood Cliffs, N.J.: Prentice Hall, 1976), 13, 22, 86. Compare, for example, the harsh realism of Marxists to the idealism of the followers of Tolstoy in Aleksandr Solzhenitsyn, *Cancer Ward*, trans. Nicholas Bethell and David Burg (New York: Bantam, 1969), 104-5.

28. *Gulag I*, 303-5, 613; *Gulag III*, 89.

29. McCarthy argued that American liberals would not like Solzhenitsyn's ethics of duty to country. Her point was well taken. Many spokespeople of American liberalism attacked Solzhenitsyn's views. McCarthy "The Tolstoy Connection," 339.

30. Solzhenitsyn saw the desire for perfect social equality as a serious problem for the United States. In a speech before the AFL-CIO he warned against attempting to establish "fine degrees of justice and even finer legal shades of equality." *Warning*, 49. See also *Zurich*, 49, 52, 65, 196.

31. Solzhenitsyn and Tocqueville both leave the meaning of "equality" vague. To be more rigorous one must say that both favor equality of opportunity (means), but are opposed to equality of results (ends), especially if government is empowered to enforce those ends. Marx, on the other hand, considered equality of results possible and desirable, once the economic arrangement is transformed. Alexis de Tocqueville, *Democracy in America*, trans. George Lawrence (Garden City, N.Y.: Doubleday, 1969).

32. Carter, *Politics of Solzhenitsyn*, 70-71; Feuer, *Critical Essays*, 13; Tocqueville, *Democracy*, 9-20, 56-57, 546-47. Compare *Rubble*, 169-70.

33. *Rubble*, 236-37.

34. "Liberal" can be used in the traditional sense to mean one who favors a limited, representative government established to protect natural rights. Solzhenitsyn seems to use the term here to describe those who favored progressive ideas.

35. *East*, 150-51.

36. Ibid., 151-53. He continues, "The way in which our Russian liberals and socialists gave way to Communists" was "repeated on a worldwide scale." Ibid., 154. See also *Rubble*, 117.

37. For an excellent account of Solzhenitsyn's attitude toward reform of Russian society see Daniel J. Mahoney, "True and False Liberalism: Stolypin and His Enemies," *Aleksandr Solzhenitsyn: The Ascent from Ideology* (Lanham, Md.: Rowman & Littlefield, 2001), 65-97

38. *Gulag III*, 91.

39. *Zurich*, 65, 212; see also "Solzhenitsyn Speaks Out," 606.

40. *Gulag I*, 353. Trotsky proclaimed, "Terror is a powerful means of policy and one would have to be a hypocrite not to understand this," *Gulag I*, 300n.

41. *East*, 151, 153.

42. *Oak*, 212, 220, 540.

43. *Zurich*, 69, 79, 146-47.

44. Ibid., 20, 57.

45. Ibid., 9, 12, 25, 30, 32, 43, 51, 73.

46. Ibid., 15, 140.

47. *Oak*, 140.

48. *Zurich*, 20, 51, 77-78, 93.

49. Ibid., 13, 22.

50. Ibid., 31, 56, 73, 76, 79, 112, 126, 174-75, 214.

51. Ibid., 143.

52. For examples of socialist self-abnegation, see Scammell, *Solzhenitsyn*, 93.

53. *Zurich*, 20, 80.

54. Ibid., 77, 96-97, 99. Solzhenitsyn gleefully reminds his readers that his hated adversary, Stalin, was introduced to the central committee by Malinovsky. Who knows, perhaps Stalin was cynical enough to have been a double agent for the tsar at one time.

55. Ibid., 68-69.

56. Ibid., 55, 90.

57. Ibid., 91.

58. Ibid., 76, 94.

59. Ibid., 56, 59.

60. Ibid., 42, 56, 60, 71, 215.

61. Ibid., 87; see also 45-46, 51, 53, 58-61, 71, 81, 215.

62. Ibid., 80, 234.

63. Ibid., 34-37. Lenin wrote in 1915, "To reject war in principle is un-Marxist. Who objectively stands to gain from the slogan 'peace'? In any case, not the revolutionary proletariat." Quoted in *Warning*, 70.

64. *Zurich*, 52, 101-4.

65. Ibid., 103-4; see also 214.

66. *East*, 20.

67. *Zurich*, 70, 214.

68. Francis Barker argues that Solzhenitsyn found no evidence of Lenin's use of terror in the first few months after the revolution. This, he claims, exonerates Lenin; he was merely reacting to the "White Terror." Francis Barker, Solzhenitsyn: *Politics and Form* (London: Macmillan, 1977), 89. Solzhenitsyn claims that the terror was begun immediately after the revolution. But perhaps it did take the Bolsheviks a few months to put the terror in place. One should not forget, however, that the suppression intensified after the White partisans were dead or defeated.

69. *Warning*, 63; "Solzhenitsyn Speaks Out," 607.

70. "Solzhenitsyn Speaks Out," 606. The law was so broad that anything either done or not done could be considered a crime. Lenin was the person who constructed the far-reaching Article 58.

71. *Gulag I*, 328.

72. Ibid., 332.

73. Ibid., 329, 372-72. Solzhenitsyn may have had his political differences with the old intelligentsia, but that does not hinder him from admiring its strengths or grieving over its loss. He recognizes that within it was a stratum of thoughtful people who reached fervently for the sublime. See especially ibid., 288-89.

74. "Solzhenitsyn Speaks Out," 606.

75. *Warning*, 61-62.

CHAPTER 4

SOLZHENITSYN ON MARX

The writings of Solzhenitsyn are most interpreted as a historical indictment of the Soviet Union. In that regard they have had an enormous influence. They discredited the legitimacy of Soviet rule among their readers in the East; they hardened public opinion in the West by clearly revealing the totalitarian character of the Soviet government; and they played an important role in undermining Euro-Communism.[1]

In addition to their importance as a history of Soviet deeds, Solzhenitsyn's writings have another, more comprehensive intention. It is the thesis of this chapter that Solzhenitsyn's works constitute a theoretical attack on Marx's philosophy. To say that Solzhenitsyn criticizes Marx is (in a dialectic way) both an understatement and an overstatement. There are few places in Solzhenitsyn's writings in which he systematically presents his differences with Marx, nor can the full measure of his objections be found by looking solely to one of his works. There is no treatise contra Marx, probably because Solzhenitsyn does not write treatises. Wherever one looks in Solzhenitsyn's works, however, there is a criticism of some aspect of Marx's ideas. This chapter shall discuss Solzhenitsyn's attack on Marx's views concerning the prediction of future trends, revolution, class analysis, the primacy of economics, history, human nature, labor, property, family relations, philosophy, atheism, and the aims of socialism—freedom, equality, and community. It is tempting to say that Solzhenitsyn wishes to discredit every important aspect of Marx's doctrine.[2]

Before beginning a discussion of Solzhenitsyn's arguments against Marx, it is appropriate to acknowledge that a great controversy rages over what Marx's philosophy actually means. Should it be interpreted to signify that the movement of history inexorably determines human fate, or is its purpose to describe a trend in historical development that individuals may or may not accept in deciding their future? The literature on Marx is so extensive and contradictory that one knowledgeable commentator seems to have thrown up his hands in despair at the prospect of ever discovering the one, true Marx. Raymond Aron writes, "The philosophy of Marx, precisely because of its intrinsic ambiguity . . . has always lent itself to many interpretations, some of which are more convincing . . . but all of which, strictly speaking, are tolerable."[3]

Because of the complexity of Marx's thought, it is with some trepidation
that an interpretation of his work, especially one so brief, is put forward. Yet in
order to understand Solzhenitsyn's criticism of Marx, it is necessary to present a
synopsis of Marx's major ideas. There seem to be two broad schools of thought
concerning Marx. The older interpretation, what we shall call here the mechanistic view, holds that, according to Marx, human life is determined by the economic structure of society. This is so because the most primary activity of human existence is labor—the labor necessary to secure one's livelihood. Since the
earliest stages of human development, the fruits of labor have not been shared
equally among those who toil. The division of labor, the means by which tasks
are most efficiently accomplished, has created social distinctions which have
hardened into social classes. Those at the top of the social hierarchy reap greater
benefits from the economic arrangement than do those at the bottom, so much
so, in fact, that the lower classes in the capitalist era are compelled to work for
subsistence wages.

Marx's analysis is more than a mere chronicle of social inequality, of
course. He builds upon G. W. F. Hegel's notion that the seemingly random
events of history have a comprehensible meaning and order. He agrees with
Hegel that each historical era has governing principles, on the basis of which
individuals within that era justify their actions. He also agrees that these fundamental beliefs vary from historical era to historical era, but that finally there will
come a time—an absolute moment—when the meaning of the movement of
history and the relation among historical eras will become apparent. Marx's contribution to philosophy is his insight that the driving force behind historical
change is not the unfolding of the Idea, as Hegel had maintained, but the struggle between social classes over the fruits of labor. Hegel, too, recognized the
ongoing conflict between master and slave, but he considered this dispute to be
primarily a war of ideas, of consciousness. Marx, on the other hand, maintains
that the ideas expressed by a particular class are merely a way of defending its
economic power and social position. Indeed, ideas and consciousness are manifestations of the economic structure. They reflect the way in which the economic
structure is organized to produce the goods and services necessary for life. Thus,
the predominant ideas tend to justify the way of life of the ruling group, for example, the hierarchical ethos of feudalism favored the aristocratic class, whereas
the values inherent in a free-market economy favor the capitalists.

According to Marx, each social system is transformed by its own inner contradictions; it falls of its own weight. For instance, it is the competitive nature of
the free market that dooms capitalism. In order to keep up with their rivals and
not be run out of business, corporations are compelled to produce goods more
quickly and efficiently while at the same time lowering the cost of production.
To accomplish these twin goals, the owners must introduce ever-more complex
machines and simultaneously reduce wages paid to workers. As a result, the
workers, numerically the largest class, become alienated from their labor and,
indeed, from their very existence. They are made to work at mindless and tedious jobs, the result of assembly-line techniques and advanced machinery, for

subsistence wages, the absolute minimum expenditure needed to keep them alive as functioning units of production. All fulfillment is lost in such labor since workers have control over neither the finished product nor the means by which those products are created.

Only after the capitalist system is fully developed do its fatal flaws become perceptible. Capitalism's very efficiency causes its downfall. It produces such a glut of material goods that consumption falls behind production, resulting in massive layoffs and, eventually, economic collapse. During these boom-and-bust cycles, a few large businesses swallow up all the rest. The inequity of a system in which the owners enjoy all the luxuries of life but do no labor and the workers labor but live in poverty becomes so evident that the workers finally seize the means of production and transform the social structure so that all share equally in its bounty.

The dispute between the two interpretations of Marx, as we shall see below, arises over whether Marx believed this process of historical change was inevitable, thereby negating human freedom, or whether he believed the worst excesses of capitalism could be ameliorated by human action. The mechanistic Marxists insist that human fate is determined independently of human will, that existence determines essence. The humanistic adherents of Marx claim that nowhere does Marx's philosophy claim that human fate is predetermined by uncontrollable economic forces. Rather, once liberated from capitalist ideology, human volition can play a role in shaping the future of society; thus, essence determines existence.[4]

The primary reason for the reevaluation of Marx's thought, which gave rise to the new interpretation of his ideas, was the publication of his early writings. A number of major intellectual figures, including Jean-Paul Sartre, Maurice Merleau-Ponty, Eric Fromm, Herbert Marcuse, and Shlomo Avineri, have brought new elements of his philosophy to light. Focusing on the goals of liberation, equality, and community that Marx deemed essential to a worthwhile human existence, these thinkers deny that Marx was a crude materialist and argue that his work is an open-ended philosophic dialogue. Marx's later writings—*Capital*, for example—which attempt to "prove" the laws of historical change, are, for a variety of reasons, discounted by these scholars. For example, Avineri contends that the mechanistic tone of Marx's later works resulted primarily from Friedrich Engels's oversimplification. To the end of his days, Avineri insists, Marx was humanistic and democratic.[5]

Solzhenitsyn criticizes both the humanistic and the mechanistic versions of Marxism, although he reserves his greatest antipathy for the latter, in part because the mechanistic view of Marx predominates in the Soviet Union and in every other nation where Communists ruled. He explains:

> Communism is as crude an attempt to explain society and the individual as if a surgeon were to perform his delicate operation with a meat ax. All that is subtle in human psychology and in the structure of society (which is even more com-

plex), all this is reduced to crude economic processes. This whole created being—man—is reduced to matter.[6]

Solzhenitsyn finds the claim that Marx is a humanist, a position expounded
primarily in the West, too fantastic to be believed. As will be shown below, he
reasons that even when the most humanistic of Marx's goals were pursued, unintended consequences followed; Marxism caused its adherents to overlook the
hard facts of political life, opening the way to injustice and incompetence.[7]

There is also an important sense in which Solzhenitsyn does not care which
interpretation of Marx is the more accurate. Solzhenitsyn applies the biblical
injunction "by their fruits shall you know them" to Marxism, with unpleasant
results for its creator. Yet Solzhenitsyn's authority for a practical criticism of
theory does not rest solely on religion. It was Marx himself in the *Preface to a
Contribution to the Critique of Political Economy* who insisted that societies be
judged by what they are and not by what they pretend to be.[8]

A word of caution must be offered before a discussion of Solzhenitsyn's
critique of Marx. It would be unfair and philosophically incorrect to maintain
that if Marx sets out saying one thing and the Soviet experience shows that
something else has occurred, then Marx's proposition is inaccurate. Indeed,
since the Soviet Union never claimed to reach the final stage of Communism,
which Marx foresaw would eliminate human conflict and injustice, no empirical
observations made about that empire can serve as a refutation of Marx. Yet
Solzhenitsyn does criticize Marx on the basis of observable evidence. Solzhenitsyn's method in this regard is to relate stories or episodes in the life of his nation
that test Marx's ideas in practice. He recounts the experiences of actual people
who were confronted with Marxian social experimentation in real situations.
What happened, for example, when Marx's ideas concerning property, family,
and equality were applied to an actual situation? How did people react? What
were the consequences?

Such a method does have serious flaws, of course. There is no strict scientific basis, mathematical correlation, or repeatable experiment to prove Solzhenitsyn's evidence necessarily leads to his conclusions. Yet Solzhenitsyn's
stories and anecdotes are worthy of serious consideration. They express the
normal human reaction to the practical application of Marx's proposals. Each
episode may have involved only a limited number of people, but the response
was shared by millions of, if not most, Russians. Indeed, the general responses
to Marxism were so widespread and similar that one must conclude that they
were universal. Thus, Solzhenitsyn's critique of Marx's philosophy proceeds by
testing that theory against the evidence of human behavior.

PROBLEM OF PREDICTION

Following the lead of Hegel, Marx claims to have understood the movement of
history. On the basis of that knowledge, Marx makes predictions about the character of future historical epochs. For example, Marx forecast that capitalism

would bring misery and poverty to the workers who toiled to produce its wealth. Solzhenitsyn points out that almost nothing that Marx foresaw has actually come true. To begin with a crucial fact, the free-market system has not impoverished the workers. Quite the contrary, Communist societies never produced "as much food, clothing and leisure" as people in the West enjoy under capitalism, Solzhenitsyn maintains. Moreover, the economic well-being of the West has not depended on colonialism (one of Lenin's additions to Marx). Only after Europe shed its colonies, Solzhenitsyn claims, was it able to achieve its post-World War II economic miracle.[9] Marx also was wrong in predicting that revolutions would begin in the most advanced industrial countries; the reverse occurred. As was the case in Russia, Marxist revolutions took place primarily in economically undeveloped nations where the proletariat was small.[10]

Marx's most inaccurate prediction, argues Solzhenitsyn, is "the picture of how the world would rapidly be overtaken by revolution and how states would soon wither away." He continues, "such a view is sheer delusion, sheer ignorance of human nature," and points out that it is precisely in those Communist nations which adopted Marxism where the state was most powerful. He casts doubt on Marx's contention that the rise of socialism would herald the decline of war. The Soviet invasion of Budapest and of Prague, the occupation of Eastern Europe and the Baltic nations, and the Sino-Soviet border clashes belied the peaceful intentions of Communist governments. Whether Marx was correct in his prognostications would be of little importance if Marx had not asserted that the inevitability of his predictions gave people a reason to revolt. But Solzhenitsyn asserts that since Marxist principles "have failed to predict a single event," he is justified in calling Marx's whole theory into question. Solzhenitsyn reasons that "Only the cupidity of some, the blindness of others, and the craving for faith on the part of still others" would allow such a "bankrupt doctrine," with such an abysmal record of accuracy, still to have adherents.[11]

REVOLUTION

At Marx's graveside eulogy, Engels paid his friend what he considered a high compliment by calling him "before all else a revolutionist."[12] Certainly no political philosopher has a greater claim to the title. At various times he called for "smashing" the machine of the state and "breaking up" the old society. He wrote of "hand to hand combat" in which "the people must be taught to be terrified of themselves." Well aware of what a revolution entails, he quoted, with approval, from George Sand's novel *Jean Ziska*, "Combat or death: bloody struggle or extinction. It is thus that the question is inexorably put." Even after the revolution, Marx foresaw that to succeed the workers would need to adopt "measures of force" and that nonproletariat classes "must be forcibly removed or transformed, and the process of their transformation must be forcibly accelerated."[13]

Solzhenitsyn maintains that "if you read Marx attentively you will there find Leninist formulations and tactics already completely outlined, with repeated calls for terror, violence and the forceful seizure of power." Elsewhere, he quotes from Marx's writings to make his point. Marx writes,

> Reforms are a sign of weakness. . . . The movement for reform in England was an error. . . . Democracy is more terrible than monarchy or aristocracy. . . . Political freedom is false freedom, worse than the worst form of slavery. . . . Given universal suffrage, revolution hasn't got a chance. . . . After coming to power—terror . . . they will begin to regard us as monsters—but we don't give a damn.[14]

Solzhenitsyn is not naive about the importance of revolutions in shaping history. He understands that to search into the origins of most political societies is to discover "revolutions and seizures of power."[15] He even agrees with Machiavelli that revolutions are sometimes good since they can induce a sense of virtue at the initial stages of upheaval.[16] However, as a means of counteracting the rebellious fervor instilled by Marxism, Solzhenitsyn reminds us of the human costs of bloody insurrections. He claims that at the present state of the development of civilization, little good can be gained through violent revolution. He opposed the use of revolution even where it was most justified by the most extreme forms of tyranny—in the Soviet Union, for example.[17]

First, Solzhenitsyn maintains that a radical uprising is likely to ruin the economy of a nation for many years. Even if the regime that comes to power is better than the one it replaces, still it would face the very difficult task of rebuilding a shattered industrial base. Thus, whatever political advantages might be gained by overturning the old order are likely to be offset by the suffering created in the ensuing economic crisis. Second, those most likely to lead a revolution are usually unfit to govern the nation afterward. How, he wonders, can the leaders of a revolution put aside their grenades and machine guns and become compassionate rulers? Internecine war rarely produces magnanimous victors. Third, even if revolutionary commanders are not ruthless people, they usually have little or no experience in the art of governing. Hence, force replaces statesmanship. Perhaps more important, revolutionaries often lack the technical know-how necessary to make the economy work. They may even be hostile to technocrats, for the expertise of such people is likely to have put them in high-paying and important posts under the old regime.[18]

One disturbing consequence of revolution is that it unleashes all the human passions. Even beyond the bitterness produced between warring factions, a great deal of lawlessness, such as assault, murder, theft, and so forth, is created when the rules of the old society are suspended and the new ones have yet to take their place. At such times, too, racial or national hostilities are easily exacerbated. Such disturbances are not fatal to a new administration, Solzhenitsyn reasons, but they are bothersome and take an enormous effort to bring under control. An added cost of revolution to an already burdened economy is the support of a large police force.[19]

In social revolution, repression must also be used to strip the old ruling class of its privilege. It is an "old, old ironical story," Solzhenitsyn muses, that rebels who liberate people from jails must set up new jails to incarcerate their enemies. It is to be expected that defenders of the old order will suffer in the wake of a social transformation; as Lenin was fond of saying, omelets cannot be made without breaking some eggs. By bringing up the point, however, Solzhenitsyn asks his readers to contemplate the nature of revolution. First, the act of suppression implies that revolutions actually are not fought for the universality of humankind, as Marx claimed. Usually one group wants to take away what another group has. Furthermore, no sooner does a new ruling group come to power than it demands special privilege to accompany its new status. Solzhenitsyn recounts that during the Gulag uprisings in which he took part, some of the leadership and many of the hit men (those who killed stoolies) demanded extra rations even though it meant their fellow prisoners went hungry. In the end, one form of oppression simply replaced another.[20]

What sorts of people are likely to enforce the rules of the new order? What sorts of people will rise to the top in a society where violence and brutality reign? Obviously, Solzhenitsyn reasons, people with harsh and brutal personalities are exactly what a new regime needs. The new leadership is likely to rely on people for whom the goals of the revolution mean very little. They are often more interested in personal rewards and pleasures, one of which could be enjoyment in seeing others suffer.[21]

Furthermore, Solzhenitsyn states that according to "a universal law," all "vast and bloody revolutions . . . invariably devour their own creators." He does not explain, however, why this universal law is binding. Perhaps, one might speculate, it is because passions run high. Or it could be, as his treatment of Stalin suggests, that dedication to ideology is so strong during a revolution that personal differences between leaders are transformed into matters of high principle that can be resolved only by one side extinguishing the other.[22]

Marx proclaimed that "a revolution . . . can succeed . . . only . . . in getting rid of all the traditional muck and . . . establishing society anew."[23] Following these precepts, Marxist uprisings were particularly pernicious, Solzhenitsyn explains, because they aimed at the destruction of the old culture. But when the old ways were gone, what was left to take their place? Reminiscent of Edmund Burke, Solzhenitsyn believes that culture takes centuries to construct. The trials and errors of many generations leave a legacy of wisdom in traditions and customs. Culture civilizes people, teaching them right from wrong, noble from base, true from false. It provides ways of coping with the natural rhythm of life—birth, marriage, aging, and death. At its highest, culture exemplifies the peak of human activity. The arts, philosophy, and literature reflect man's endeavor to capture the elusive essence of beauty and truth.

Marx would have us sweep all this "muck" aside and create a new culture ex nihilo. Solzhenitsyn argues that the labor of generations is nearly impossible to replace. In fact, when tradition is destroyed, a vacuum is created into which flows the coarsest kind of human thinking. Chapter 1 of this book showed how easily the thieves' philosophy spread from the camps to Soviet society. The destruction of culture does not mean that people's creative talent will be unleashed, Solzhenitsyn concludes. Rather, it is far more likely to result in the degeneration of morals and manners to the lowest level of common humanity.[24]

CLASS ANALYSIS

One of the worst aspects of Marxism, Solzhenitsyn complains, is its faulty understanding of society and the division of classes. According to Marx, human suffering, at least in the industrial age, originates in the bourgeois way of life, in capitalism. Marx asserts that the "absolute general law of capitalist accumulation 'establishes' the irreconcilability of class antagonism." At one end of the division are riches and opulence, at the other, poverty and degradation. To reach this conclusion, Marx begins with the premise that the most fundamental human activity is to provide for one's physical needs, and all that come after is influenced by this endeavor. He explains that, "life involves above all eating and drinking, shelter, clothing. . . . This is the first historical act . . . which must be fulfilled . . . today as well as a thousand years ago." From this premise Marx postulates that the way in which people gain their livelihood affects everything else they do. In a real sense, he claims, that people are what they produce and the way they produce it. He reasons:

> The way in which a man produces his food . . . his mode of production . . . is . . . a definite way of expressing . . . life. As individuals express their life, so they are. What they are, therefore, coincides with what they produce and how they produce. The nature of individuals thus depends on the material conditions which determine their production.

Naturally, it follows that if people are conditioned by circumstances external to themselves, their opinions and actions will be shaped by those circumstances. About people, he writes that "their personality is conditioned and determined by very definite class relationships . . . A nobleman, for instance, will always remain a nobleman and a commoner always a commoner . . . a quality inseparable from his individuality." If the way people orient themselves to the world is fully determined by their class origins, then antagonisms cannot be ameliorated since people can never transcend the principles of their particular class. Once it is admitted that the basis of human opinion, hence motivation, lies in the structure of society and outside the control of human beings acting as independent agents, then the only possible way to resolve differences between people is to abolish those things (classes) that make them different. It is as if a person meeting a member of a different class were encountering an alien being. The class structure makes their life experiences utterly different from one another, and since this experience is the basis of their opinions and ideas, these too are utterly incompatible. People from different classes cannot compromise because they share no common ground on which compromise can be based. As Marx formulates it, there cannot be "an equilibrium between forces . . . contradictions . . . must be overthrown."[25]

Solzhenitsyn objects to this analysis on several grounds. First, he reminds us that by denigrating compromise, Marx made his followers into self-righteous zealots. They saw no need to temper their judgments and, in fact, held that any agreement with other classes was illegitimate. They were left with no alternative but to deceive, arrest, terrify, and murder their opponents.

Second, Marx's class theory proclaims that people ought to be judged good or evil, not on the basis of anything they have done—undermining the socialist regime, for instance—but on the basis of their social standing at birth. Individual innocence or guilt has no place under such a principle; the Communist state is empowered to suppress "socially dangerous" elements on the basis of their "class origin." M. I. Latsis, a member of the Soviet secret police, made this perfectly clear. "In the interrogation," he instructed his colleagues, "do not seek evidence and proof that the person accused acted . . . against Soviet power. The first question should be: What is his class, what is his origin, what is his education and upbringing?"[26]

When Marx called for the suppression of the bourgeoisie, perhaps he meant no more than to have the social structure overturned. Solzhenitsyn brings home the stark reality that in practice the abstract idea of transforming class relations translates into the "annihilation" of a "concrete two-legged individual possessing hair, eyes, a mouth, a neck and shoulders."[27]

He bitterly mocks Marx's notion that social background is the single constituent of human motivation. If that were true, Solzhenitsyn argues in a satirical chapter of *Gulag II* entitled, "Zeks as a Nation," the prison population constituted not only a distinct class within Soviet society, but should have been considered a different nation. Its citizens had their own particular mode of production—slave labor—a separate language, a common history, and their own set of customs. Since they had no control over the means of production and did not share in the fruits of their labor, they had, given Marxist dialectics, a historical mission to overthrow their oppressors, the Communist state.[28]

For Solzhenitsyn, class background is only one of the elements that make up the human personality. People have far more things in common (for example, culture) than can be discovered by looking at their status in a social hierarchy. Since they share a capacity for speech and reason, human beings are able to resolve their differences through deliberation. Moreover, they are open to "spiritual conversion." Even in the absence of a universal revolution they can rise above the narrow interests of class or party and act for the common good.[29] Finally, he argues that the very concept of rigid class stratification is inaccurate.

Classes are fluid, their composition continually changing as people move up and down the social ladder.[30]

Marx's most famous contribution to the history of thought is his teaching that people's social activity originates in economics. It follows that political institutions and practices derive from economic conditions and that the state is a mechanism by which the ruling class holds its superior position. The ruling class's oppression may not be overt, however. People in subordinate classes may even choose the government under which they live, since they accept the ruling ideology of their particular historical epoch. Moreover, the ruling class is not necessarily cynical. Its members in all likelihood would believe that the government is just and that the social hierarchy is ordained by nature or God. Only after the productive forces change do the stark inequities of a social or political system become apparent. Whatever form the regime takes, it does little to influence the underlying productive forces that dominate and control human life. Marx provides the following example:

> Property, etc., in short, the entire contents of law and state is the same in North America and in Prussia, with few modifications. In North America the republic is a mere form of the state as monarchy is here. The content of the state remains outside these constitutions . . . the material state is not political.[31]

If the problems confronting people are economic, Marx hypothesizes, then the solutions too must be economic. Reform can occur only when the productive forces are changed. Furthermore, after the means of production finally fall into the hands of the proletariat (when everyone owns everything) the political arrangement will not matter. The cause of oppression will have disappeared so that the mechanism of oppression, the state, will wither away. As Dante Germino comments, "Man, from being a dwarf will become a giant, and the new man will have no need of the institutions that served as fetters in his prehistory."[32]

The antidote to such idealism, Solzhenitsyn counsels, was the reign of Stalin. There is little doubt that Marx would have been appalled by Stalin's despotism; he specifically rejects the "cult of personality." Yet Solzhenitsyn questions the responsibility of a teaching that makes no provision for governing, establishes no institutional checks against tyranny, and lays down no limitations on the exercise of power. For example, he comments that in the Soviet Union, "the legislative, executive and judicial authorities [are] at the mercy of a telephone call from the one and only, self-appointed authority." When compared to Western countries, protection of natural rights under "advanced Soviet jurisprudence [was] barbaric." "In our country," he complains, "everything [was] permissible."[33]

In this instance Solzhenitsyn criticizes Marx not for what he proposed, but for what he failed to propose. By presenting no scheme for the proper arrangement of political life and by refusing to consider people's natural ambition, Marx committed a sin of omission. He left those countries that accepted his principles unprepared for the political squabbles and contests for power and influence that are inevitable in social life. Ignorance of the true springs of human action may not be sufficient cause to blame Marx for the ascent of Stalin, but surely it can be considered a necessary cause. Or is it better to say that by providing no political check on ambition, Marx allowed Stalin and all the many other Communist dictators to emerge?

Marx did not think it necessary to formulate an institutional arrangement for future society, however. He preferred democracy, but one unfettered by past democratic institutions. He foresaw universal, free, and spontaneous association of all individuals. Putting aside for the moment the impracticality of such a goal, one might ask how Marx's goals are supposed to come into being. After the revolution, he insisted, a transitional form of the state would be required, a unified centralized administration resting, in the short run at least, on the "revolutionary dictatorship of the proletariat."[34] But would not some have to be more equal than others during the period of transition? Or did Marx really believe that all the workers would suddenly begin to think and act alike?

In the real world, no revolution can succeed without leadership. Once in command, Solzhenitsyn contends, human beings, even the vanguard of the proletariat, are confronted with the temptations of power. Power is intoxicating, he explains. Those who possess it come to have a certain aura about them. They are feared and respected by others, and they are likely to expect greater privilege to go along with their higher rank. Most often they become proud of their distinction, since, as he puts it, pride "grows in the heart like lard on a pig." Once gained, power is very difficult to relinquish; people tend to cling to it to protect their privileges. Who wants to be demoted back to the masses?[35]

Marx had expected that love of honor, privilege, distinction, and domination would disappear once private property was abolished. But Solzhenitsyn shows that human behavior is not that easily transformed. Economic arrangements may change, but people's desires and passions remain. Indeed, nowhere was desire to attain and hold power more evident than in Communist countries, proving once again that certain traits are synonymous with human existence and not intrinsic to a particular mode of production.[36]

There is an even greater danger in the exercise of power. Solzhenitsyn contends that lurking within the human soul is a desire to lord it over others, to make them completely dependent on one's will, and to watch them suffer. This dark tendency emerges when a person gains total control over the life of another. Using the example of the camps, he shows how the guards—the Dog Service, he calls them—were utterly corrupted by the complete control they wielded over the prisoners. They quickly became arrogant, smug, lascivious, greedy, and cruel. They used zeks as slaves and concubines. They stole the prisoners' meager belongings and saw prisoners' suffering as entertainment. He writes, "Human nature, if it changes at all, changes not much faster than the geographic face of the earth. And the very same sensations of curiosity, relish, and sizing up which slave-traders felt at the slave-girl markets twenty-five centuries ago . . . possessed the Gulag bigwigs." Could such creatures really be, Solzhenitsyn muses, "the heirs" of the "universal human culture" that Marx predicted?[37]

Marx's disregard for the importance of politics led him to misunderstand one of the most elemental of human desires. When one ruling class is overthrown, the leaders of the revolution are bound to take its place. Privilege is rarely abolished; it is merely passed from one elite to another. "The prohibition of all privilege," Solzhenitsyn explains in response to a proposal by Andrei Sakharov, "is . . . a mere cry from the heart, and not a practical task. . . . In Russia such prohibitions, reinforced by powder and shot, have been known in the past, but privilege popped up again as soon as there was a change of bosses." The Bolshevik Revolution did little more than exchange an avaricious bourgeoisie for an even more avaricious Communist bureaucracy. Solzhenitsyn makes the point in an artistic way in *First Circle* where he explains the role of the security chief in the prison facility where the action of the novel takes place. He writes,

> From the half barren office, in which the only instruments of production were steel cabinets containing the prisoners' files, a half dozen chairs, a telephone and a buzzer, Lieutenant Colonel Klimentiev—without any visible clutch, drive, or gear box—supervised the outward course of 281 lives and the service of 50 guards.

So much for the primacy of economics over politics.[38]

HISTORY

Exactly how Marx thought history moved, and whether he believed it was activated by a causal chain initiated by human production, is a matter of academic debate. What is clear, however, is that Marx left the impression that history was moving inexorably toward its culmination in the proletarian revolution and the Communist epoch. Indeed, there is a great deal of evidence to support such an interpretation. Marx begins by asserting that man is primarily a producer, since he must produce to survive. As people create their means of subsistence, so they establish the rest of their social life. All is contingent on the mode of production used to maintain people's physical well-being. Humans are capable of changing history, but not in the way one would usually think, that is, by a conscious act of will. Rather, Marx claims, "by . . . acting on the external world, and changing it, [man] at the same time changes his own nature." This interpretation resolves two seemingly contradictory statements by Marx: "circumstances make men just as much as men make circumstances," and "Are men free to choose this or that form of society for themselves? By no means. Assume a particular state of development in the productive forces of man and you get a particular form of commerce and consumption . . . and a corresponding organization of the family, of orders, of classes, in a word, a corresponding civil society." As economic arrangements change, so does the nature of society, as Marx expresses in his oft-quoted remark: "The hand-mill gives you society with the feudal lord; the steam-mill, society with the industrial capitalist." Thus, the history of human-kind can be understood only by investigating the material forces that lie behind and move events.[39]

Marx's reflections on historical change led to the conclusion that notions of morality and rights change from one era to another in line with the reorganiza-tion of productive forces. "The class that is the ruling material power of society is at the same time its ruling intellectual power," he states. "The ruling ideas are nothing more than the ideal expression of the dominant material relationships grasped as ideas. . . . The dominant idea . . . is expressed as an 'eternal law.'" He further rejects the proposition that people are endowed with natural rights. For example, he states, "The ideas of religious liberty and freedom of conscience merely give expression to the sway of free competition." It is exactly those rights that the bourgeoisie claim are natural, he contends, that have tied the masses to the slavery of wage-labor.[40]

It is a matter of some controversy whether Marx agreed with Engels's asser-tion that all morality is variable according to its time and place in history. Engels's formulation, written before Marx's death and claiming his authority, is as follows:

> We therefore reject every attempt to impose on us any moral dogma whatso-ever as an eternal, ultimate and forever immutable ethical law. . . . We maintain on the contrary that all moral theories have been hitherto the product . . . of economic conditions of society obtaining at the time.[41]

Solzhenitsyn points out that all four of these propositions—history moves inevitably toward a workers' state, individuals do not control history, human beings are endowed with no intrinsic rights, and morality is variable—were ac-cepted as the correct Marxist-Leninist doctrine wherever Communists held power. Marx's views anointed party decisions with the infallibility of historical inevitability. Hence, party authority became absolute.

In practice, Marx's ideas allowed party leaders to adopt any position what-ever if they felt it would contribute to the success of the movement. (Recall, for example, what Krylenko said on the expediency of Soviet criminal proceedings.) Taking full advantage of the latitude it enjoys, the party on more than one occa-sion found it useful to ally itself with and even to aid some of the more reaction-ary forces of history; Stalin made a pact with Adolph Hitler. In the search for the most opportune course, party chiefs, in line with Marxist principles, gave little thought to the "fetters" of past morality and ethics. After all, if traditional moral-ity and ethics were merely the discredited remnants of an antiquated mode of production, was it not correct that Communist leaders adopt new, proletarian norms of behavior? As it turns out, Solzhenitsyn contends, the new standards were little more than an expression of the leader's unrestrained individual will, or, as was once said about Stalin, his "iron will."[42]

While the practical result of Marx's teaching was to liberate party leaders from moral limits, it had the opposite effect on the vast majority of the party rank and file. In their case, individual choice was sacrificed to the historical necessity of party discipline. For example, Solzhenitsyn recalls that party loyalists never opposed Stalin. His commands were enthusiastically obeyed and his excesses blamed on someone else, usually some "puppet" of the reactionary forces of history. Even when party members were themselves arrested, they refused to resist, complaining only of the "mistake" that had led to their personal misfortune. They did not evince a will of their own, accepting in all things the current party line. Solzhenitsyn holds that loyal party members hardly ever objected to anything that the party did because to do so would have cast doubt on the inevitable victory of socialism and made their entire life's work meaningless.[43]

The willingness of party members to do whatever their leaders asked of them resulted in the rulers having almost unlimited power. Perhaps this, more than any other fact, accounts for the totalitarian nature of Communist societies. Old-style despots may have had the most grandiose schemes in mind, but they could count on only a few diehard supporters, and whomever else they could buy, to carry them out. Communist tyrants enjoyed the vigorous cooperation of people convinced of the rightness of their cause who did not ask questions about the ethics of their actions. Unlimited power in the hands of unrestrained will, it seems, was the consequence of Marx's teaching about history.

Not only does Solzhenitsyn criticize Marx for the effects of his philosophy of history, but he doubts whether those ideas have much validity. For example, if Marx was right, then no changes would have occurred in party policy after Stalin's death. In contradiction to the progressive laws of economics, however, under Khrushchev the government did change, if only for a short while. With the fall of Stalin's last and most vicious chief of state security, Lavrenti Beria, the Soviet regime loosened its grip just a bit. The worst excesses of the terror ended, and the number of people interned was reduced. Is this not proof, Solzhenitsyn asks, that individual human beings, for reasons having little to do with the productive forces, can control the movement of history? Nowhere had Marx claimed that individual leaders could individually redirect the course of history. But what else is the "personality cult" if not an admission that individuals can and do influence events?[44]

Solzhenitsyn makes the point with almost vindictive glee. He explains that the Stalinists who were in the Gulag did nothing to oppose their beloved leader. They accepted their fate and Stalin's brutality as ordained by sacred history. Later, when the "cult of personality" was exposed—that is, the party line changed—they were disgraced for not having resisted Stalin, just fate, Solzhenitsyn suggests, for those who decide to abandon individual conscience to the vagaries of history.[45]

Solzhenitsyn makes the point another way. If everything in society changes along with the mode of production, why does not language change? Since language does not change radically at each turn of history, perhaps the human capacity for speech—hence, reason—is independent of changes in the economic structure, a conclusion that casts doubt on Marx's theory of historical development.

Solzhenitsyn recognizes, of course, that language can be modified. In fact, he holds that one of the most calamitous effects of Soviet rule was the degradation of the Russian language. But the abolition of private property seems to have had little to do with this change. Rather, it was the awkward and mediocre mind of Stalin, along with the incessant sloganeering of the party, that invaded even the highest regions of expression and poisoned a language rich in tradition and subtlety. Again, it appears that individuals took a leading role in the creation of history.[46]

HUMAN NATURE

In his analysis of human existence, Marx begins with a rudimentary, yet most important, fact: people must provide for their physical well-being. The distinguishing characteristic of the human species is its capacity to fulfill its needs through the activity of conscious production. Marx states, "Man is distinguished from the animals by consciousness, religion, or anything else you please. He begins to distinguish himself from the animals the moment he begins to produce his means of subsistence." In an effort to make life better and easier for themselves, people discover new ways of doing things; they create new modes of production. In transforming the economic structure, they also change the superstructure. Ideas about "morality, religion, metaphysics and all the rest of ideology" are modified, for these things are not "independent" but rest on "material relationships." Consciousness itself derives from economic causes. Marx argues:

> The production of ideas, of conceptions, of consciousness is directly interwoven with the material activity and of the material relations of men; it is the language of actual life. Conceiving, thinking, and the intellectual relationships of men appear here as the direct result of their material behavior. . . . Consciousness does not determine life, but life determines consciousness.[47]

CRIME

Since the social and economic environment is the source of ideas, and ideas are the basis of actions, it follows that people's actions are products of the environment in which they live. It also follows that people do not have free will; they do not choose their way of life. Their surroundings choose it for them. Thus, although Marx does not make this explicit, people are not responsible for their actions. Individual guilt (and innocence) is rejected by Marx as an antiquated bourgeois concept. Crime is the consequence of social inequality. Whether Marx meant for his ideas to be carried to their logical conclusion is unclear, but his followers had no doubt about his meaning. For example, Krylenko reasoned that, "every crime is the result of a given social system"; thus, for a long time the party considered common criminals as socially friendly elements.[48]

By relieving human beings of responsibility for their behavior, Marxism excuses any act of savagery or terrorism as long as it is aimed against the bourgeoisie. Such acts are rationalized as a liberating revolt against the "fetters" of historically reactionary societies. Even when violence is not consciously political, it is thought to be caused by, and is justified as resistance against, the oppressive strictures of capitalism.[49]

Furthermore, Solzhenitsyn argues, because Marxism fails to recognize that evil resides in human beings and not exclusively in their environment (how else can Stalin be explained? He had the right social origins), it has the tendency to create criminals. For example, the Soviet Union was slow to admit that it had a crime problem. The party hid the whole issue from public view because it was embarrassed. In particular, it did not want the West to gloat over this apparent contradiction in Marxist principles. Only capitalist countries, racked by poverty and degradation, were supposed to have lawlessness. Because the Soviet Union was a socialist society, it should have been immune to crime. The conspiracy of silence made it easier for criminals to ply their trade. Honest Soviet citizens were never warned of the dangers facing them; thus, they rarely took adequate precautions to protect themselves. A life of crime became attractive. Outlaws found easy prey among the unwitting populace. They were rarely caught, and even when they were, their jail terms were relatively light. By not placing suitable barriers against base passions, Solzhenitsyn argues, the Soviet government encouraged those passions to be unleashed; criminals in spirit became criminals in fact.[50]

ESSENCE AND EXISTENCE

Solzhenitsyn strenuously rejects the idea that human beings are determined. He objects again and again to the Marxist claim that essence is determined by existence. He does not doubt that some people allow themselves to be pushed here and there by circumstances. Such people live, he says, by the "swinish principle" that existence determines consciousness. Even if some people allow themselves to be determined by their circumstances, this fact does not prove that Marx's theory is correct, but it shows only the lack of spiritual strength in some individuals. "For people of strong minds and spirits," Solzhenitsyn maintains, "a similarity of paths in life and a similarity of situations" does not give rise to "a similarity of characters." Even under the harshest and most extreme conditions, some inhabitants of the Gulag refused to sell their souls for a piece of bread, choosing instead to maintain their inner spiritual freedom. There were many such people in the camps, more perhaps than will ever be known, since most of them perished. Solzhenitsyn recounts many stories of their tenacious spirit and noble resistance.[51]

It is true, no doubt, that most people make concessions to necessity—this is only human and natural. But Solzhenitsyn criticizes Marx's contention that people cannot help but be reduced by hunger to the level of animals. His character

Ivan Denisovich Shukhov best embodies that resilience of character that allows people to survive without being degraded. Despite racking starvation, Ivan Denisovich eats his meager ration slowly, so it can be properly digested. He retains a formality in table manners and even refuses particularly unappetizing parts of his soup. In all things it is Shukhov, and not his hunger, in control, showing that people need not be debased by their needs.[52]

Solzhenitsyn attacks Marx's suppositions concerning human existence in another way. He argues that if existence dictated consciousness, everyone in the camps would have, and should have, become a revolutionary. Conditions in the Gulag were much worse than in the sweatshops and factories of the West. The oppression, suffering, and degradation were immensely greater. Doesn't that mean, according to Marxist doctrine, that socialism sowed the seed of its own destruction? Despite having this revolutionary kernel within it, the Soviet state was not overthrown during its most oppressive stage, partly because not everyone became resentful after their years as slave laborers. Loyal Communists among the camp dwellers, who should have been attuned to social inequities, repudiated any hint that their beloved party might have been unjust and should be overthrown, and no experience could change their minds.[53]

TRANSFORMATION OF HUMAN NATURE

Marx wrote that "the whole of history is nothing but a continual transformation of human nature." On this postulate rests his hope for the future of humankind. Without it, the promise of a better world is impossible. "For the success of the cause," he writes, "the alteration of man on a mass scale is necessary."[54] Marx championed the transformation of human nature, for to look backward into the past of the human race was to see a species incapable of forming a perfect society. Marx recognized the truth of Hegel's claim that history was a slaughter bench, but he hoped to change that. Beginning with the premise that people are determined by the environment, he calculated that when the environment changed, so would human nature. A better future was possible because all the faults and limitations of the past could be overcome. Marx thought less of people in the present—they were neither free nor responsible for their errant ways—because he expected more of them in the future; they would be reformed when the economic structure was perfected.

If the sordid history of the attempt to institute socialism in the Soviet Union proves anything, Solzhenitsyn maintains, it proves that human nature cannot readily be transformed. The same urges—greed, lust, and ambition—that have motivated people since time immemorial are still with us no matter what the social configuration. A theory that does not take this truth into account is destined to make tragic errors when put into practice. An attempt to "alter man on a mass scale" solely by restructuring economic relations is foolish.[55]

WHAT IS HUMAN NATURE?

For Solzhenitsyn, Marx's conception of man is too narrow. He holds that there is always something in human beings that cannot be fathomed by class analysis or causal reasoning, something that is forever surprising. "The bounds of a human being!" he writes. "No matter how you are astounded by them, you can never comprehend." People, "never fit into . . . previously set grooves." Human nature cannot be understood through "simple linear formulations, flat solutions, [and] over simplified explanations," for it "is full of riddles and contradictions; its very complexity engenders art."[56]

LABOR

Marx's view of labor is actually twofold. Labor is productive in the sense that human beings go about changing and shaping the world in order to satisfy their creative urges. Labor is necessary in the sense that human beings must satisfy their bodily needs. Marx is actually more interested in the first aspect of labor, humans as creative producers, although he is normally associated with the second, people driven to revolt by oppression and scarcity. Human labor began, he asserts, as a response to physical necessity. Once begun, labor quickly became an expression of individual freedom and creativity, a way of conquering nature and putting it to one's advantage. The task of subduing nature obviously was beyond the capacity of single individuals, and therefore the community of human beings was formed—as Marx calls it, man as a "species being." For convenience and efficiency, the chores of a community were divided according to those who could best accomplish them. No sooner was this division of labor put in place, however, than it began to create problems. People relinquished part of their labor and lost a corresponding amount of control over their lives. Social stratification arose since people with particularly useful skills demanded greater compensation. These distinctions hardened into classes as wealth and privilege passed from one generation to the next.[57]

The antagonisms established as social strata developed became more acute over time, according to Marx. The individual, as worker, had an ever-decreasing influence over what he produced, until, in the final stages of capitalism, he was reduced to an appendage of the machine. The assembly-line worker has a fragmented consciousness because his productive activity consists of nothing more than repeating the same mechanical operation again and again. And since he has little control over the finished product, he gains no gratification from its creation.

As the society becomes more developed, the worker enjoys fewer and fewer of the fruits of his labor. His labor power, as Marx calls it, is wrenched from him by the owners. The meager wages the worker receives are dictated by the market. The owners, in a mad dash to beat their competition and make a profit, must reduce costs by lowering wages and investing their profits (surplus value) into ever more complex machines. The new machines simplify the tasks of labor even more, thus further condemning the workers to mindless repetition and cheapening the value of their labor by eliminating any need for mechanical expertise. Technological innovations glut the market with goods. In spite of the enormous wealth all around them, workers are reduced to abject poverty since, as Marx claims to have discovered in his theory of surplus value, capitalism cannot exist without appropriating all the value of the labor except that minimum necessary to sustain their lives.[58]

LABOR THEORY OF VALUE

Solzhenitsyn argues that the theory of surplus value is a "superficial" account of economics that has gained wide popular acceptance only because few people bother to read Marx's works carefully. Marx argues that capitalism "rivets" workers to the "agony of toil, slavery, ignorance, brutality [and] mental degradation . . . more firmly than the wedges of Vulcan did Prometheus to the rock." Solzhenitsyn argues that Marx's theory is flawed because "it declares that only workers create value and failed to take into account the contribution of . . . organizers, engineers, transportation, or marketing systems." In other words, Marx overlooks the role of technical expertise and managerial skill. Moreover, Marx considers only the commodity market in a free-market system; he fails to recognize that a competitive labor market also exists which helps to raise the wages of laborers. Little wonder Solzhenitsyn calls Marx's economics "primitive."[59]

ALIENATION OF LABOR

Solzhenitsyn partly agrees and partly disagrees with Marx's views on the alienation of labor. He recognizes that people can be degraded by the labor they perform, yet he objects to Marx's assertion that this is an immutable law, necessarily true in every case. Even in the camps, he explains, where people received no benefit at all from their work and had no control over the means of production, occasionally they still found labor rewarding. He makes this point through his character Ivan Denisovich. Ivan Denisovich is consoled by his work despite the harsh reality that all the value of his labor is being extracted from him—he is on starvation wages—and in spite of the fact that he has utterly no creative control over the things he is forced to produce.[60]

Interestingly, Solzhenitsyn's novel, which circulated widely during the brief Khrushchev thaw, was attacked by loyal Communists. In line with the Progressive Doctrine, they argued that Ivan Denisovich could not have enjoyed work under such adverse conditions and that he should have refused to work and joined the "true" party members in the camps who were leading the struggle against the cult of personality. Solzhenitsyn scoffs at the latter position and recalls that for loyal Communists, even in the camps, Stalin "remained an uneclipsed sun." To the former assertion he responds that something in human nature finds the process of labor rewarding. He explains:

[S]uch is man's nature that even bitter, detested work is sometimes performed
with an incomprehensible wild excitement. Having worked for two years with
my hands, I encountered this strange phenomenon myself: suddenly you become absorbed in the work itself, irrespective of whether it is slave labor and
offers you nothing. I experienced those strange moments at bricklaying. . . .
And so surely we can allow Ivan Denisovich not to feel his inescapable labor as
a terrible burden forever, not to hate it perpetually?[61]

As further proof of his contention, Solzhenitsyn considers the difference in
the quality of work done in former times with that produced in the modern
world. In such a contest, he claims, the past is superior even though present-day
workers are often better compensated. The workers of old may have "ground
their teeth and cursed" at the difficulty of their tasks, but their toil gained meaning from the excellence and beauty that it attained and from the purpose to
which it was put. Contemporary work, in line with the spirit of equality, aspires
to be little more than functional; it serves the greatest number. By failing to
reach for the sublime, it loses its capacity to elicit great effort and becomes
shoddy and common.[62]

Nor does Solzhenitsyn consider the division of labor to be alienating. Ivan
Denisovich, for instance, feels a certain pleasure in the unison of a group effort
although he considers his own work superior to the rest. In general the division
of labor may actually help satisfy the human desire to create, since more can be
accomplished in a group than by individual effort. Furthermore, the division of
labor can be viewed as a manifestation of the complexity of the human species.
Solzhenitsyn reasons that some people such as Ivan Denisovich have the dispo-
sition and conditioning to excel at manual labor. He knew two trades and "could
pick up a dozen more just like that," while others became exhausted by the same
effort. In part the division of labor reflects the differences in ability and talent
with which nature endows the human race. For all his talk of the variety of social activities that will become available to people after the revolution, Marx's
critique of labor does not adequately express the range and depth of human motivation.[63]

Solzhenitsyn also questions Marx's insistence that work is satisfying only
when the individual is able to perform many different tasks. He agrees that there
may be some truth in this assertion, as the example of Ivan Denisovich shows,
but there is also a great deal of satisfaction in doing one thing very well. If people spread their talents over many occupations instead of concentrating on just
one, might this not lead in the direction of dilettantism and away from the development of human excellence?[64]

LABOR AS THE CREATOR OF THE HUMAN SPECIES

According to Marx, the human race is distinguished from animals by its capacity
for conscious production. This activity does not merely serve to satisfy human
needs; it constitutes the very essence of the species. Through labor, the human

race creates itself. Marx writes, "Since for socialist man . . . the entire so-called world history is only the creation of man through human labor and the development of nature for man, he has evident and incontrovertible proof of his self-creation, his own formation process."[65] Solzhenitsyn takes exception to both of Marx's points. He argues that the distinguishing characteristic of the human race is not that people are conscious producers, but that they are conscious. To be a conscious producer, one must first have consciousness. "Man," Solzhenitsyn alleges, restating an argument of great antiquity, "has separated himself from the animal world by thought and speech."[66]

Solzhenitsyn bitterly attacks Marx's claim that labor created man, for it was this premise that became the justification for the Gulag. Since labor constituted man, it was deduced that only labor could reconstitute, or reforge, social deviants. Thus did the Soviet state find a rationale for forced-labor camps. He writes of Engels's discovery, "The human being had arisen not through the perception of a moral idea and not through the process of thought, but out of happenstance and meaningless work (an ape picked up a stone—and with this everything began)." Marx further compounded the error by declaring that labor could reform people. Solzhenitsyn explains that for Marx,

> [T]he one and only means of correcting offenders . . . was not solitary contemplation, not moral soul-searching, not repentance, and not languishing (for all that was super structure)—but productive labor. He himself had never in his life taken a pick in hand. To the end of his days he never pushed a wheelbarrow, mined coal, felled timber, and we don't even know how his firewood was split—but he wrote that down, and the paper did not resist.[67]

To prove his point, Solzhenitsyn gives many examples of people who repented their past lives and reformed their ways. None of them were reclaimed by labor. Indeed, the heavy physical labor of the camps in which people replaced machines and from which "the human being" was "once created . . . from the ape," often had the opposite effect, "inexplicably transforming him back into the ape again." Solzhenitsyn mocks the Progressive Doctrine for having ushered into the world the cruelty of the corrective (destructive) labor camps. He compares the exploitation in the camps to that which existed during the old regime and in the capitalist West and shows that under Communism far worse conditions prevailed. He ironically suggests that only under the aegis of the Progressive Doctrine did exploitation reach its full potential. To build socialism, people were forced to work at or below subsistence level.[68]

Nothing in the bourgeois world could compare to the level of abuse that occurred under Communism. Western governments could not marshal sufficient support to force their publics to endure the intolerable conditions that existed in the Gulag. Citizens of the West would simply have stopped obeying, using their "false" bourgeois right of liberty to fend for themselves. Or they would rise up and demand a more equitable share of the nation's resources, which is exactly what occurred during the labor unrest of the twentieth century.

Under Communism, however, power was centralized, making possible a higher stage of oppression. Particularly in the camps, where prisoners could be shot without warning, full extraction of labor was possible at little or no material costs. Prisoners' "piece work" consisted of being starved and having higher rations dangling before them to reward greater effort. Of course, this method had its drawbacks; after about three months, prisoners could no longer perform any useful labor, and most died. Not even in the darkest days of serfdom had there been exploitation on such a scale.[69]

An even closer relationship exists between Marxism and the Gulag, Solzhenitsyn maintains. The camps, he says, are the foundation of Marxist economics. He reasons as follows: Socialism could never have been established in the Soviet Union (or elsewhere) without the assistance of forced labor. How else could people be made to toil and receive nothing in return? The nation was too poor to afford the capital necessary for the vast industrialization the party envisioned. It is doubtful whether the state could ever have raised sufficient capital to modernize, since its economic policies crushed individual initiative. To fulfill its promise of material advancement, it had no other option but to conscript labor. Was there another way it could elicit the talents "of highly skilled specialists who were willing in addition to live for years in conditions unfit for dogs"?[70]

An objection can be raised that Russia was not an industrial nation, as Marx's theory had predicted it would be, when it was overtaken by a premature revolution. Hence, Marx cannot be held accountable for the horrors of modernization that took place in Russia. He had argued that no such development would be necessary. This proposition is true enough, although it must be recognized that successful Communist revolts primarily took place in underdeveloped countries. In addition to this discrepancy, Solzhenitsyn unearths an even subtler connection between Marxism and forced labor.

Marx insists that alienation will end only when the necessity for labor no longer exists. He envisages a mode of production that "does away with labor" and asserts that "the question is not the liberation but the abolition of labor." He sees a time when science will fully conquer natural necessity, when man and nature will be one. Labor, instead of a hated torment, will be transformed into a "free manifestation of life." Solzhenitsyn responds that nature is not so easily brought to heel. Its complexities and mysteries are beyond the human capacity to fully unravel. A concerted effort to bring nature totally under human command is likely to backfire, resulting in an ecological disaster of some sort. Nature can never be fully transcended because human beings did not create existence and have no means of abolishing death; the beginning and the end of being are beyond their control. Yet Marx maintains that alienation would cease and true happiness would reign only through the conquest of nature. Those under Marx's influence, those who accept his goals, attempted to achieve this feat.[71]

Insofar as nature cannot be overcome, Communism, no matter where it existed, was always in the process of being built. Since Communism's economic system was so poor at generating wealth, especially investment capital, it could not build the machines required to transform the world without forcibly extracting the profits from somebody's labor. It is by this chain of reasoning that Solzhenitsyn forwards his claim: The essence of Marxism is the camps.

Marx uses the term "Asiatic despotism" to describe the most primitive form of social organization, virtually the first stage of historical development. Solzhenitsyn sarcastically adopts the same expression to characterize the form of labor that was spawned as the result of Marx's philosophy. The choice of terms is more than coincidental, since Marx said that the attributes of Asiatic despotism consisted of "the private arbitrariness of particular individuals," and a centralized state that constructed and maintained a complex and costly waterworks system—a rather accurate description of one of Stalin's pet projects, the Belomar Canal.[72]

LOVE OF ONE'S OWN

In an address before the AFL-CIO, Solzhenitsyn said that the *Communist Manifesto* "contains even more terrible things than what has actually been done." Apart from historical analysis and some proposals for minor reforms of society, the *Manifesto*'s major prescriptions involve the abolition of private property, the transformation of the family, and the communism of women. Marx's suggestions for change strike at those things that people hold most dear—property, family, spouse.[73]

DEFENSE OF PRIVATE PROPERTY

Marx's name and the endeavor to abolish private property have become almost synonymous. In a sense, Marx views private property as the root of all evil. To abolish it would be to rid society of injustice. To be sure, Solzhenitsyn agrees, private property is a kind of selfishness because it gives personal gratification to its owner. However, the abolition of private property will not free the human race from selfishness and greed. In fact, the confiscation of property is likely to jeopardize some very valuable things, including important attributes of the human character. "The fundamental concepts of private property and private economic initiative," he writes, "are part of man's nature, and necessary for his personal freedom and his sense of normal well-being." But why is this so?[74]

First, and given the history of Soviet Communism, perhaps most importantly, private ownership of property acts as a shield or buffer against the arbitrary and capricious whims of those in power, including well-intentioned bureaucrats. Personal property allows individuals to act as independent agents. Because they are free to secure their own livelihood, they are not exclusively or directly dependent on the government for their well-being or life. Moreover, the separation of political and economic power inhibits the government from tightening its grip. It loses a powerful tool of coercion. Since it is not fully in control of the economy, it cannot use the threat of starvation—by taking away a person's job, for example—as a way of compelling obedience. Finally, the separation of political and economic activity creates autonomous centers of power that, in the nature of things, tend to keep each other in check.

Second, private property increases the likelihood of competence, even excellence, in the professions. In Solzhenitsyn's novel *Cancer Ward*, Dr. Oreshchenkov defends private medical practice against socialized or state medicine. Although the views of Dr. Oreshchenkov are not necessarily those of his creator, the arguments that he presents are so compelling that they cannot readily be dismissed.

Oreshchenkov maintains that a doctor, and by implication members of other trades and professions, "should depend on the impression he makes on his patients, he should be dependent on his popularity."[75] Since patients are likely to seek out the best care available for themselves, such a scheme weeds out incompetent or untalented people. Who wants to pay for poor health care? At the same time, it rewards the adroit with renown and, of course, material gain. The good doctor, it seems, is an advocate of consumer sovereignty.

Obviously, anyone holding such a view is being inconsistent. He is entrusting the care and well-being of others to the personal selfishness of doctors. He is arguing that in one man's breast can exist both a love of others and a love of self. Despite the logical inconsistencies of this position, it does seem to accurately reflect a tension that occurs, to a greater or lesser degree, within every human being. People can and do act selflessly, but it would violate reason to say that altruism is their only motive. A proper regard for oneself is not unnatural or even ignoble; it merely reflects the desire of every individual for well-being and may even express an impulse toward the perfection of one's ability and character.

Not compensating people for their hard work or superior ability is likely to lead to mediocrity. The talented may begin to wonder if they should bother developing their skills. If the reward for work of a high caliber is no different than for low, will not the able and diligent throw up their hands in disgust and join the crowd? One does not have to bow down to the perfection of the marketplace to see that a rough justice is achieved when people are compensated for a job well done.[76]

Solzhenitsyn shows a strong sympathy for Dr. Oreshchenkov's views. He argues, for example, that the peasants' desire for land was an expression of the dual nature of human striving. He explains, "The peasant masses longed for land and if this in a certain sense means freedom and wealth, in another (and more important) sense it means obligation, in yet another (and its highest) sense it means a mystical tie with the world and a feeling of personal worth."[77] He further points out that farmers who worked their own land during the N.E.P. produced more than they did either for their former landlords or for the communal farms. They were even likely to learn the most advanced techniques of agriculture.[78]

Returning to Dr. Oreshchenkov's argument, the free market, to a great extent, protects patients (and, by implication, consumers). First, it allows for free choice. Except in a dire emergency the ill can seek out a doctor they prefer, choosing one they trust. Private doctors are likely to be more solicitous than those working for the state because they are dependent for their livelihood on what their patients think of them. A personal rapport is likely to develop in which their patient comes to be treated as a whole person rather than just a sickness or an injury.

Under socialized medicine doctors are under little compulsion to care about the private concerns of individuals; rather, they are pressed to turn out a certain amount of work. A patient is treated as one case in a long line of cases. In rare instances, such a system produces exceptionally qualified physicians. More often, it encourages no more than technical competence. And at its worst, it engenders apathy, since the doctor's salary is paid, regardless. The free market may turn the members of every profession into wage earners, as Marx suggested, but socialism transforms them into something worse, insensitive bureaucrats.[79]

Solzhenitsyn does not subscribe fully to the vagaries of free-market economics, however. For instance, he does not condone that excessive thirst for wealth that leads some people to oppress others or to sell state secrets to their nation's enemies. He seems to argue that the free market works best when the size of businesses is limited and when economic relations between people do not become entirely impersonal. The question that immediately comes to mind is whether such limitations on commerce and industry are practical. What of economies of scale? To this point Solzhenitsyn gives two responses. First, he advocates a "small technology" and a decentralized economy, which, although less efficient, may be more conducive to the human good than large corporations that rapidly exploit and consume natural resources. Second, he argues that the ills of the free market can be mitigated if people understand that there is something higher than the quest for material reward—morality should place a check on avarice.

Let us return once again to Dr. Oreshchenkov. Surprisingly, he argues that private medicine is less expensive than socialized. In the first place, he points out, socialized medicine is not free, but is paid for by a levy that government places on people's earnings. If that money were not taken from them, they could use it to pay for medical care, even if that meant having to forgo some other expense. The cost of medical care could be kept down because private medicine is less wasteful than socialized medicine. It is not encumbered by the salaries of a large, bureaucratic support staff. Moreover, people are less likely to seek unnecessary care or consultations when they are made to pay for it. However, Dr. Oreshchenkov does not fully endorse a free-market approach to medical care. He believes that truly costly medical treatment is the responsibility of the community.

Solzhenitsyn seems to concur with his artistic creation. In contrast with Marx, he asserts that the communism of property is wasteful. When things are held in common, there is no accountability and less care given for how things are used. To illustrate this point, Solzhenitsyn recounts the story of a *Potemkin* sailor, one of the mutineers crucial to the Bolshevik Revolution, who had escaped punishment and made a good life for himself as a farmer in Canada. When the revolution came to his beloved homeland, he sold everything except a tractor and returned to his native region. With his tractor and his money he hoped to help build socialism. He enlisted in one of the first communes and donated the tractor for common use. The tractor was driven any which way by whoever happened along and was quickly ruined. The money was rapidly squandered on foolish expenses. Finding himself working harder and all the while growing thinner, the farmer escaped from the land of shared wealth and returned to Canada to begin life over again.[80]

Private ownership, on the other hand, encourages respect for the value of things, since the responsibility rests squarely with the owner and because the owner must pay for ruined equipment out of his own pocket. Ivan Denisovich values the best trowel because he is proud of his superior bricklaying. Even though he would not have to replace it, he fears entrusting it to others. So he meticulously hides it at the end of each workday.[81]

Finally, Solzhenitsyn maintains that abolishing private wealth does away with the possibility of exercising the virtue of generosity. If the state owns everything, then obviously people cannot give away their possessions. From a realistic perspective, no doubt, this loss of the virtue of magnanimity may be counterbalanced by the gain to common humanity that socialism entails. Yet, to Solzhenitsyn, this is just one more example of how Marxism undermines the development of human character and the exercise of virtue in its rush to provide for man's material welfare.[82]

CONFISCATION OF PROPERTY

As is the case with many of Marx's other forecasts, the confiscation of property did not work as he predicted. Marx expected that small businesses would be swallowed up by huge capitalist enterprises prior to the revolution taking place, and thus there would be no small businesses left for the state to confiscate. But that is not what happened. Under Communism, small holdings were confiscated along with large industries. This was so, Solzhenitsyn argues, because the desire to hold property is widespread among all people. Hence, expropriation of property is likely to injure not just a few bloated capitalists but a large segment of the population.

Solzhenitsyn presents a particularly poignant illustration of this fact in relating the plight of Russia's peasants. Confiscation of their property began as early as 1918 with an edict issued by Lenin. "Those guilty of selling, or buying up, or keeping for sale in the way of business food products which have been placed under the monopoly of the republic . . . [are to be] imprisoned for a term of not less than ten years, combined with the most severe forced labor."[83]

The N.E.P. gave a respite to the peasants, many of whom used seven-years to enrich themselves and their villages. In the strange tangle of Marxist logic, however, it was these people who suffered most. Solzhenitsyn estimates that fifteen million kulaks paid an extreme price—death——for their ambition, industry, and skill as farmers. On the other hand, the Progressive Doctrine took poverty as a sign of solidarity with the workers. Those who "drank down everything" in vodka and saved nothing were immune from "the peasant plague." Sometimes the profligate were even given important posts on collective farms. Others simply did not want to work. They loved possessions no less dearly than the next fellow, but they had too little control over their passions to use them wisely.[84]

Confiscation of property also has a tendency to destroy artisans and tradespeople, Solzhenitsyn claims. He tells of a former peasant who, by his hard work, was able to open a small sausage factory. When collectivization came, the tax man hounded him unmercifully until finally he had little left of any worth. When a survey of the peasant's holdings revealed that some rubber plants in a tub would have to be taken, he hacked them to pieces in disgust. He was subsequently arrested for destroying state property. The tale does not end there, however. The peasant ended up in the camps working in a sausage factory. This sausage factory was not confiscated, since its only customers were party higher-ups.

Finally, Solzhenitsyn maintains that expropriation of property excuses and intensifies the low passion of envy. Those who are jealous of the success of others and "incapable of making anything of themselves except activists" are the ones most likely to carry out expropriation. The urge to expropriate is nourished by contempt for human excellence.[85] For example, the property of the monks at Solovestsky Island was confiscated by people acting on the Progressive Doctrine's assumption that priests do no more than prey on others. The monks' cloister had been remarkably successful at agriculture and had discovered and fished a particularly flavorful variety of herring. The monks were completely self-sufficient, growing all their own food and exporting fish to pay for religious relics. Who were they hurting? How did their private holdings oppress anyone? Only a desire to show the monks up and to exhibit the superiority of socialism could have compelled the Bolsheviks to throw these people off their land. However, the socialist commune that took over the monks' property could not grow crops in such an intemperate climate, and no one could find where to catch the herring.[86]

REEMERGENCE OF SELF-INTEREST

The stated goal of Marxist revolutions was to abolish bribery, corruption, oppression, and the whole tawdry mess associated with the cash nexus. Yet no sooner had these revolutions been completed, explains Solzhenitsyn, than the age-old vices reappeared. As early as 1918, the commissioners of supply for the Eastern Front were discovered to have siphoned millions of rubles into their pockets. They used the money to buy big houses, rode around on expensive horses, and engaged in orgies with women their money had impressed. Even the

Cheka was not immune from greed. One very successful agent arrested people at piece rate.[87]

These incidents all took place early in the Russian Revolution. It could be that they reflect the psychology of a bourgeois background and were the initial errors of what Marx calls "crude Communism." The problem with Marxian analysis, Solzhenitsyn vividly shows, is that the quest for material gain and economic privilege became more pronounced as time passed. By 1937 the entire party had become infected with an oligarchic disdain for the life of ordinary Soviet citizens. Party members sentenced to the camps refused to share any of their extra rations or packages from home with the other zeks. They mouthed the slogans of equality and community, but they would actually have none of it. Their private automobiles, special closed stores, and fine dachas had corrupted them.[88]

Part of the problem was created by Stalin. Trained by vicious bureaucratic struggles and cynical to the core, he understood that money is a temptation few can resist. He preyed on this weakness, paying party officials high wages and then, when his trust in them soured, using their wealth as the basis for an indictment against them. On the theory that soldiers would fight harder if it were in their self-interest to do so, he allowed the Red Army to plunder the defeated Germans in World War II. Top NKVD officers were rumored to have amassed vast personal fortunes in this way. In spite of the fact that it did no productive labor, Stalin's favorite institution, the secret police, never lacked for material comforts. Its vigilance in uncovering fresh cases was enhanced by the high pay and benefits its members received. Prison chiefs in remote areas virtually lived as ancient potentates, harems and all.[89]

For most of the time that the party held power, special privileges were accorded to high party officials. The top echelon enjoyed elaborate apartments, stately summer homes, chauffeured limousines, and the finest clothes and food. Brezhnev even used a lake as a private game reserve.[90]

Disclosures made after the collapse of Communism in the Soviet Union and Eastern Europe show that Solzhenitsyn was correct about rampant corruption in the party ranks. Few people—especially party members, it seems—can live up to Marx's principles. Such principles defy common attributes of human nature by asking that people work with no thought of material advantage. Marxist principles demand that self-interest disappear. But self-interest will never disappear. Indeed, wherever a Marxist revolution took place, self-interest reappeared with a particular vengeance; the stage of Marx's "crude Communism" has never been transcended.[91]

As further evidence of his point, Solzhenitsyn reminds us that wage incentives had to be reintroduced into Communist economies as a way of getting people to work. The Soviets merely appropriated the piecework method, once common to capitalism, and renamed it socialist competition. Insofar as the government did succeed in squelching private initiative, it resurfaced as the "second story" economy, black market labor in which craftsmen bartered their skills and thereby avoided the impenetrable bureaucratic tangle that accompanied all state-owned enterprises. Evidently, laziness is more a part of human nature than Marx had predicted; it is best overcome by material incentives.[92]

PROPER LIMITS OF PRIVATE PROPERTY

Solzhenitsyn labels Marx's hope that the longing for private property can be expelled from the human soul a fantasy. The consequences of that fantasy were visible in the Soviet terror. First an attempt was made to banish the desire for property by exterminating those classes who were thought to be the standard-bearers of private interest. Later the fantasy reemerged in the rule of people who espoused the ideals of Marx, while presiding over one of the least equitable economic systems on earth. Somehow, under the influence of Marx, people twisted and warped reality so much that they were no longer aware of what their actions meant. How else, Solzhenitsyn makes us ponder, can one explain the fact that party officials, entrusted with teaching the masses about the ideology of Marxism-Leninism, would not "lift a finger . . . without payment?"[93]

No doubt Marx would be outraged to learn that his teaching has been put to such use. He had hoped that once property was held in common, people would pursue more humane, nonmaterialistic endeavors. But Solzhenitsyn wonders if events could have turned out otherwise than they did. In spite of all Marx's talk about the transcendence of property, he does not differ from the bourgeoisie except in one respect. The philosophy that inspired both capitalism and Marxism encouraged the idea that material well-being can somehow make people happy. Indeed, Marx goes a step further than capitalism in stressing the link between material pursuits and creation of a perfect social arrangement. The real difference between Marx and capitalism is not so much about the ends of life—prosperity is the goal pursued by both—but rather about the means of attaining those ends. Under capitalism, individuals are responsible for their own well-being; for Marx, the welfare of individuals is a communal activity. In truth, Marx's teaching concerns not so much the abolition but the communal ownership of property.

Little wonder, Solzhenitsyn remarks, that Marxism encouraged materialism. "We only have one life" is the motto that has sprung up under its banner, "and we must live it to the fullest." Marx's mistake was that he presented no teaching that would restrain greed; he left that to the good graces of history. He and other socialists assumed that people would become selfless once property was held in common. As Solzhenitsyn explains, "In no socialist doctrine . . . are moral demands seen as the essence of socialism—there is merely a promise that morality will fall like manna from heaven after the socialization of property."[94]

The root of Marx's dilemma lies in the assumption that human beings will evolve into something better once universal prosperity is achieved. But what is that something better? Will they become generous, moral people with admirable characters? If that is the end, as many of the purified Marxists hold, then why is material prosperity necessary at all? After all, Solzhenitsyn and his friends developed their characters while in the camps. It is apparent from everyday life, moreover, that people can strengthen their character in spite of suffering the most severe poverty. Indeed, it seems that a certain amount of hardship contributes to spiritual strength. Without adversity, people can be lulled into a false sense of security. They resist confronting their mortality and squander their time on earth in petty pursuits.

What Marx thought to be essential—prosperity—Solzhenitsyn holds, in the most important sense, to be superfluous. Only after everything is lost, he believes, can one comprehend the depths of his own spirit and enjoy the blessings of complete freedom. He writes of his dawning awareness in the camps, "Own nothing! Possess nothing! Buddha and Christ taught us this, and the Stoics and the Cynics. Greedy though we are, why can't we seem to grasp that simple teaching? Can't we understand that with property we destroy our soul?" By losing things, one gains the ability to think, to perceive existence clearly and impartially. He explains:

> A free head—now is that not an advantage in the Archipelago? And there is
> more freedom: No one can deprive you of your family and property—you have
> already been deprived of them. What does not exist—not even God can take
> away. And this is a basic freedom.[95]

Only a person who has suffered unjust imprisonment and survived can truly value "the right to move about without waiting for an order; the right to be alone; the right to gaze at the stars that were not blinded by the searchlights. . . . Yes there were many, many more rights like these." Perhaps those who have been forcibly denied the ability to pursue wealth can better appreciate the sublime pleasures of the mind, those "mysterious flights of the soul which physiologists have never explained."[96]

Solzhenitsyn here seems to contradict what was said above about the virtues of private property. There is a contradiction, but one that reflects human nature and not Solzhenitsyn's oversight. The theory that one can be happy only after one has lost everything is an extreme position. It would be acceptable to people if they had no concern for their daily bread or no care for the welfare of their bodies. If everyone adopted this selfless attitude, the human race would soon die out from want of food. There is little probability of that, however. Most people, most of the time, are deeply interested in their personal welfare. A teaching that expects them to be otherwise is a fantasy. But this is not to say that people's physical cares ought to be their only, or even their most important, concern. They need to be reminded occasionally, by the example of individuals who have no tangible goods but who possess great spiritual strength, that the most necessary requirements in life are not necessarily the highest aspirations to which human beings should aspire. If for no other reason, moral teachings are needed to show people the limits of acquisition. At its highest, a moral perspective can even lead them to full development of their potential.

Marx's philosophy places no limits on humankind. It reasons that once people have everything, they will be happy. However, experience does not bear this

out. Stalin had everything, but he wasn't happy. Nor does private wealth necessarily lead to happiness, as the lives of some celebrities demonstrate. Solzhenitsyn's character Shulubin in *Cancer Ward* explains:

> Happiness is a mirage. . . . When we have enough loaves of white bread to
> crush them under our heels, when we have enough milk to choke us, we still
> won't be in the least happy. . . . If we care only about "happiness" and about
> reproducing our species, we shall merely crowd the earth senselessly and create
> a terrifying society.[97]

Solzhenitsyn's endorsement of private property and material acquisition is a
qualified one. Human beings should be restrained by moral considerations and,
as the passage cited above suggests, by natural limits. On this point he even acknowledges a difference with bourgeois philosophy, since it too has "no incentive to self-limitation." Indeed, its ideas about private property

> would be beneficial to society if only . . . the carriers of these ideas had limited
> themselves, and not allowed the size of their property and thrust of their avarice
> to become a social evil, which provoked so much justifiable anger. It was as a
> reply to this shamelessness of unlimited money-grabbing that socialism in all
> its forms developed.

In a backhanded way he accepts that Marx may have done some good. Solzhenitsyn explains that if nothing else, the October Revolution and the "inhuman
experience" that followed taught ruling classes elsewhere to make concessions
to the laborers in their midst.[98]

Solzhenitsyn's position on property can be summarized as follows. He insists that people be allowed to acquire property, since this is a natural desire
growing out of their physical existence. Yet he is equally adamant that material
well-being not be their only concern, since the most important part of a human's
being is not physical. The dual nature of human existence is perhaps best expressed by the erstwhile defender of the free market, Dr. Oreshchenkov, of
whom Solzhenitsyn writes:

> He had to take frequent rests nowadays. His body demanded this chance to re-
> coup its strength with the same urgency his inner self demanded silent contem-
> plation free of external sounds, conversations, thoughts of work, free of every-
> thing that made him a doctor. Particularly after the death of his wife, his inner
> consciousness had seemed to crave a pure transparency. It was just this sort of
> silent immobility, without planned or even floating thoughts, which gave him a
> sense of purity and fulfillment. . . . The image he saw did not seem to be em-
> bodied in . . . work or activity. . . . The meaning of existence was to preserve
> unspoiled, undisturbed, and undistorted the image of eternity with which each
> person is born. Like a silver moon in a calm, still pond.[99]

FAMILY

Marx never actually calls for the abolition of the family. He simply observes in the *Communist Manifesto* that "the bourgeois family will vanish."[100] His opposition to the family is not accidental, however. Communism, by its nature, demands a loosening of family ties. Attachment to family weakens concern for the well-being of universal humankind. It turns people's loyalty inward toward blood ties rather than outward toward the common good. It promotes a sort of injustice, since family members want their loved ones to advance, even at the expense of others and sometimes to the detriment of the general welfare of society. Taken to an extreme, love of family supports nepotism.

A strong connection also exists between family and property. Parents want to give their children all the advantages that their wealth allows. They may wish to perpetuate their family line by providing for posterity after they have died. The desire to secure immortality through family lineage leads to inequality, since the advantages of wealth are passed from generation to generation. That Marx understood this to be a hindrance to equality can be seen in his prescription for the "abolition of the right of inheritance."[101]

All governments must confront people's natural attachment to family. To a greater or lesser degree, every society demands that family members broaden their perspective by looking to the general good of the community. If they did not, society would devolve into factional strife based on blood ties. Communism takes an extreme position, however, since it requires that people be at least as interested in the welfare of humanity as they are in that of their own kin.[102]

Solzhenitsyn makes a number of observations about Communism's treatment of families. Although he acknowledges a certain nobility in the fervent attachment to humanity, he wonders whether there may not be something indecent about a commitment that entails neglecting one's own relations. He tells of a local party secretary, who, as the secret police searched her house prior to her arrest, was more troubled about the incomplete state of the minutes of party sessions than she was about never seeing her children again. The interrogator conducting the search had to remind her to bid them farewell.[103]

Another Communist, a prisoner in the camps, received a letter from her daughter asking whether she was guilty. "Mama," the fifteen-year-old wrote, "are you guilty or not? I hope you weren't guilty, because then I won't join the Komsomol, and I won't forgive them because of you." Unable to bear her daughter not joining the Communist youth organization and hating the Doctrine of Universal Brotherhood, the mother, who was as guiltless as millions of her fellow prisoners, responded, "I am guilty. . . . Enter the Komsomol!"[104]

Solzhenitsyn also protests the idea that children should be raised communally, which in practice translates into being raised by the state. Marx did not specifically recommend that children be reared in common, yet this proposition can be inferred from his assertion that all human relations, including of course those within families, should become collective. In an ironic way, Solzhenitsyn contends that the camps were a sort of testing ground for Communist proposals.

Many infants were born there outside marriage. Camp authorities discouraged lasting relationships, so fathers rarely were able to see their offspring. Mothers were allowed to stay with suckling babies until they were weaned. After that, parent and child were separated, and the state assumed responsibility for rearing the youngsters. Solzhenitsyn reports that these children were often maladjusted and soon returned to the camps as juvenile offenders.

There was another example of the communal raising of children. This occurred among those young people who found themselves cast into the camps on some trumped-up pretext. It was no small-scale social experiment. In 1927 nearly half of the population of the Gulag was between the ages of sixteen and twenty-four. By 1935 Stalin had decreed that anyone over twelve years old could be sentenced as an adult.[105]

These young people were not reforged either by the communal life they were made to lead or by the human-creating labor they were forced to perform. Instead, they were quickly infected by the poisonous attitude of the camps. Without parents to guide them, they became uncontrollable. They lost all capacity to subdue their immediate desires. They could perceive "no demarcation line between what was permissible and what was not permissible, and no concept whatever of good and evil." Perhaps most revealing of all, their capacity for speech was diminished, so that they could clearly express only their immediate physical desires.[106]

Obviously, rearing children in the camps is not analogous to a more sympathetic and humane program of cooperative nurturing. Still, Solzhenitsyn's presentation makes the point that children need the love and direct supervision of parents if they are to mature into decent and normal human beings. The family is the medium by which civility is transmitted through generations. Any scheme that undermines the integrity of the family is also a threat to civility. Since the family is a necessary component of social life, every government (and the ideas on which it is based) must accept certain limitations on what it can achieve. For instance, equality of conditions is impossible because people are naturally attached to their own and seek to pass their privileges on to their children.

The Soviet Union is a perfect example of the tension between equality and family. Solzhenitsyn describes how people in the upper class, party members or highly paid experts, used their position to advance the careers and fortunes of their progeny. The Soviet elite was concerned with the same problems that confront parents everywhere—providing their offspring with a good education, finding them a suitable mate, and securing them a rewarding job. Ironically, in a regime governed by the ideas of Marx, the children of the Soviet well-to-do were more likely to be given social perks than children in other societies, since almost everything in the Soviet Union was achieved on the basis of patronage. Once again it seems Communism underestimated the immutability of human nature.[107]

There is an even greater irony concerning the relationship between the Marxist state and the institution of the family. Solzhenitsyn claims that it was the threat posed to people's families that kept the regime in power. For example, a favorite trick of interrogators was to elicit confessions by threatening to haul people's families in for questioning. Prisoners were kept in line by the fear that their loved ones would be persecuted. In fact, Soviet society was generally immobilized by the fear of reprisals against people's families.[108]

Interestingly, Solzhenitsyn points out, the people most able to resist the despotic edicts of the state were either those with no families, hence nothing to lose, or those with such strong family ties that everything outside the clan was met with hostile resistance. Enough has been said about the former, but he presents an amusing and revealing anecdote about the latter.

After he was released from the Gulag, Solzhenitsyn was exiled to Kok Terek, where he became a schoolteacher. One of his students, Abdul, was a Chechen, whom Solzhenitsyn describes as a group of people who "never sought to please, to ingratiate themselves with the bosses, their attitude was always haughty and indeed openly hostile.[109] They viewed all laws, except their own, with contempt; they simply refused to corrupt their daughters by obeying the rules concerning mandatory education.

The story begins when Abdul's brother killed an old Chechen woman while robbing her. When his act was discovered, he coldly turned himself in to the state security police to escape the reprisals of her family. Under the harsh Chechen law, the dead woman's clan had to take vengeance on some member of the murderer's family. As the next oldest male, Abdul was singled out to stand in for his criminal older brother; he was to be executed. Surprisingly, no one seemed able to stop the vendetta—not the teachers, not the headmaster, not the district party committee, not even the mighty state security police. At last, only the Chechen elders were able to avert bloodshed by sentencing the elder brother to death in absentia. And Abdul "learned all over again that the greatest force on earth is the law of vendetta."[110]

While "Europeans" might scoff at "this savage law, this cruel and senseless butchery," Solzhenitsyn claims that the Chechens can teach an important lesson. A few of them fell victim to the vendetta, but not so many, and those left behind were strengthened by the harsh example. The law of vendettas created "a force field of fear" around the Chechens, frightening strangers and enemies alike. "Strike your neighbors, that strangers may fear you! The ancestors of the highlanders in remote antiquity could have found no stronger hoop to gird their people," he writes and then wonders, "Has the socialist state offered them better?"[111]

For Solzhenitsyn there is something noble in the fierce attachment to family that ancient cultures foster. If such cultures do not breed sociable, law-abiding citizens, at least they do not produce passive ones. Their people rarely drink from the well of justice, but they are refreshed, instead, at the springs of spiritedness. In such societies one's own good or that of one's clan is always favored over that of the community, the particular over the general. Hence, these societies rarely enjoy an easy peace. On the other hand, the horrors of mass murder, in which millions meekly march to their graves, are equally unknown.

Of course, Solzhenitsyn does not give unqualified support to the ancient law of blood feuds. Such a tradition negates anything higher in humanity than an individual's, or a family's, point of view. It leads to anarchy, if not in politics, then surely in morals. Although he is sympathetic to the bonds of kinship, he also recognizes principles of a higher kind. Again his position is inconsistent, but again it reflects the inconsistency found in human existence. People love their own and they love the common good, or simply some concept of the good. Sometimes the tension between the two loves cannot be easily reconciled.

The object of literature, of a work of art, is to infuse theories with life. The dual nature of human attachment is brought to life in Solzhenitsyn's characterization of the peasant Spiridon. Spiridon is an inmate in the Marvino Sharaska, a research institute inhabited by zeks that serves as the setting of *The First Circle*. He has been incarcerated for happening to fall behind German lines during World War II. Over the years his fortunes have risen and fallen with the various turns in party ideology and the tumultuous events occurring in his native land. Both in good times and in bad, Spiridon seems unaffected by the ideas and principles of those in power, be they tsarist, Leninist, or Stalinist. His one overriding concern in life, which he pursues with toughness and cunning, is the security and well-being of his family. Solzhenitsyn writes:

> What Spiridon loved was land. What Spiridon had was family. The concepts of "country" and "religion" and "socialism," which seldom turn up in everyday conversation, were evidently unknown to Spiridon. His ears were closed to them; his tongue would not speak them. His country was—family. His religion was—family. Socialism was—family.

Despite his first love, Spiridon expresses a due regard for something higher. When questioned by the devotee of Socratic inquiry, Nerzhin, who proposes that no one "can really tell who is right and who is wrong" since "life changes," Spiridon answers simply, "The wolfhound is right and the cannibal is wrong."[112]

Solzhenitsyn's final position on family may be summarized as follows. In his zeal to equalize social conditions, Marx endeavored to undermine attachment to family. By doing so, he advanced ideas contrary to the natural affections of most people. Moreover, he overlooked the ability of families to transfer morals and manners from one generation to the next. A philosophy that disdains the bonds of family either will not be obeyed or will be obeyed to the detriment of humanity. Recognizing the need for families puts a limit on what can be expected in social life, especially as regards the equality of conditions. People may be drawn to the common good, or to some higher principle, but love of family draws them away from ever fully endorsing it. A decent government can be measured by how sympathetically it endeavors to resolve this crucial tension at the root of our social lives.

COMMUNITY OF WOMEN

It is not clear exactly what form of marriage Marx will take in the final stage of Communism. In the short run, at least, Marx argues that the "hypocritically concealed community of women" of the bourgeoisie would be replaced by an "openly legalized one" of the proletariat. Moreover, he suggests that in the future epoch, humans will have less exclusive relationships than those commonly practiced in previous historical periods.[113]

It should come as no surprise that Solzhenitsyn tests Marx's ideas in the experience of the camps. He finds that, rather than liberating people from the fetters of an obsolete morality, the community of women served only to degrade them by unleashing the admittedly natural, yet low, passion of lust. He presents the example of Krivoshchek Camp, where five hundred women lived together in a barracks. Officially, men were prohibited from the area, but everyone ignored the ban. Women, especially the pretty ones, were propositioned, bribed, and threatened into satisfying men's urges. Since it was a common barracks, the acts were performed in the open, which served to arouse passersby, some of whom were only juveniles. The only defense a woman had was to pick a man who could defend her "from the next in line, from the whole greedy queue, from the crazy juveniles gone berserk, aroused by everything they could see and breathe in there."[114] The community of women devolved into little more than debauchery.

Solzhenitsyn implies that although monogamous relationships between the sexes may not be natural in the sense of satisfying natural desires, they are certainly more decent, especially to women. The superiority of exclusive relationships derives, first, from their being the basis of family life, and, second, from their being a source of self-restraint. Prohibitions against open sexual unions build a healthy sense of shame in people. Such rules teach people to govern their desires rather than be governed by them. In a sense, strictures against sex are the first lessons by which adults learn to subdue their desires and impulses so that they can command their own destinies. Finally, while remaining faithful to one's spouse is undoubtedly a difficult task, Solzhenitsyn considers it a sign of a certain integrity and even nobility of the soul even when, as in Nerzhin's case, that nobility is futile.[115]

Solzhenitsyn implies that Marx's misunderstanding of the relationship between the sexes stems from his belief that in the capitalist world, "all passions and all activities [are] submerged in avarice." Hence, the sexual union becomes prostitution.[116] For Solzhenitsyn, Marx's analysis puts the cart before the horse. Eros is a far stronger and more enduring passion than avarice. If avarice drives women into the cash nexus of prostitution, the opposite is even truer, for Eros drives men to become profligate with their money. Solzhenitsyn tells of one fellow who claimed to have had sexual relations with "209 plus" women. To attract them he let "wild money [pass] through his hands." Even the strict discipline of the Organs was easily defeated by the power of Eros. Prostitutes in the camps became "rich as never before" from plying their trade among the guards.

Perhaps even more significant is the lengths to which prisoners went, at times risking danger and even death, in order to satisfy their desires.[117]

The obvious conclusion one draws is that Eros does not depend on the economic structure. Rather, it expresses itself in ways that may be detrimental to economic rationality. This seemingly insignificant and commonsense observation has particularly troubling consequences for Marx's theory. If Eros is outside the causal chain of economic reasoning, may it not be said that it could significantly alter the course of history, and in a particularly spicy way? For example, if a capitalist becomes infatuated with a worker, might not the relationship soften the desire of the capitalist for gain by allowing him to understand the workers' plight? Could this mean that in order to secure better working conditions, the proletariat, instead of forming unions or readying themselves for the revolution, might choose the most attractive individuals from their ranks and send them as lures to engage in physical unions with the bourgeois as a way of blunting capitalists' greed? The scenarios are infinite and humorous to imagine. In any case, Solzhenitsyn argues that there is a fundamental flaw in Marx's calculation of the driving force behind human action.

If Eros slips past Marx's reasoning from below, love escapes it from above. As is often true, Solzhenitsyn makes his case with an example. After the camps adopted the practice of separating the sexes, he explains, relationships sprang up based on no more than a few quickly uttered words whispered through a wall, or on love letters secretly passed between fences. Sometimes these chance meetings germinated, and people fell in love even though having never seen each other. Among them were some Lithuanian Catholics who took their religion seriously. They were married through the walls by priests, their vows irreversible and sacred.

A Marxist analysis might explain such behavior in terms of social (religious) background which would see these people as motivated by the ideology of bourgeois (and remnants of feudal) society. Objectively, from the perspective of material analysis, their vows were really a way of keeping women in the bondage of monogamy so that they would produce offspring who in turn would become fodder for an industrial society. A more reasonable explanation however, would hold that their actions had nothing whatever to do either with historical necessity or with economic preconditions. They did it for love.[118]

Solzhenitsyn disagrees with Marx because in Marx's utopian speculations people are punished for a natural love of their own. A decent regime must accept as a limitation on the yearning for perfect social justice this pull of people away from the common good. By teaching people to disregard these limits, Marx is responsible for inculcating rash and even cruel expectations in his followers. Lest we forget that no Marxist regime ever existed without repressing its own people, Solzhenitsyn reminds us that imperfect human nature does not fit into a perfect mold. There will always be those who cannot measure up or those who resist. There will always be a need for some place to put them. Again, it seems, the essence of Marxism is the camps. He explains:

:hipelago was, the Archipelago remains, the Archipelago will stand for-
_____ ithout it, who can be made to suffer for the errors of the Vanguard Doctrine? For the fact that people will not grow into the shapes devised for them?[119]

PHILOSOPHY

An objection can be raised that Solzhenitsyn sets up a straw man when he criticizes Marx. Solzhenitsyn attacks Marx by presenting the statements of Krylenko, Lenin, and Latsis. Clearly, these spokesmen for the Progressive Doctrine
were never on an intellectual level with Marx. It is doubtful whether Marx
would have endorsed the crude materialism of Krylenko; nor would he have
condoned the excesses of Lenin, not to mention Stalin. Perhaps, as Avineri suggests, his ideas were too subtle and complex even for his collaborator, Engels, to
comprehend fully. Can Marx be held responsible for his ideas being put to bad
use?

The misunderstanding and vulgarization of Marx's philosophy could be
forgiven if it were not for his insistence that to have validity, philosophic principles must be put into practice. Prior to Marx, all philosophers saw their task as
understanding the truth about existence. Political philosophy, a subspecies of the
broader philosophic pursuit, did endeavor to affect human behavior. However,
political philosophers maintained that there would always be a gulf between the
best regime that could be constructed in theory and that which could actually be
achieved. The goal of political philosophy was to suggest what was desirable,
but not to mislead as to what was possible. Marx denigrates previous philosophers for making a distinction between thought and action. He proposes that
whatever differences exist between theory and practice must be settled in favor
of practice—praxis. Marx writes, "You cannot transcend philosophy without
actualizing it . . . by the negation of philosophy as philosophy. The philosophers
have only interpreted the world in various ways; the point is to change it." Indeed, he goes so far as to argue that for something to be true, it must occur in the
world of phenomena and not just in the mind.[120]

Immediately a dilemma arises. Just who is to bring Marx's philosophy into
being? True philosophers with original minds are scarce. For the most part, the
human race is made up of those second-rate—or worse—minds who misunderstand the nuances of philosophy. It is exactly the Krylenkos and Latsises, the
Lenins and Trotskys, and—yes—even the Stalins, who populate this world. If
Marx's philosophy has been incorrectly applied, is it not his fault for failing to
recognize the capacities of the people asked to do the applying? Solzhenitsyn
acknowledges the gulf between Marx's ideals and the practices of the Soviet
Union, yet he does not excuse Marx on that account. He maintains that Marx's
principles were bound to be badly applied, for Marx's historical analysis led him
to the imprudent conclusion that he need not be concerned about the limitations
of his followers.

For example, consider the idea of premature revolution. Those who forward this argument hold that Lenin perverted Marx's teaching by leading an industrially backward nation into revolution. The Bolsheviks, of course, did not see it that way. They reasoned that if a nation was given the opportunity to skip the capitalist stage of history, with it attendant horrors and oppression, it should do so. They came to that conclusion because they believed history to be moving inevitably toward the victory of socialism; hence, seizing the reins of power was a legitimate means of lessening human suffering. But was it not Marx who began this faulty chain of reasoning by writing, in his most frequently read work, that the bourgeoisie's "fall and the victory of the proletariat are equally inevitable"?[121]

Marx's union of thought and action is also deadly to thought, claims Solzhenitsyn. By insisting that all things of importance can be settled at the level of praxis, Marxism reduces human beings to laborers without the leisure to think. Marxism denigrates all that is finest in humanity because it distracts people. It stresses the everyday tasks of life instead of the development of reason, the uniquely human characteristic. Of course, Marx argues that once natural necessity is overcome through the communism of the means of production, people will use their free time to pursue any of a number of nonmaterialistic endeavors. But by his emphasis on labor as the truly human activity, Solzhenitsyn suggests, Marx may have limited the possibility of achieving those higher ends.[122]

Whether Marx intended for the highest reaches of thought and philosophy to disappear after the arrival of Communism is difficult to say. However, he does set out to demolish all philosophy prior to his own. When material reality is depicted accurately, he reasons, "philosophy as an independent branch of activity loses its medium of existence." From this premise he downgrades the importance of philosophy by asserting that for man, "the species being," the metaphysical questions that give rise to philosophic inquiry are unimportant. He advises that investigations into the origin, purpose, or end of life are not fruitful because such questions are mere abstractions that assume the nonexistence of man and nature. He continues:

> Give up your abstractions and you will give up your questions. . . . Do not think, do not question me, for as soon as you think and question, your abstraction from the existence of nature and man makes no sense. Or are you such an egoist that you assert everything as nothing and yet want yourself to exist.[123]

As Solzhenitsyn points out, humans do ask such questions, for even the humblest people are egoistic enough to wonder about their own death. Thus, not only is Marx's refusal to face the deepest issues of existence profoundly unphilosophic but his dismissal of the questions also belies the experience of virtually every living human being.

Even beyond that, Solzhenitsyn explains, however, Marx's negative attitude toward philosophic speculation led his followers to repudiate the whole notion of discussion and debate. When it is in their interest, Marxists reserve the right to quash all speech on the grounds that "there are some questions on which a definite opinion has been established, and they are no longer open to discussion." Solzhenitsyn writes that Marxism "uses the neat device of declaring all serious criticism 'outside the framework of possible discussion.'" Communism "is so devoid of arguments that it has none to advance against its opponents. . . . It lacks arguments and hence there is the club, the prison, the concentration camp, and insane asylums with forced confinement."[124]

Communism's approach to freedom of speech is a perfect example of the bastardization and inversion of Marx's philosophy. Given Marx's stand on the need for *praxis*, no philosopher in history, Solzhenitsyn compels us to believe, deserves his fate more than Marx.

ATHEISM

At one point Solzhenitsyn calls Bolshevism "unbridled atheism and class hatred."[125] Communist atheism can be traced directly to Marx who asserts that belief in God diminishes humankind. "The more man attributes to God," he claims, "the less he retains for himself." Since the human race created the idea of God, it must also destroy that idea. The human species is the highest thing in the universe, and in order for it to fully express its creativity and worth, it must owe its existence only to itself.[126]

To prove God's existence is not a simple matter. Perhaps this is why Solzhenitsyn concentrates primarily on the consequences of atheism. He argues that atheism serves not to elevate people but to coarsen them. While it may be true that under an atheistic regime everything is permissible, this fact neither enhances human freedom nor encourages noble achievements. On the other hand, religion supports the idea that every individual has personal worth, a divine spark. Without such a concept, human beings can come to be thought of as merely "material" or "matter" (Recall Lenin's use of the term, insects) that can be used and discarded in building the future epoch.[127]

A particularly troubling consequence of atheism is its tendency to slacken people's self-control, Solzhenitsyn insists. They are less likely to restrain their desires and passions because they see little moral reason for doing so. By unleashing these urges, atheism results in a breakdown of civilization's mores, the mechanism by which society is held together peacefully. Moreover, it is unlikely that people will have the capacity to engage in creative pursuits if they cannot bring their lowest passions under control.

The most dangerous aspect of this disintegration occurs when people are entrusted with power. Without internal moral checks and lacking the concept of divine retribution or reward, their heady position overwhelms and corrupts them. They use their authority for personal gain or for the pleasure they receive from lording it over others. Solzhenitsyn explains:

> Power is a poison. . . . But to the human being who has faith in some force that holds dominion over all of us, and who is therefore conscious of his own limi-

tations, power is not necessarily fatal. For those, however, who are unaware of a higher sphere, it is deadly poison. For them there is no antidote.[128]

Liberating human beings from the fetters of religion does little to foster creativity. Instead, most people use their newly acquired freedom to indulge their basest urges.

AIMS OF SOCIALISM

Solzhenitsyn is critical not only of Marx's analysis of society but also of the aims or ends of socialism. Refusing to ride the tide of scholarly opinion, Solzhenitsyn claims that Marxism is not humanism, but rather that everything associated with that doctrine is antihumanism.[129] Obviously, these assertions run counter to a great deal of enlightened opinion in the West, which looks favorably on Marx, not so much for his analysis of economics—in that most agree he was in error—but for the goals he espouses: freedom, equality, and community.

FREEDOM

Exactly what the ends of socialism are Marx never makes clear. The lack of clarity may be due to the prudent caution one should exercise when predicting the future. A reason more consistent with his analysis may be that future society will be so different from any known to people of the past that its forms are impossible to foretell. Marx insists that whatever shape the new society takes, it will be good for people. Hence, they should positively embrace it. The future era will solve "the riddle of history," and bring a true resolution to "the antagonism between man and nature, between man and man . . . between existence and essence . . . freedom and necessity, individual and species."[130]

Marx's words are appealing, but are such things possible? Solzhenitsyn wonders why the ideals of socialism should be adopted when, in practice, they have never been seen or known to exist. Why, for instance, is socialism a worthy choice? Marx's doctrine does not prove that socialism and the good are the same. Marx merely criticizes all previous epochs, while insisting that history is moving toward socialism. But what grounds does he have for arguing that life will improve after the revolution? Saying that a thing is inevitable does not necessarily make it beneficial. For example, given statistical probabilities and the vagaries of auto travel, either the author of these lines or the reader of them will inevitably get into an auto accident. Does that make it a good thing? Marx contends that the division of labor has existed since the beginning of human history. That being the case, how does he know that its end will make people happy? Marx's materialism, which begins by insisting that only empirical reality is valid, ironically concludes by calling for a social arrangement that has no empirical basis whatever.

Solzhenitsyn goes on to challenge all socialist thinkers on the same account.[131] They all ask that we buy an imagined future sight unseen. Given their lack of clarity, he questions the wisdom of sacrificing the good of present generations for the promised good of an unknown future.

Marx has been interpreted to be, above all else, a proponent of liberation—liberation from the cruelty and oppression of capitalism and liberation from the burden of labor itself. As Engels wrote, man must move from the realm of necessity to the realm of freedom. Solzhenitsyn does not accept this standard view of Marx, however. Solzhenitsyn seems to take Marx's surprising statement in *Capital III*, "The true reign of liberty can only flourish insofar as it is founded on the reign of necessity," as Marx's mature position, and reasons that "the Marxist concept of freedom" is the "acceptance of the yoke of necessity."[132] In other words, Marx argues not merely that leisure is a precondition of the good life but that only after the realm of necessity is conquered by the entire human race can the realm of freedom reign. Solzhenitsyn argues that such a claim dooms people to unceasing labor since it is impossible fully to overcome the demands of natural necessity. Indeed, if Marx were to have his way, human "species-beings" would contentedly labor to produce what they need, with no thought but of the continued existence of the race—like cows happily grazing.

Solzhenitsyn balks at this vision of humanity's future. He maintains that a life dedicated to nothing more than the quest for physical well-being reduces people to matter. He describes the hope that prosperity can buy happiness and the desire to exchange personal autonomy for the collective well-being as the temptation of the Grand Inquisitor.[133] Even if such a condition of material bliss could come into being, he doubts whether it would be good for people. Perhaps, people would find a world of universal contentment grotesquely devoid of passionate striving.

The more traditional commentaries on Marx insist that he was genuinely dedicated to the liberation of humankind. Accepting, for the sake of argument, that Marx does endorse freedom, Solzhenitsyn asks: Freedom to do what? Freedom is analogous to an empty container; it must be filled with something. It is the end or purpose to which freedom is put, he explains, that determines whether freedom will bring happiness. To enjoy the freedom to act is certainly a good thing, but to hold that such freedom is happiness is to mistake a precondition of happiness for happiness itself. Moreover, he reasons that human beings do not need to be liberated, since they possess an inner freedom from birth that they can exercise regardless of external circumstances.[134]

EQUALITY

Perhaps no aspect of Marx's thought stands out more than his commendation of equality. It is because he is an advocate of equality, not because of his analysis of society, that his writings caught the spirit of the age and propelled his philosophy into prominence.

Although it is not altogether clear, Marx seems to accept the possibility of equality of results or ends. He rejects bourgeois natural rights on the grounds that they secure only equality of opportunity. Thus, he claims that natural rights

actually encourage inequality of results, since the talented, and, more importantly for him, the well born, will always rise to the top. He suggests that differences in ability might diminish as conventional inequality, in the form of property and class privilege, is abolished. His final formulation, "from each
according to his ability to each according to his need," leaves open the issue of
whether natural talents would interfere with the egalitarian goals of Communism.

Solzhenitsyn understands people' attraction to the idea of equality. In *The
First Circle* he pictures a young, idealistic Communist making the following
address in an attempt to convince a friend of the virtues of the Bolsheviks,

> The main thing is they are for equality! Imagine it: universal, complete, abso-
> lute equality. No one will have any privileges others don't have. No one will
> have an advantage either in income or in status. Could there possibly be any-
> thing better than such a society? Isn't it really worth all the sacrifices?[135]

Despite expressing sympathy with the idea of treating people fairly, Solzhenitsyn maintains that Marxist equality is implausible. It attempts to achieve
equality of results, as expressed in Lenin's remark that every cook or housewife
should be able to run the state. It overlooks what nature has given us, both the
talents and the limitations.[136] It stresses what is most common among people,
thereby ignoring the impulse toward individual excellence and providing little
incentive for the elevation of humanity.

Solzhenitsyn also observes that the egalitarian spirit of Marxism nurtures
envy within the lower classes. For example, in the early stages of the Bolshevik
Revolution, some members of the lower classes came to see the destruction of
privilege and distinction as their duty. They became so caught up in the urge to
level humanity that they increasingly vented their wrath against natural, in addition to conventional, inequality. In fact, natural differences in ability frustrated
the egalitarian struggle more because they were more difficult to eliminate than
conventional inequalities. Solzhenitsyn tells of incompetent people who, solely
on the basis of their proletarian background, demanded important posts for
which they were demonstrably unsuited. Every sort of skill, especially the technical prowess of engineers, was attacked in the impulse to level Russia's classes.
The consequence, as noted earlier, was the reign of incompetence which ruined
the economy for years.[137]

Regardless of the initial gains that might be made in an egalitarian revolution, Solzhenitsyn says, the results are never long lasting. The purpose of a mass
movement may be to institute equality, but human beings remain determined to
seek distinction, position, privilege, and money for themselves. He tells of many
instances in which Communists craved honor for their dedication to the common
people. Inequality of rank became as pronounced under Communist rule as it
had been under the old regime. However, there was one important difference
between the two, according to Solzhenitsyn. Under the old order the upper class
had some notion of what a true aristocracy was, both with regard to privilege

and to duty; hence, at least a semblance of justice prevailed. The new elite had little awareness of the character of human excellence; it quickly abused its power and thereafter protected its position solely by the application of its superior force.[138]

COMMUNITY

According to Marx, the human race can fully resolve its conflicts only by uniting in a universal, spontaneous, and homogenous community.[139] Evidently, he had more in mind than human beings living and occasionally acting in common. He argues that individuals gain significance when they act upon others and are acted upon by others. If people engage in self-interested actions that lead to conflict, alienation ensues, since the losers in the struggle will be made to adopt behavior they did not freely choose. Only when every single person on earth acts in unison can social harmony be achieved, the relationship between master and slave be resolved, and the full potential of the species finally be reached.

Marx places enormous importance on social unity because he argues that a person's social relations provide the only source of meaning in existence. There is nothing beyond or above the individual that gives him significance; hence, he must look laterally, to his fellow human beings, to realize his purpose. In common humanity one discovers the greater whole of which he is a small part.

Solzhenitsyn is critical of Marx's notion of community for a number of reasons. First, he argues that although Marx's communitarianism may make him a humanist of sorts, it is a humanism founded on the lowest common denominator of the race. The only possible means by which all humanity could be united is on the basis of their physical—material—needs; those things that every individual body shares in common. How else could all the differences in politics, language, religion, custom, and culture be overcome? For Solzhenitsyn there is little noble or even worthy about a devotion to common humanity. He argues that people need principles that elevate them above their mere physical existence. This is true even if the price they must pay for holding those principles— since inevitably they will differ from nation to nation or religion to religion—is social and political discord. What sort of humanism is it, Solzhenitsyn wonders, that reduces people to beings interested primarily in their survival and in the comfort of their bodies? Is this concern also not the primary interest of beasts?

Second, Solzhenitsyn criticizes Marx's notion of community because it is based on materialism. Marx claims to be both a materialist and a communist. Solzhenitsyn knows that the two goals are incompatible. He points out that Marx asks us to share the one thing we cannot share—the pleasures and pains of our bodies. It is true, of course, that we can fulfill each other's desires—in the most intimate of circumstances, for example. Yet we cannot share the actual physical sensation of each other's pleasure. Even more problematic is pain, the most solitary of all experiences. Pain drives our thoughts inward to the self, to our personal distress. Solzhenitsyn captures this truth in his remark, "nobody groans when another man's tooth aches."[140]

Marx even diminishes the importance of death. He argues that the individual may die, but the species lives on. He insists that questions about life and
death, existence and nonexistence, are fraudulent and egotistical, and therefore
should not be asked. Solzhenitsyn rejects Marx's communal perspective of life
and death. People may be part of a collective while they are alive, he reasons,
but they die alone. The continued existence of the species provides little comfort
to an individual whose life is about to be extinguished.[141]

Third, Solzhenitsyn questions Marx's assertion that communal action can
be both spontaneous and centralized. Once again, it is impossible to say exactly
what form of association Marx foresaw when the final stage of Communism had
come into being. However, in the intermediary stage of Communism, he clearly
asserts that all political, economic, and social functions will be centralized.[142]

Solzhenitsyn's story *For the Good of the Cause* centers on some students
who voluntarily construct a new science building for their school during their
summer vacation. When the job is completed, however, the government takes
over the facility for another, more pressing, purpose. Everyone involved in the
construction is disheartened.[143]

Solzhenitsyn's point seems to be that centralization of power inevitably results in a conflict between the whole and the parts. In such a contest, the more
powerful central government nearly always emerges the victor. Seeing their fate
dependent on a distant, somewhat alien, force and not on their own efforts, people are likely to lose their initiative. If the interference in people's lives becomes
too great, they may even become corrupted by it, choosing to live their lives as
passive tools of the state. Rather than making people spontaneous, centralization
has the tendency to make them dependent and subservient.

Fourth, Solzhenitsyn attacks Marx's hope that the unity of humankind can
be made a practical reality. Marx asserts that once class antagonisms, the material basis of conflict, are put to rest, political differences will also vanish. Such
an expectation, Solzhenitsyn argues, is foolishly naive. True, human beings act
on the basis of their material interest, but there is also a natural division of opinion within humanity predicated on nothing more than different ideas. Marxism is
a bad representation of reality because it rejects the independence of human
thought.[144]

The worst consequence of Marx's erroneous claim that divergent opinions
will disappear after the revolution is that Marxist rulers expected views divergent from their own to disappear. Guided by this premise, they crushed free
speech and any form of opposition that arose within their countries. "Anyone
who is the least bit familiar with Marxism," Solzhenitsyn proclaims, "knows
that 'classless society' implies that there will not be any parties." He continues,
"On the very same day," that Communists agree "there will be a multi-party
system [they] suppress every [other] party."[145]

Fifth, Solzhenitsyn questions whether "unity" is actually good for people.
Marx asserts that "only in community do the means exist for every individual to
cultivate his talents in all directions. . . . Only in the community is personal free-

dom possible."[146] Although Solzhenitsyn does not reject the goal of community per se, he does challenge the assumption that it is ultimately satisfying. For instance, life in the camps was totally communal, but it was not good for people since they hardly had time to think. At one point, he calls the communal existence he once endured in the camps as life in "a herd." He further claims that Communism attempts to "abolish the human essence and deny all individuality to man [by] the forced living in communes, and the incessant dinning of slogans and dogmas." Since Communism is a threat to the individual, it is also a threat to human creativity. The creative process is an individual endeavor, grounded on the deep insights one gains through solitary reflection. To expect the mass, or any large group of people, to suddenly become original, he concludes, reflects ignorance of nature of thought.[147]

Solzhenitsyn sets forth his objections to communal life in the play *Candle in the Wind*. He says that the assertion that people should live for the sake of community results in the ridiculous conclusion that "I live for you and you live for me." As appealing as this sentiment of reciprocal affection may sound on first hearing, one is forced to wonder whether it answers the deeper question of why we are alive at all. Solzhenitsyn wants us to ponder the formidable issue of the ends or purposes of human life. If people live solely for the sake of the community, have they done any more than insure the continued existence of the species? Does there not have to be something in life that lifts it above mere survival? After all, what is the meaning of all the eating, sleeping, and procreating that people do? If these functions are the purpose of life, then human beings are no different from animals.

Solzhenitsyn holds that socialism is particularly lax in answering these fundamental questions about existence because it defines justice as the equal enjoyment of material well-being. Despite its avowed antipathy toward commercialism, socialism is as guilty as capitalism of making people want material goods. Indeed, it holds that people are unhappy because of scarcity and will be made whole because of plenty. It postpones consideration of what is good for human beings, other than equitable distribution, in the hope that people with full bellies will be better able to answer the question. It diverts people from consideration of moral and ethical issues by making equality of circumstance the one and only moral or ethical principle. Of course, every ethical doctrine holds that those of equal merit should be treated equally. Socialism insists that the only basis for making ethical judgments is the physical needs and desires of the many. For Solzhenitsyn, to pursue the satisfaction of one's physical urges, with no thought for the proper limits of those desires, is not a mark of morality but, rather, of the lack of morality. Thus he concludes that, "there can be no moral form of socialism . . . [because] ethical principles are not only not inherent in socialism, but are opposed to it."[148]

Solzhenitsyn's blanket rejection of socialism, including the softer variety in the West, seems more than a little harsh, especially to those brought up on the idea that socialism is the only path to social justice. Surely concern for one's fellow man must be thought of as a moral principle. Can those who wish to use government programs to provide for the security of all be lacking completely in moral commitment? In response to Solzhenitsyn, a socialist might say that people cannot develop their souls if they are without the rudimentary necessities of life. It might be correct for Solzhenitsyn to argue that socialists are naive in what they expect from such programs or deluded about the possibility of social reform, but are they lacking in morals?

Clearly Solzhenitsyn and socialists have different definitions of morality. For socialists, morality is primarily a devotion to the bodily well-being of others; for Solzhenitsyn, it is devotion to principles thought to be eternal, which have the effect of making people interested in the development of their individual character. Solzhenitsyn argues that by stressing what is, in fact, a mere precondition of the good life, socialists have misled people into believing that materialism—equally distributed—*is* the good life.

Finally, Solzhenitsyn holds that Marxism does not really lead to community. He argues that it is impossible for any community to treat all its members alike. Theorists of socialism prior to Marx confessed to this lack of universality by admitting that some jobs are so burdensome that no one would volunteer to undertake them. They reasoned that for the good of society a special class would have to be created whose primary function was to perform distasteful labor. The Gulag, says Solzhenitsyn, is the realization of this prophecy.[149]

In fairness to Marx, it should be said that he envisaged no need for an underclass within the community, because he expected the complete conquest of nature to transcend labor. As yet, however, nature is far from defeated. Difficult menial tasks remain. Thus, although Solzhenitsyn's criticism of Marx on this point may not be warranted on the basis of theory, it is justified on the basis of practical reality.

Solzhenitsyn argues that Marx's goal of a global community is implausible, since internationalism cannot become a true foundation for unity. While acknowledging the nobility of the ideals of internationalism, Solzhenitsyn believes that human affections have limits, beyond which even the highest ideals are likely to become empty rhetoric. The most secure bonds of community are fastened through personal relations. If people know and like their fellows, they are less likely to hurt or take advantage of them. In such a community the harsh demands of duty are softened by feelings of friendship. It seems that in his short story "Matryona's House" Solzhenitsyn wishes to remind his readers that small communities based on kinship and virtue can have an endearing quality of civility about them, just as they did when the Greeks first sang their praises more than twenty centuries ago.[150]

Solzhenitsyn is not naive about the chances of restoring the simple life of small communities. He recognizes that the modern world has made such a return impractical. Nevertheless, he refuses to agree that the nation should be replaced by a larger political unit. He argues that if devotion to a particular political community is not, strictly speaking, natural to humans, it is certainly a commendable second nature. Within nations grow unique cultures that become the basis of a shared life. National culture is the medium through which people communicate, resolve their differences, and learn to live together. It is culture that teaches people to restrain their passions and to make sacrifices for the common good. The irrational and unpremeditated love of one's country is a passion in favor of the common good that counterbalances the all-too-human tendency of people to pursue nothing but their own interests.

While the goals of internationalism may exhibit a certain "spiritual beauty," Solzhenitsyn wonders whether humankind can ever reach such heights. Too often, he claims, internationalism destroys civic responsibility by undermining whatever national ties exist between people. People with global consciousness frequently neglect their local duties. Their sense of sacrifice and duty becomes so broadly dispersed that it is lost in a mass of undistinguished humanity. They are thrown back on themselves, become isolated, and pursue only what serves their own interests.[151]

The Marxist movement made particularly grievous errors in the name of internationalism, Solzhenitsyn argues. It suppressed indigenous cultures in an attempt to supplant them with the enlightened ideals of socialism. We have already seen the barren results of that effort. Party slogans and propaganda do not constitute a culture, and societies without secure bonds, Solzhenitsyn says, can be held together only by force.

Indeed, the Communists' hatred for the nation has backfired more than once. During World War II, for example, slogans of the Progressive Doctrine suddenly disappeared in the Soviet Union to be replaced by messages extolling the virtues of Mother Russia. Almost overnight the old ways were resurrected, and the Orthodox Church even emerged from the relentless suppression to which it had been subjected.

Why this sudden change in the course of history? Solzhenitsyn explains that most people cannot be roused to fight or made to sacrifice for the cause of internationalism. It is too ephemeral a goal. He reports that during World War II, when a young zek was asked to enlist in the defense of socialism, he responded, "The proletariat has no fatherland!" Solzhenitsyn notes dryly, "Marx's exact words, I believe."[152]

Of course, the Russian people did respond to the call of duty, honor, and country, despite its being raised, in part, to bail out Stalin and his colleagues. Caught as they were in the tragic situation of having to choose between the two worst dictators in history, Russians heeded the call of their country, which is exactly what many of them had refused to do for the cause of international socialism.[153]

Notes

1. Paul Johnson, "Solzhenitsyn: Hero of Our Time," *Washington Post, Book World*, 2 September 1984, 1, 11. The influence of Solzhenitsyn's *Gulag Archipelago* was espe-

cially strong in France. Georges Suffert, the editor of *Le Point*, remarked that it had "forever eclipsed the beacon of communism." Quoted in Scammell, *Solzhenitsyn*, 877n.

2. Although he may not have been entirely systematic in presenting the differences between his ideas and those of Marx, Solzhenitsyn is well acquainted with Marx's views. See Scammell, *Solzhenitsyn*, 87, 94, 104-5. Solzhenitsyn seems to have read the many volumes of Marx's *Collected Works*, for he derives all his citations from that source. For the convenience of readers I have used the most readily available contemporary editions of Marx's works wherever possible.

3. Raymond Aron, *Marxism and the Existentialists*, trans. Helen Weaver, Robert Addis, and John Weightman (New York: Simon & Schuster, 1970), 4- 5. See also Herbert Marcuse, *Reason and Revolution* (Boston: Beacon Press, 1969), 327.

4. Compare Lenin, *Collected Works*, with Marcuse, *Reason and Revolution*, and Erich Fromm, *Marx's Concept of Man* (New York: Ungar, 1961).

5. Shlomo Avineri, *The Social and Political Thought of Karl Marx* (Cambridge: Cambridge University Press, 1968), vii, 258. Two points can be raised against Avineri's interpretation. First, Engels graciously and rightly conceded that he was not the leading member of the partnership with Marx. If Engels was saying something wrong about Marx's ideas, one can only wonder why, in a collaboration that lasted nearly forty years, Marx did not find the time to straighten him out. Second, if Marx's closest friend and confidant (their exchange of letters is voluminous) could not rightly understand his mentor, one must wonder whether Marx wrote too incautiously. Perhaps he wanted to be misunderstood, if that would help bring an end to capitalism. If, after all, the humanist interpreters of Marx are correct, and human beings are free, then there is nothing certain about the victory of socialism. Marx may have wanted to assure the enemies of capitalism that their cause would ultimately triumph. What surer way is there of turning philosophy into praxis?

6. *Warning*, 56-57. See also Aron, *Marxism*, 6.

7. See Solzhenitsyn's "Letter to the Soviet Leaders" in *East*, 75-142. Although Marx's writings were an embarrassment to Communist rulers because so little has worked out as planned, for seventy years the Soviets doggedly held to Marxism as an explanation of life. Until the end of the Soviet regime, even Mikhail Gorbachev accepted it.

8. Compare *East*, 89-90, and Karl Marx, *Critique of Political Economy* (Moscow: Progress Press, 1976), preface. See also Aron, *Marxism*, 8.

9. Karl Marx, *Capital* (New York: Modern Library, n.d.), 45. Compare *East*, 121; *Rubble*, 4.

10. See, for example, Marx's defense of moving the international socialist movement headquarters to New York City. Robert C. Tucker, ed., *Marx-Engels Reader* (New York: W. W. Norton, 1978), 523 (hereafter cited as Tucker, *Marx Reader*).

11. *East*, 121-22; *Warning*, 56.

12. Robert C. Tucker, *The Marxian Revolutionary Idea* (New York: W. W. Norton, 1970), 3. Avineri argues that because Marx rejects "Jacobin subjectivism," the view of him as a revolutionary is overblown. Avineri, *Social and Political Thought*, 258.

Perhaps Marx did reject "Jacobin subjectivism," but before deciding one should know exactly what is meant by that term. How, for example, does the term differ from the generic word, Jacobinism—a term coined during the French Revolution and defined as the irrational use of violence? More important, how does it differ from Jacobin objectivism, which, given Marxist terminology, means that if objective conditions are correct, the use of Jacobin violence (Jacobinism) is justified? Avineri proves too much and too little by his assertion. Marx never disclaimed violence; he objects to its uses only when history had not provided the proper opportunity for it to advance the cause of the proletariat victory. To paraphrase Lenin, Avineri takes the revolutionary heart out of Marx. On this point Lenin's scholarship seems superior. See Arthur Mendel, ed., *Essential Works of Marxism* (New York: Bantam, 1965), 103-5, 115, 117, 121, 126, 129, 131 (hereafter cited as Mendel, *Essential Works*). See also Tucker, *Marxian Revolutionary Idea*, 3-48; Marcuse, *Reason and Revolution*, 288.

13. *Writings of the Young Marx*, 253, 357; Tucker, *Marx Reader*, 219, 543. On rare occasions Marx concedes the possibility of peaceful change. But he saw peaceful change as the exception rather than the rule. For most of his life he fought against the idea of a "peaceful process of dissolution," believing that the nonrevolutionary route sapped the Communist movement's strength. Compare Tucker, *Marx Reader*, 522, with 553. In his speech before the Workers International, he may have toned down his remarks because he faced an audience of workers less than imbued with revolutionary fervor.

14. "Solzhenitsyn Speaks Out," 606; *Warning*, 57.

15. *Gulag I*, 355.

16. In *The Discourses*, Machiavelli argues that people must occasionally be thrown back to the origin of political society to remind them of the need for virtue. Niccolò Machiavelli, *The Prince* and *The Discourses* (New York: Random House, 1950), 166, 400, 478, 480. Compare Solzhenitsyn's discussion of sexual restraint during the camp uprisings at Kengir. *Gulag III*, 306.

17. He makes this assertion despite his own—implied—use of violence at Kengir. Compare *Oak*, 222, where he hopes to "start something" in his own country.

18. *Gulag I*, 335, 338, 382; *Gulag II*, 51.

19. *Rubble*, 5; *East*, 29, also 25, 130-31; *Gulag I*, 33; *Gulag II*, 427-28. One wonders if this lawlessness does not contradict Machiavelli's point (see note 16 above). However, since these crimes were committed before power had been solidified, there would be no force capable of sufficiently frightening people into probity.

20. *Gulag III*, 240n. Marxist theory does distinguish between the final stage of Communism, in which all political and economic differences are abolished, and the intermediate era of the dictatorship of the proletariat, in which the workers use the power of the state to sweep aside the vestiges of the old class system. Thus, Solzhenitsyn's criticism of the revolutionary phase of a Marxist struggle is only partly justified. Still, his practical critique of Communist revolutions is quite apt, for until 1989 no Communist revolutionaries gave up power voluntarily. Even then Communists were forced from power by mass protests. Communists traditionally used whatever methods were available, from intimidation to propaganda, to maintain their position of dominance. Only after there were no enemies of Communism left in the world, they claimed, could the party safely be able to relinquish its power.

21. Solzhenitsyn says of one of them: "It is evident from his face how he brimmed with vicious, human hating animus." *Gulag II*, 88. See also *Gulag II*, 319.

22. *Mortal*, 14, Carter points out that Solzhenitsyn's views are somewhat heretical in the United States, which is itself steeped in a revolutionary tradition. Solzhenitsyn was remarkably silent on the American Revolution, perhaps because he understood that because of it some Americans feel sympathy for struggles of national liberation. Or perhaps he reasoned that in America the conflict was fought over independence, not social transformation. Carter, *Politics of Solzhenitsyn*, 93.

23. *Writings of the Young Marx*, 431.

24. *Gulag I*, 137, 188, 262; *Zurich*, 215. See also Solzhenitsyn's prose poems "Easter Procession," "A Journey along the Oka," and "City of Neva," and his short story

"Zahkar-the-Pouch" in Aleksandr Solzhenitsyn, *Stories and Prose Poems*, trans. Michael Glenny (New York: Bantam, 1973) (hereafter cited as *Stories*); and "The Nobel Lecture" in *East*, 3-38. For a discussion, see Clement, *The Spirit of Solzhenitsyn*, 186; Dunlop, *Critical Essays*, 102, 252.

25. Tucker, *Marxian Revolutionary Idea*, 53, 136; Mendel, *Essential Works*, 104; *Writings of the Young Marx*, 19, 149, 409, 458.

26. *Gulag I*, 96. See also *Gulag II*, 46, 282, *Gulag III*, 350-55; *Rubble*, 241.

27. *Gulag II*, 46.

28. Ibid., 502-33.

29. *Gulag I*, 325n. Usually Bolsheviks did not accept that people could convert. In at least one instance they did. A young man killed his father, a priest, out of class hatred. He was punished, but he later rose quickly through the party ranks. *Gulag II*, 64-65.

30. Krylenko discovered this fact, much to his chagrin, while questioning some high-ranking engineers at the Promparty Trial in 1930. In the quest to make reality fit theory, Krylenko felt compelled to uncover the motivation for the engineers' anti-socialist activities in their social origins. But Solzhenitsyn comments that he dug too deep. It turned out that all eight on trial had worked their way up from poor families. *Gulag II*, 387-88.

31. *Writings of the Young Marx*, 575.

32. Dante Germino, *Beyond Ideology* (Chicago: University of Chicago Press, 1976), 58.

33. Tucker, *Marx Reader*, 521; *East*, 135; *Gulag I*, 101; *Warning*, 80; *Gulag II*, 375.

34. Mandel, *Essential Works*, 32. See also *Writings of the Young Marx*, 460-61; Marcuse, *Reason and Revolution*, 288.

35. Solzhenitsyn himself was not uncorrupted by power. See *Gulag I*, 1-23, 147, 160-64. One of the reasons the Organs were always inventing cases against innocent people was to justify their privilege and high pay. During World War II it was particularly attractive to uncover plots. It meant that the Organs were vigilant in the battle against a fifth column, and, of course, it kept them from the front. *Gulag II*, 377-78.

36. *Gulag I*, 146-52.

37. Ibid., 567. See also ibid., 511-12, 539-63; *Gulag II*, 553. Solzhenitsyn mentions Dostoyevsky when speaking of the human propensity to enjoy cruelty and seems to consider him an authority on the darker side of the human soul. See Fyodor Dostoyevsky, *House of the Dead*, trans. Constance Garnett (New York: Dell, 1959), 240-41.

38. *Rubble*, 15-16; *First Circle*, 173, see also 394-96, 402, 426-29. Marx was warned that this phenomenon would occur. In *Statehood and Anarchy* (1873) the anarchist Mikail Bakunin held that the ruling members of the proletariat would "start looking down on all ordinary workers from the heights of the state. . . . He who doubts this simply doesn't know human nature." Quoted in Tucker, *Marx Reader*, 542-48. Marx's point by point rebuttal is fascinating. It shows that Marx was oblivious to the possibility of an entrenched workers' dictatorship. He really did expect that a change in the economic foundations would make prudence unnecessary.

39. Tucker, *Marxian Revolutionary Idea*, 15; Aron, *Marxism*, 13; *Writings of the Young Marx*, 409, 412, 432; *Capital*, 177. See also Tucker, *Marx Reader*, 144, 170; letter from Marx to P. V. Annenkov, 12 December 1848, quoted in Leo Strauss and Joseph Cropsey, eds. *History of Political Philosophy* (New York: Rand McNally, 1972), 7; Karl Marx, *The Poverty of Philosophy* (Moscow: International Publishers, n.d.), 127.

40. *Writings of the Young Marx*, 438; Mendel, *Essential Works*, 31. A fuller discussion of natural rights is found in *Writings of the Young Marx*, 233-41.

41. Tucker, *Marx Reader*, 726- 27.

42. Aron, *Marxism*, 13. Solzhenitsyn explains, "Principles are principles, but some-times it is necessary to be elastic. There was a period when Ulbright and Dimitrov in-structed their Communist Parties to make peace with Nazis and even support them. Well, we have nothing to top that; that's dialectics!" *Gulag II*, 345n. Taken to its logical con-clusion, Marx's position leads to the assertion that truth itself is impossible to establish. The human capacity to comprehend reality and perception may be questioned, as it was by Vyshinsky. See also *Gulag I*, 100-101, 433; *First Circle*, 108, 226-27.

43. *Gulag II*, 58, 331-38. According to Marxist doctrine, the party could bring about only progressive change. When, in reality, Communist rule all but ruined the economy and worsened most people's standard of living, blame for this regressive fact had to be placed elsewhere. Thus, Soviet society suddenly became infested with "wreckers." See also *Gulag I*, 402-18.

44. *Gulag I*, 322-41; *Gulag II*, 22, 78-80, 418; see especially *Gulag III*, 224, where Solzhenitsyn laments the loss of immutable notions of good and evil. Why else would people of the twentieth century, more than people of previous ages, be willing to carry out every order—no matter how inhumane?

45. *Gulag II*, 34; *Gulag III*, 279, 421-22.

46. Marx suggests language does change. *Writings of the Young Marx*, 42. Compare *Gulag I*, 188, and *First Circle*, 112. Solzhenitsyn's writings were an effort to enhance his people's consciousness by restoring the Russian language using an intricate style and an enriched vocabulary. See also Carter, *Politics of Solzhenitsyn*, 50.

47. *Writings of the Young Marx*, 409, 414-15, see also 295, 419.

48. *Gulag I*, 319; *Gulag II*, 149.

49. The theory of liberating violence was made popular by Frantz Fanon in *Wretched of the Earth*, trans. Constance Farrington (New York: Grove Press, 1968).

50. *Gulag II*, 68, 74, 144-45, 431-34; *Cancer Ward*, 506-7; Kodjak, *Aleksandr Solz-henitsyn*, 69-70.

51. *Gulag II*, 412, 539, 627. Solzhenitsyn tells of one, Aric Arvid Anderson, a Brit-ish officer of Swedish nationality, who sympathized with the ideals of Marx. He was kidnapped after World War II and brought to the Soviet Union in hopes of making him an outspoken defector. He refused, however, even when he came face-to-face with Andre Gromyko. He was kept in solitary confinement for a year, but, he still refused to proclaim the merits of Communism in radio broadcasts to the West. By his refusal, Solzhenitsyn comments, "he made existence contingent on consciousness." Finally, Anderson was given a twenty-year sentence in the Gulag. He expected to be released in a few years, but he never was. Solzhenitsyn says he misunderstood the strength of Communist totalitari-anism, a common mistake among Westerners. *Gulag I*, 553-54.

52. Marx writes:

> For the starving man food does not exist in its human form but only in its ab-stract character as food. It could be available in its crudest form and one could not say where the starving man's eating differs from that of animals. The care-laden, needy man has no mind for the most beautiful play. *Writings of the Young Marx*, 310.

Compare *Gulag I*, 209, in which Solzhenitsyn recognizes the power of necessity, but writes, "all your Progressive Doctrine is . . . built on hunger, on the thesis that hungry people will inevitably revolt against the well-fed." See also *Gulag I*, 540n, and Aleksandr Solzhenitsyn, *One Day in the Life of Ivan Denisovich*, trans. Ronald Hingley and Max

Hayward (New York: Bantam, 1963), 2, 16-17, 54, 86-87, 168-72, 200, 202 (hereafter cited as *Ivan Denisovich*).

53. *Gulag II*, 336, 503-22; *Gulag III*, 17-19, 78.

54. Tucker, *Marxian Revolutionary Idea*, 5; Tucker, *Marx Reader*, 193. See also *Writings of the Young Marx*, 240-44, in which Marx quotes Jean-Jacques Rousseau approvingly.

55. *Gulag III*, 292-93, 422.

56 *Gulag II*, 47, 563; *Warning*, 125. See also *First Circle*, 296-98. It is not surprising that Solzhenitsyn most clearly gives us a glimpse into the riddle of human existence in a work of art—*First Circle*.

57. Tucker, *Marx Reader*, xxxi; *Writings of the Young Marx*, 293, 450-12.

58. See Marx's statements about "the laws of surplus value." *Capital*, 708-9.

59. *East*, 120; *Warning*, 54.

60. *Ivan Denisovich*, 54.

61. *Gulag II*, 259, 335, 336-37, 610. See also *First Circle*, 40, in which the zeks "were so wrapped up in their work, which brought them no return."

62. *Rubble*, 12-13, 21. Solzhenitsyn also compares the artistic creations of the past, as expressed in Bach, Rembrandt, and Dante, to pop culture. He wonders whether a listener from outer space, upon hearing the former, would ever imagine that the same species had produced the latter. His prose poem "The City of Neva" compresses the quest for the sublime into artistic form. *Stories*, 205.

63. Compare *Ivan Denisovich*, 106-7, 110, 114, and *Gulag II*, 265-66, with *Writings of the Young Marx*, 424-25.

64. Compare *Writings of the Young Marx*, 424, with *First Circle*, 236, in which Solzhenitsyn writes, "Once a single great passion occupies the soul, it displaces everything else." Some of Solzhenitsyn's other characters, Dr. Oreschenko in *Cancer Ward*, Sologdin in *First Circle*, and Captain Vorotyntsev in *August 1914*, do one thing well. They might be compared to Rusanov in *Cancer Ward* and Yakanov in *First Circle*, who do more than one thing, but not well. For a discussion of Solzhenitsyn's criticism of Marx's ideas on labor see Clement, *Spirit of Solzhenitsyn*, 49-54.

65. *Writings of the Young Marx*, 314.

66. *Oak*, 494.

67. *Gulag II*, 143. Perhaps I am reading too much into "the paper did not resist," but I interpret this remark to mean that Marx was not a materialist at all and that he did not ground his theory in praxis, as he had insisted. Thought, unlike action, put up no resistance to the physical world. One can think, thus write, anything at all, no matter how incorrect. Practical reality will not contradict thought until, of course, one tries to apply it. That Marx's ideas were used in a way he would never have intended shows the power of thought, thought's independence from praxis, and the danger of attempting to bring theoretical speculation into being.

68. *Gulag II*, 254-55. This argument does not necessarily contradict the one supporting Ivan Denisovich's enjoyment of labor. Solzhenitsyn argues that the kind of labor that Marx says created man can become so burdensome as to make "conscious production" impossible. People had to be conscious before they could be producers. Whatever the origins of the species, the labor intended to reforge criminals was so grueling that it became deadly. Compare Marx's statement on exploitation in *Writings of the Young Marx*, 459.

69. *Gulag II*, 113, 149, 155, 201n, 209.

70. Ibid., 260; see also 187.

71. Compare Tucker, *Marxian Revolutionary Idea*, 74, 78; Mendel, *Essential Works*, 83-100, 199-206; Marcuse, *Reason and Revolution*, 292; *Writings of the Young Marx*, 281, with *Rubble*, 137; *East*, 95-101. Solzhenitsyn reports that exotic tropical trees were once planted at the Solovetsky Islands on the Arctic Circle in an effort to exhibit to the world that the "Soviet Republic was remaking the world and building a new life." *Gulag II*, 39. As if to prove Solzhenitsyn's point, the Chinese Communists also attempted to conquer nature during the Cultural Revolution of the 1960s. In accordance with the spirit of Marx, it was decided that the local crop yields around Peking could be increased if birds were kept from eating the newly sown seeds. The birds were ordered killed, and incessantly stirring up the creatures and not letting them sleep did the deed. No sooner was this progressive feat of natural engineering accomplished than the city was inundated with insects. Without natural predators they multiplied geometrically. Reacting decisively to rid the city of this new vermin, the party sent out Peking's nine million citizens to yank up every shrub, tree, and blade of grass in sight. With nothing to eat, it was reasoned, the insects would soon starve. At last nature was brought under control. There were no birds, no insects, and no vegetation. A dusty, barren landscape remained. Without flora to clean the air, Peking's pollution became seven times worse than that of Los Angeles. When the Cultural Revolution ended, a leadership more oriented toward the free market came to power and replanted the trees. Insects reappeared, along, of course, with the birds. Michael Weisskopf, "Spring in Peking Is Birdless, Shrubless," *Washington Post*, 26 April 1982, A24.

72. Tucker, *Marxian Revolutionary Idea*, 67. *Writings of the Young Marx*, 312. See also Solzhenitsyn's "The Duckling" and "We Will Never Die" in *Stories*, 200, 217-18. Clement, *Spirit of Solzhenitsyn*, 26; Kodjak, *Aleksandr Solzhenitsyn*, 58.

73. *Warning*, 54. Marx's reforms, such as a graduated income tax and free education, are taken for granted. Other proposals, such as the public ownership of banks, transportation, and communication are more controversial, but still not radical. Labor armies saw their day during the Great Depression (CCC).

74. *Rubble*, 137. Compare *Writings of the Young Marx*, 310; Mendel, *Essential Works*, 26.

75. *Cancer Ward*, 424.

76. Ibid. 411-18. See also *Gulag III*, 352-54; Allaback, *Aleksandr Solzhenitsyn*, 145. Marx was aware of the problem of laziness, but he insisted that it would vanish when private property was abolished and human nature transformed. See Mendel, *Essential Works*, 28.

77. *Rubble*, 19-20. At *Gulag III*, 354, Solzhenitsyn tells of a person who rebuilt the mill he once owned before it was destroyed in the rush to collectivize simply to make his neighborhood more beautiful. See also *First Circle*, 453-56.

78. *Gulag I*, 343. Russia exported food before World War I. The Soviet Union was always plagued by food shortages. One wonders whether the economic system was at fault or whether, as the official annual reports suggested, there were seventy years of bad weather.

79. *Cancer Ward*, 423-24.

80. Compare *Writings of the Young Marx*, 467-68, with *Gulag I*, 149n. See also Aristotle, *Politics*, trans. Games Lord (Chicago: University of Chicago Press, 1984), book 2, chapters. 5-7.

81. *Gulag II*, 153; *Ivan Denisovich*, 61.

82. *Gulag I*, 61.

83. Ibid., 33, in which Solzhenitsyn adds, "A peasant keeps grains for sale in the way of business. What else is his business anyway?"

84. *Gulag II*, 437-42, 570. Solzhenitsyn tells of a fellow named Krokhalyov who embezzled about 8,000 rubles a month. He notes that this "should be understood as an amendment to the Marxist thesis that the lumpen proletariat is not a property owner. Of course he isn't! Krokhalyov didn't use his eight thousand to build himself a private home; he drank them or lost them at cards." *Gulag II*, 437n,

85. *Gulag III*, 357-59. See also *First Circle*, 169, 172.

86. Solzhenitsyn quotes Marx, who calls priests, "leeches on the capitalist structure," and places them in the same category as lawyers, police, and notaries. *Gulag I*, 313. See also *Gulag II*, 30-31.

87. *Gulag I*, 311, 314-16.

88. Compare *Writings of the Young Marx*, 302, with *Gulag II*, 335.

89. *Gulag I*, 10, 22, 95, 129, 138, 146, 152, 154-55, 489; *Gulag II*, 543, 578, 587-88; *Gulag III*, 23, 222, 311, 377. See also *First Circle*, 118, 267-68, 438.

90. *Rubble*, 4; *Stories*, 198-99.

91. *Gulag II*, 220, in which Solzhenitsyn admits to having a prisoner's bias against the power of money.

92. Ibid., 92, 113, 259-85, 568n; *Rubble*, 13.

93. *East*, 178; *Gulag I*, 516.

94. *Rubble*, 12; see also Kodjak, *Aleksandr Solzhenitsyn*, 106.

95. *Gulag I*, 516; *Gulag II*, 607.

96. *Cancer Ward*, 150-51. See also *First Circle*, 584, in which Rubin "was soaring aloft on the wings of the spirit." I acknowledge a debt to Delba Winthrop for helping me to wonder at the significance of those mysterious flights.

97. *Cancer Ward*, 443.

98. *Rubble*, 121-22, 137.

99. *Cancer Ward*, 427-28.

100. Mendel, *Essential Works*, 29.

101. Ibid., 32.

102. *Gulag III*, 402-5. See also *First Circle*, 225, in which Rubin, the good Communist, is said to have "lived the life of all mankind as if it were his own family life." See also *Gulag II*, 238, 242.

103. *Gulag II*, 327-28. For Solzhenitsyn's views on the relationship of the individual to humanity in general, see his statement that Amnesty International is "nobly conceived"; his sympathetic treatment of Rubin in *First Circle*; and his admission that there were "good communists" in the camps, individuals who genuinely were interested in the welfare of others. "Solzhenitsyn Speaks Out," 605; *Gulag II*, 323-25.

104. *Gulag II*, 327, in which he comments, "that is the price a man pays for entrusting his God-given soul to human dogma."

105. Ibid., 243, 448-49.

106. Ibid., 457, 459-60.

107. *Cancer Ward*, 396-411. Solzhenitsyn claims that love of one's family is not necessarily a sign of goodness if, in other things, one acts despicably. But paternal love may achieve some good things. He portrays the children of party members in a surprisingly sympathetic light at times. They seem to be far more humane than their parents. *Gulag I*, 172; *Cancer Ward*, 396-411; *First Circle*, chapter 39.

108. *Rubble*, 249; *Gulag I*, 106, 397; *Gulag II*, 317; *First Circle*, 636-37; Winthrop, "Emerging," 9.

109. *Gulag III*, 402.

110. Ibid., 405.

111. Ibid.

112. *First Circle*, 461, 466.

113. Mendel, *Essential Works*, 30. Marx's statement that "relations between man and woman" would become "natural functions" suggests a certain spontaneity. Tucker, *Marx Reader*, 83. This interpretation is given credence by Herbert Marcuse, *Eros and Civilization* (New York: Vintage Books, 1962).

114. *Gulag II*, 233.

115. *First Circle*, 600. Sologdin, who claims to be in complete control of himself, yields to the desires of the flesh. He may not be in as much control of himself as he thinks. His invention may have put him in the same situation as the pliable Colonel Yakanov. See *First Circle*, 532.

116. Tucker, *Marx Reader*, 96; Mendel, *Essential Works*, 30.

117. *Gulag I*, 199; *Gulag II*, 67.

118. *Gulag I*, 199, 530; *Gulag II*, 53, 67, 231, 247-49. To which Solzhenitsyn adds: "I hear a choir of angels. It is like the unselfish, pure contemplation of the heavenly bodies. It is too lofty for this age of self-interested calculation and hopping-up-and-down jazz." *Gulag II*, 249. See also Clement, *Spirit of Solzhenitsyn*, 63-97.

119. *Gulag III*, 505.

120. *Writings of the Young Marx*, 256, 402.

121. Mendel, *Essential Works*, 25. Compare *Gulag II*, 414; *Gulag III*, 340; *First Circle*, 146-47.

122. "Solzhenitsyn Speaks Out," 609; *Gulag II*, 194, 266; *First Circle*, 31, 108, 574; *Oak*, 494.

123. Karl Marx, *The German Ideology*, ed. R. Pascal (New York: International Publishers, 1933), 14-15; *Writings of the Young Marx*, 313-14. Eric Voegelin writes, "Marx . . . does not permit a rational discussion of his principles—you have to be a Marxist or shut up." Eric Voegelin, *From Enlightenment to Revolution* (Durham: University of North Carolina Press, 1975), 298.

124. *Cancer Ward*, 135; *Warning*, 57, 142.

125. *Rubble*, 124.

126. *Writings of the Young Marx*, 227, 250-51, 290, 312.

127. *Gulag I*, 538-39; *Gulag II*, 87, 104, 375.

128. *Gulag I*, 147.

129. *Warning*, 58-59.

130. *Writings of the Young Marx*, 304. The early writings suggest that Marx thought that Communism would be good for people, thus a worthy goal for them to pursue. The later Marx is more scientific and wishes only to explicate the "laws" by which Communism will come into being. This is one of those vexing points that divide commentators on Marx.

131. Solzhenitsyn explains, "Thomas More, Campanellas, Winstanlye, Moirelli, Deschamps, Babeuf, Fourier, Marx, and dozens of others." *Warning*, 143.

132. *Rubble*, 136. Compare Karl Marx, *Capital III* (Moscow: Progress Press, 1976), 820.

133. *Rubble*, 230. See also "The Puppy," in *Stories*, 206.

134. Compare Tucker, *Marxian Revolutionary Idea*, 18, 20, 31, 50, 85-86; Marcuse, *Reason and Revolution*, 292-95, with *Rubble*, 16, 20, 23, 137; *Gulag I*, 595; *First Circle*, 24, 127; and *Stories*, 197.

135. *First Circle*, 146-47.

136. Ibid., 109. Solzhenitsyn notes that thieves seem to be born to their fate, while he contends that artists have their abilities "breathed" into them at birth. *Gulag I*, 516;

East, 22. Of course, he does not reject the idea that conditioning and circumstances play an important role in the development of personality. For a fascinating exposition of the difference between natural and conventional inequality, see *Gulag II*, 489-91n; see also *First Circle*, 61, 569-70. *August 1914* is, in part, an artistic recognition of the inequality of natural abilities.

137. *Gulag I*, 337-38, 388-89, 392; *Gulag II*, 353-56; *Gulag III*, 353.

138. *Gulag II*, 84, 325-26, 329, 343, 435, 574; *First Circle*, 25; *Rubble*, 240-43.

139. *Writings of the Young Marx*, 292-94.

140. *Gulag III*, 344. It is not coincidental that Solzhenitsyn is talking about the failure of post-World War II socialist parties in the West to condemn the horrors of Soviet Communism.

141. Compare *Writings of the Young Marx*, 307, 313-14, with *Cancer Ward*, 137.

142. Mendel, *Essential Works*, 32.

143. *Stories*, 43-101.

144. Solzhenitsyn implies that the error was begun by Thomas Hobbes. *First Circle*, 365.

145. *Warning*, 69.

146. *Writings of the Young Marx*, 45.

147. *Gulag III*, 515; *Warning*, 64. For example, compare the creative Sologdin, who "got into a quiet side-stream [at the research institute], was never checked on, had enough free time at his disposal, and [was] without supervision," to the uninventive Rubin, who found loneliness "unbearable" and who "did not allow his thoughts to mature in his head, but finding even half a thought there . . . hastened to share it." *First Circle*, 191, 198, 216.

148. "Solzhenitsyn Speaks Out," 609.

149. *First Circle*, 267; *Gulag II*, 187.

150. "Matryona's House," in *Stories*, 1-42.

151. See Solzhenitsyn "The Nobel Lecture," in *East*, 3-36. What ties all humanity together is not the community of material well-being but the appreciation of artistic creation. See also *Rubble*, 262-64.

152. *Gulag III*, 365.

153. *Mortal*, 34, 39-43; *Warning*, 134-35. See also Scammell, *Solzhenitsyn*, 132.

CHAPTER 5

THE CONSEQUENCES OF MARXISM
IN THE SOVIET UNION AND ELSEWHERE

The previous chapter discussed many of the theoretical problems raised by Marx's teaching. This chapter completes Solzhenitsyn's criticism of Marx by presenting the practical consequences that occurred when Marxist governments held power. Solzhenitsyn's criticisms were made before the collapse of Communism in the Soviet Union and throughout most of the rest of the world. The breakdown of Communism seems to contradict some of Solzhenitsyn's contentions about its fearsome strength. His views are therefore considered in light of those momentous events.

IDEOLOGY

It is debatable whether Marx would approve of his philosophy being used to answer all of life's mysteries. It is true, nonetheless, that many Communists accepted Marxism as a complete description of how life should be lived. Indeed, Marxism was the reigning ideology of the twentieth century. Its theories were the horizon under which a large portion of mankind lived.

Solzhenitsyn is extremely critical of ideology in general and of the ideological commitment people have made to Marx's ideas in particular. He argues that Communism encouraged people to stop thinking.[1] Committed Communists accepted party doctrine on faith and refused to consider rational arguments that point out its contradictions.[2] Instead of critical analysis, they adopted the belief that "what is real is rational." They denied the evidence of their own senses in an attempt to make reality conform to theory. How else can one explain the unwavering support for Stalin and all the other Communist tyrants? How else can one explain a seventy-year commitment to collectivized farming despite its devastation of agriculture?[3] Some Communists were so blinded by the promised perfection of society that they refused even to ponder the ugly reality that appeared before them. Indeed, "socialist realism" is an "art form" that depicts people as they should be, not as they actually are.

A commitment to Marxist ideology had two other portentous consequences, Solzhenitsyn maintains. First, people under its influence rejected "all absolute concepts of morality and scoffed at any consideration of 'good' and 'evil.'" They replaced these principles with the more relativistic concepts of progressive and regressive. Whether an action was progressive depended on the "circum-stances and the political situation." Hence, "murder, even killing hundreds of thousands, could be good or could be bad." But who determined what was pro-gressive? Obviously the people as a whole could not "get together and pass judgment." Rather, "a handful of people" decided, and the rest were expected to follow. Solzhenitsyn argues that when people were "deprived of the concept of good and evil," nothing was left "but the manipulation of one another." Loyalty to the Marxist cause also entailed loss of humanity, since members of the cadre, instead of making their own moral judgments, entrusted their leaders with that responsibility. It is ironic that a doctrine which sprang from utter skepticism about the moral superiority of any ruling class should have turned over absolute authority to a political party. Relativism inexorably became absolutism, for reli-ance on party dictates was the only measure for determining whether an action would lead to the progressive betterment of humankind.[4]

An even more dangerous attribute of ideological fervor, according to Solz-henitsyn, was that people come to believe that their own views were entirely correct. They became haughtily self-righteous in rejecting the views of others. Indeed, ideology encouraged its adherents to find a scapegoat for all human ills. "The same old atavistic urges—greed, envy, unrestrained passion, and mutual hostility" were explained by faulting a certain class or group.[5] If only those few evildoers over there were eliminated," committed ideologues insisted, the world will be perfect. "If it were so simple," Solzhenitsyn responds,

If only there were evil people somewhere insidiously committing evil deeds, and it were necessary only to separate them from the rest of us and destroy them. But the dividing good and evil cuts through the heart of every human be-ing. Who wants to destroy a piece of his own heart?[6]

According to Solzhenitsyn, William Shakespeare's characterization of Iago in *Othello* inaccurately depicts the root of malicious behavior. Iago seems to revel in his own evil—he is black and born to hate. But Solzhenitsyn maintains that in the past immoral acts were mitigated by the need to provide a justifica-tion for those actions. Most people did not wish to admit their own profligacy. It was difficult to justify breaching widely held moral principles, and this provided a check on behavior. True, many violated moral edicts, then as now, but they knew their actions were a departure from the norm; hypocrisy was vice's nod to virtue. There were, of course, great villains who went beyond all ethical bounda-ries, but even they did not attempt to revise the moral code to fit their deeds.

Adherents of ideology have no inner restraints on their behavior because they earnestly believe their every action is commendable. "To do evil," Solz-henitsyn writes, "a human being must first believe that what he is doing is good, or else it is a well-considered act in conformity with natural law." The blind acceptance of a creed was how "the agents of the Inquisition fortified their will," just as European colonizers, Nazis, and Jacobins accepted the infallibility of their own ideals. But it has been in the twentieth century, a time when belief in traditional morality has dwindled, that the contagion of ideology has been most virulent. Is there a better explanation of the mass carnage? "Ideology—that is what gives evildoing its long-sought justification and gives the evildoer the necessary steadfastness and determination."[7]

Evidently attachment to ideology can utterly destroy the human soul and with it the capacity to do good. Solzhenitsyn claims that most people vacillate between good and evil. But there is a threshold beyond which people cannot go and still return to humanity. The threshold is passed when, in the name of the cause, evil deeds are committed to an "extreme degree" or when power over the fate of others is held absolutely.[8]

The ideologue is animated by the goals of his cause; he is continually busy in defense of its ideals. Because he has little time to think, the capacity for deep reflection is lost. He misses the wisdom that came to Solzhenitsyn as he lay "on the rotting prison straw . . . the line separating good and evil passes not through states, nor between classes, not between political parties either, but right through every human heart."[9] This wisdom led him, "to understand the falsehood of all revolutions in history. They destroy only the carriers of evil contemporary with them. And they take to themselves as their heritage the actual evil itself, magnified still more."[10]

MARXISM AND THE SOVIET UNION:
TOTALITARIAN DICTATORSHIP

Perhaps the most contemptible repercussions of Marxism were its unvarying propensity to create governments. From what been said thus far, there can be little doubt that the Soviet Union fell prey to this calamity during Stalin's reign. However, there is an ongoing intellectual debate as to whether the heirs of Stalin moved the Soviet system away from the totalitarian camp.

Much of the academic opinion in the West from the 1960s up until the collapse of Communism in 1989-1990 held that the Soviet Union was a totalitarian regime only under Stalin. Sovietologist Jerry Hough presented the most cogent argument for this view. He argued that the totalitarian structure initiated by Stalin was transformed by Khrushchev and subsequent leaders. In *Soviet Leadership in Transition*, published in 1980, Hough stated that "few scholars today think the totalitarian model is an accurate summary of the contemporary Soviet Union." Indeed, it seemed that "many will not even use the word totalitarian. . . . The term most often used," he commented in a parenthetical remark, "is . . . authoritarian, which denotes a more conservative and limited repressive regime."[11] The image of the Soviet Union Hough presented was that of a bureaucratic state, which was slow to change, slow to act, and reluctant to alter the status quo.[12]

Solzhenitsyn's description of the Soviet Union under Brezhnev placed it squarely in the totalitarian camp, although he recognized that there are better and worse forms of totalitarianism. Repression softened after the grisly reign of Stalin, Solzhenitsyn reasoned, but not enough to transform the character of the state. He suggested that Marxist regimes pass through stages. At first the leaders of the revolutionary struggle fought to equalize social conditions, resulting in great upheavals within society. A second stage featured the strengthening of the state with the ascendancy of a dictator who insisted on being worshiped by his followers. Finally, the tasks of government became routine, and less emphasis was placed on upheaval and change.[13]

Solzhenitsyn's position is reminiscent of the views of Hannah Arendt, who was the first to recognize that the revolutionary fervor of totalitarian states eventually cools. She remarks that once faced with "the everyday business of government," totalitarian governments would gradually lose their revolutionary momentum and utopian character. Practical reality would "destroy the fictitious world of their organizations."[14]

Despite the fact that Leonid Brezhnev's government was not as obviously cruel as its predecessors, Solzhenitsyn argued that all the main ingredients of a totalitarian state were still in place. The state's ideology attempted to control people's minds as the secret police did their bodies. The party exercised complete control over every aspect of a Soviet citizen's life. There were some outward signs of greater freedom, but whenever that freedom acted in a way detrimental to the party's total control, or to enlarge the people's sphere of independent action, it was quickly crushed.[15]

Commentators such as Hough argued that the Soviet Union changed because the top leadership lost faith in the ideology. According to this theory, Marxism continued to be the official doctrine primarily because party leaders could continue to justify their high-paying jobs and special privileges only if they remained representatives of Marxist ideals. Solzhenitsyn acknowledged that the party had been corrupt and self-seeking. He pointed out how the obvious discrepancy between Soviet rulers' actions and their espoused beliefs made them cynical. He depicted a party of about three million people, controlling all the means of oppression and propaganda, looming above a crushed populace. The upper caste did not actually have to *own* anything since its members were granted every privilege: special stores, secret payments of hard currency to purchase foreign-made goods, the best houses and apartments, private medical facilities, and free access to health resorts. In exchange for these benefits, party members were required to give "unquestioning and obsequious service"; at any hint of disloyalty all the perks disappeared. At the center of this group was the ruling elite, "an oligarchy," numbering about a hundred thousand. They enjoyed unlimited access to material comforts, perhaps living better than had the ruling class under the tsars. Moreover, their special position allowed them to pass on privileges to their children.[16]

How could such people still have claimed to be Marxist egalitarians? Solzhenitsyn speculated that in order to justify their high position and the contemptible treatment inflicted on ordinary Soviet citizens in order to maintain it, party members clung ever more steadfastly to the ideology. Ironically, deviation from pure Marxist principles actually strengthened the power of the ideology over society. If Marxism had been abandoned, the party could not have claimed special benefits, and, more important, past crimes committed in the name of the cause might have been uncovered and the perpetrators punished.

The devotion to ideology may have weakened, Solzhenitsyn wrote in the late 1970s, "but its malignant poison floods our souls and all our life. Ideology is dead, but it still makes us slaves." Even if the leadership no longer believed in Marxism, it was forced to behave as if it did. Why else continue to pursue policies such as collective farming, reckless industrialization, and a centrally planned economy? Why else arm terrorist groups everywhere in the world? "If no one believes and yet everyone submits," he reasoned, "this demonstrates not the weakness of an ideology but its frightful, evil power." He concluded that "Marxist ideology is the fetid root of today's Soviet life. Only by cleansing ourselves from it can we begin to return to humanity."[17]

He complained bitterly that the ideology forced everyone to live in a sort of fabricated world. Lies were the bedrock of existence within the Soviet Union, since the truth of life did not fit into the ideological principles. "A universal spiritual death" touched the Soviet population. People were compelled to dismiss what they knew to be true in order not to provoke the wrath of the state. Fear of retribution clutched the population so tightly that some proclaimed their loyalty to the lie openly, thereby violating the first tenet of personal integrity. Indeed, what some feared most was "to lag behind the herd and to take a step alone."[18]

The obligatory ideological lie disclosed the insidious nature of Soviet society. Unlike authoritarian governments, past and present, which required of their citizens little more than supine acceptance of official directives, the Soviet state expected its citizens to make a positive commitment to the ideology. Attendance at ideological training sessions, membership in "voluntary" party associations, and continual public displays of loyalty were the only security against losing one's job, or worse. Furthermore, the lie concealed the violence by which the regime governed. "Violence quickly grows old," Solzhenitsyn explained. Since human beings lose confidence in a government supported by violence, "in order for it to maintain a respectable face it summons falsehood as its ally—since violence can conceal itself with nothing except lies, and lies can be maintained only by Violence."[19] Thus the Soviet state asked more than mere compliance—it sought to possess people's souls.[20]

Another proposition put forward to support the idea that the Soviet Union had altered its nature held that the leaders were more "liberal." Their main concern, it was said, was to build a healthy economy at home and to avoid a tragedy similar to that which their nation suffered during World War II. Solzhenitsyn rejected this view as bad scholarship. The system, he argued, encouraged a brutal and despotic leadership. Soviet rulers wrapped themselves in the cloak of progressivism, but in truth they had learned how to treat people under the heavy hand of Stalin. Before Gorbachev, at least, all the top leaders had gained promotion by stepping on the backs of their superiors. Their first successes came by crushing the opposition or by mercilessly carrying through the harsh edicts of collectivization.

Solzhenitsyn maintained that it was naive to expect a softer variety of Soviet ruler. The bureaucracy from which any leader arose was replete with patronage and corruption. The processes by which one came to dominate such an organization, therefore, had to be vicious. People of good character were inevitably excluded. He explained: "Never has the Politburo numbered a humane or peace-loving man among its members. The Communist bureaucracy is not constituted to allow men of that caliber to rise to the top—they would instantly suffocate there."[21] Moreover, he argued, because Soviet rulers gained advancement and maintained their position through such stern measures, they were really all the same. There may have been a struggle for power among them, based solely on personal ambition, he wrote, "but on essentials they all agree."[22]

In the Brezhnev era, no less than in Stalin's time, Solzhenitsyn charged, despotic rule filtered downward so that each province, each factory, and each labor union became the petty fiefdom of some party official.[23] Even beyond that, the style of leadership left its mark on the mores of the Soviet populace. The ruthlessness with which the party retained its privilege and position taught many an important lesson: might makes right. Little wonder that crime was so rampant in Soviet society and so difficult for post-Communist governments to control. The example Communist leaders set was interpreted to mean: if you can get away with it, do it. Only the massive force of the state kept this impulse at bay. Particularly troubling to Solzhenitsyn were the youth, many of whom seemed to learn little from their Soviet education except to take pleasure in cruelty toward the meek and downtrodden.[24]

Solzhenitsyn acknowledged that Stalin's heirs did make some changes—the excesses diminished. However, he maintained that the Soviet state could not have survived without massive repression. The Gulag remained open and functioning, with zeks toiling to provide natural gas for the West; insane asylums were filled with people crazy enough to doubt the Progressive Doctrine's definition of an ideal life, believing instead what their own eyes and ears told them; and the secret police was the most powerful branch of government. As Solzhenitsyn puts it:

> Rulers change, the Archipelago remains. It remains because that particular political regime could not survive without it. If it disbanded the Archipelago, it would cease to exist itself.[25]

But what of Khrushchev's reforms of the 1960s? Khrushchev did not agree with his predecessor. He even denounced Stalin. Solzhenitsyn was a beneficiary of Khrushchev's thaw, and he grants that the volatile leader was an exception. This, Solzhenitsyn maintains, is why Khrushchev was so quickly removed from office and why he became a forgotten man in the nation he once governed. Moreover, Khrushchev used the secret police, the camps, and the other forms of repression to restrain opposition to his form of rule. But if Khrushchev's leadership did make a difference, even for a time, then Solzhenitsyn cannot be correct in saying that those in power are all alike.[26]

Even more troubling for Solzhenitsyn's position was the era of Gorbachev. Solzhenitsyn made few direct comments about the Gorbachev reforms during the 1980s, and the statements he offered may have intentionally overstated the evils of the Soviet regime in order destroy it. Tomas Venclova, a visitor to Solzhenitsyn's Cavendish, Vermont, home during the Gorbachev era, reported that Solzhenitsyn followed "developments with interest and not without hope."[27] Gorbachev's policies led to *glasnost* (openness) and *perestroika* (restructuring), two terms actually used by Solzhenitsyn in a 1969 letter objecting to his ouster from the writers' union. Gorbachev permitted publication of Solzhenitsyn's *The Gulag Archipelago*, *Kolyma Tales*, by Varlam Shalamov, whom Solzhenitsyn had asked to coauthor *The Gulag Archipelago*, and other reports of cruelties committed by previous Soviet leaders. Gorbachev gave Soviet media a freer hand to print what it wished, including battlefront coverage of the once-taboo topic of the war in Afghanistan. Public demonstrations in independent republics of the Soviet Union, calls for independence in the Baltic states, and protest marches in Moscow itself were presented on Soviet television. Gorbachev's noninterventionist foreign policy led to the collapse of Communist rule in Eastern Europe. During Gorbachev's reign, Communist party meetings in the Soviet Union regularly aired disputes among members. All of this reform indicated that, contrary to Solzhenitsyn's assertions, there could be true differences among Communists. Especially worthy of note was the election of the late Andrei Sakharov to the Soviet legislature. Solzhenitsyn was even asked to join a council that planned to build a monument to commemorate the victims of Stalin.[28]

Despite the dramatic changes that occurred under Gorbachev, Solzhenitsyn was correct about the possibility of reforming Communist systems: They did not change, they collapsed. Gorbachev faced formidable obstacles: an entrenched and powerful bureaucracy, a recalcitrant party, a stagnant economy, and, perhaps most difficult of all, long-simmering disputes among the nationalities that comprising the Soviet Union. Gorbachev was finally forced from power by entrenched interests without his reforms having fundamentally altered the character of the Soviet system.[29]

Solzhenitsyn's analysis was a more accurate prediction about the impossibility of reform than those made by many Western pundits because it was based on past performance. It is plausible to make such forecasts by postulating the effects that governmental structures have in choosing a nation's leaders. The closed, secretive, bureaucratic, and corrupt selection process of the former Soviet Union had little hope of choosing truly humane leaders. In fact, Gorbachev was elevated to power by the KGB, the Soviet secret police, in an effort to re-fashion an economic system that was near ruin. As we shall see in what follows, the policies of the post-Stalin leadership nearly bankrupted the nation. Gorba-chev was chosen, not for the humanitarian reason of providing a better life for the Soviet people but merely to protect the nation from an economic collapse and the party from international humiliation.

The period of openness under Gorbachev showed that Solzhenitsyn's views were all too accurate. By providing an arena for airing grievances against the party, *glasnost* undermined the regime. The complaints made against the Com-munist party—its crimes against the Soviet people—disclosed that the Soviet Union was more like the picture painted by Solzhenitsyn than that presented by Western scholars. Once the truth spread, Communism quickly became a discred-ited doctrine with virtually no public support; it collapsed almost without a struggle.

As this text is being written only a few countries still cling to Communist ideology. The most strident are Cuba and North Korea, both nations are tyran-nies governed by egotistic dictators. Saparmurad Niyazov, the Communist ruler of Turkmenistan, made himself president for life, created a cult of personality around himself, and staged Stalinist show trials to punish opposition leaders. Although he came to power as a social democrat, Robert Mugabe has taken an ever-more ideological stance in an effort to implement Marxist ideals in Zim-babwe. He has also become a tyrant, repressing opposition and negating the election of 2002 that would have turned him out of the presidency. China, nomi-nally a Communist country, has abandoned Marxism entirely or has utterly dis-torted Marx's principles with its free-market policies, best exemplified by the slogan "to become rich is glorious." There are few certainties in political life and fewer correlations in social science with a coefficient of one. However, the evi-dence indicates that wherever a strong commitment to Marxism exists on the part of leaders of a country, tyranny will surely follow. It is perhaps the one per-fectly accurate correlation in social science.[30]

FURTHER CONSEQUENCES

According to Solzhenitsyn, life under the Marxist-inspired post-Stalin leadership was bleak and dismal. First, government policies impoverished the nation. Solz-henitsyn claimed that 40 percent of the population lived in a state of poverty. Food was normally rationed in some way. There were persistent shortages. Many people lived on inferior diets high in starches and low in nutrients.[31]

Lack of private initiative was perhaps the most important explanation for the Soviet economy's abysmal record. The farming population, bound to the land by the internal passport system, existed in a condition of virtual serfdom. Without proper incentives, collective-farm labor was done in a slipshod manner. Perceiving little hope for advancement, the young sought to leave the kolkhoz by whatever means possible. In sum, the collective-farm system was so inefficient that it could not produce enough food for the nation.[32]

The economy as a whole was organized in such a way as to stifle excellence and innovation, except in government-sponsored projects such as the military, where scientists were given a free hand to copy Western technology. Large industries had such ponderous plants, the consequence of government overinvestment, that they could not readily adapt to new technology. Even small businesses such as trades and services were nationalized, making minor household repairs a bureaucratic nightmare. As a result, an illegal, but officially overlooked, "second story," or underground, economy flourished. Since shortages in one commodity or poor coordination of goods in another often resulted in economic dislocation throughout the entire nation, the underground economy thrived. The Soviet people were compelled to resort to lawlessness as the modus operandi of their economic life.[33]

Adding to the problems of an already beleaguered economy was the cost of training and supporting the KGB, once the largest police force in the world. Despite having lost some numbers from its zenith under Stalin, the KGB managed to secure a healthy portion of the Soviet budget. Moreover, the KGB's wards, the zeks, added to the inefficiency of the system. As Solzhenitsyn made poignantly clear, slavery is not a cost-effective means of production.[34]

The state's lack of success at producing material goods was not for lack of trying to do so. Quite the contrary: The overwhelming compulsion of the Marxist ideal was to insure physical well-being through increased industrialization and productivity. The consequences of this intense urge to modernize were to dramatically increase pollution of all kinds, to strip the nation of its natural resources with no thought for the future, to press women into the labor force and compel them to perform the most backbreaking and tedious jobs, and to disfigure cities in a foolish attempt to "plan" urban life.[35] Little wonder that post-Communist governments have nearly sunk under the daunting task of repairing what Communism wrought.

Solzhenitsyn also declared that Russia's priceless cultural heritage was continually under attack during Communism. The arts were scrutinized to an unprecedented degree. Not only were artists prohibited from expressing certain ideas, they were expected to take an active role in propagating the doctrines of the party. Worst of all, sterile party pronouncements replaced the once rich Russian language.[36] The language of Pushkin, Gogol, Tolstoy, and Dostoevsky was debased because, unlike the old regime, the Soviet state left no breathing space for creativity. Moreover, the traditions and folkways of the villages, which for centuries had taught the ordinary people how to live, were ridiculed by local party officials. People were distracted from developing their spiritual potential by the constant blare of radios and loudspeakers. Propaganda stunted their minds; "voluntary" ideological sessions took up their precious leisure time. They were taught to believe in the sanctity of materialism. They were kept from pondering the meaning of life—and of death.[37]

Despite its troubles at home, Solzhenitsyn argued, the leadership spared no expense to stir up trouble abroad. Although he recognized the need for national defense, he maintained that the vast Soviet military capability served no rational purpose except as an offensive tool. The West did not threaten Russia and would have quickly reduced its arms, he correctly predicted, if the Soviets showed some initiative.

The source of the Soviet Union's expansionist policies, he explained, was none other than the ideology that proclaims that "socialism" is truly possible only on a worldwide scale. Hence, the leadership sought, wherever feasible, to expand its power, influence, and territory. It supported any terrorist group that might be used to undermine the stability of the West. It exacerbated local and regional conflicts to gain a foothold for its ideology everywhere in the world.[38] Tragically, it did all this by depriving its own citizens of the necessities of life. Solzhenitsyn concluded that "the forces of the entire Soviet economy are concentrated on war," a statement made prior to the revelations that up to 70 percent of the Soviet state budget was spent on armaments.[39]

Only the naïveté of the West supported the idea that détente could reform Soviet foreign policy. In the Soviet Union there was no détente. Out of the main cities, in the places from which the Western press was excluded, the media continually presented war propaganda.[40] The obvious intent was to frighten the population into making sacrifices for the future socialist victory over the forces of imperialism. The less obvious intent was to secure loyalty; fear of war is a powerful means of attaching people to the regime. Solzhenitsyn warned the West that such a government could not be trusted. He insisted that a government that did not obey its own constitution would not keep its pledges to disarm or to observe its treaty agreements.[41]

Solzhenitsyn considered the Soviet Union the worst regime in human history. Hitler, whose reign is most often held to be the pinnacle of evil, was a mere disciple of Stalin. In fact, Stalin actually helped the Nazis establish their power by circumventing the Treaty of Versailles and training German officers. Once Nazism and the whole Fascist movement burst onto the world stage and its barbarity was recognized it quickly vanished. Communism was better disguised. Although it murdered a far greater number of people, Marxist doctrine remains attractive even after the fall of Communism, especially among Western intellectuals.[42]

Solzhenitsyn argues that, among regime types, only other Communist dictatorships have rivaled the Soviet Union in evil. By comparison, the authoritarian societies of the right were mere juvenile delinquents of terror. He points out that since they could not fully control the flow of information, their atrocities eventually met with resistance at home and condemnation abroad. For instance, he compares the sentences meted out for suspicion of terrorism in South Africa, once the pariah of the international community, to those administered in the Soviet Union. In South Africa, which he acknowledges was an unjust society before the end of apartheid, any person suspected of fermenting social unrest was likely to be detained without trial for three months; in the Soviet Union a similar offense might have netted one an incarceration of from three to ten years.[43] On this point Robert Conquest writes in support of Solzhenitsyn's analogy, "To compare the suffering of Greek [prior to the restoration of democracy in the 1970s] and other right-wing governments with those of the Soviet Union is something in the nature of saying a gross and unprovoked assault, such as punching someone on the nose, is the same as boiling him in oil."[44]

Solzhenitsyn even contends that authoritarian societies of the right may nurture important spiritual principles within them. He infuriated liberal opinion in the West by praising Franco's Spain for preserving its Christian heritage. In 1975 he warned that reforms should proceed gradually in that nation and that at all costs revolution should be avoided. There is little doubt now that Solzhenitsyn was correct in his appraisal, especially if one considers the slow but steady gains Spain has made to reach democracy.[45]

THE WORLDWIDE MARXIST MOVEMENT

In a statement many in the West might once have considered either naive or an antiquated holdover of Cold War mentality, Solzhenitsyn claims that Communism is radically hostile "to mankind as a whole" and that it is "irredeemable . . . there exist no 'better' variants." He continues, "it is incapable of growing 'kinder' . . . it cannot survive as an ideology without using terror . . . consequently to coexist with Communism on the same planet is impossible. Either it will spread, cancer-like, to destroy mankind, or else mankind will have to rid itself of Communism."[46]

Prior to the opening of secret police files in the former Soviet bloc, such statements were disparaged in the West as anti-Communist hysteria. Sophisticated critics argued that Communism was far from monolithic; it showed a divergence of views as varied as governments in the West. Solzhenitsyn was aware of the differences among the followers of Marx, yet he argued that in the most important ways they were "frightening" in their "unity and cohesion."[47] A fundamental goal of Communist parties, wherever they existed, was to destroy the social order of the West, he maintained. Even where they acted as minority parties in constitutional democracies, their real purpose was to attain power and abolish all opposition. Their seeming loyalty to the nation was a ploy, made expedient by their lack of strength.[48]

Once in command, "all Communist parties . . . have become completely merciless."[49] Their aim, Solzhenitsyn wrote, "whether in the U.S.S.R., in China, or in Cuba is to force the people to serve them unfailingly as a work force, or, if need be, as a fighting force."[50] It is as if Communist leaders were compelled by the inexorable logic of their ideology to proceed through the various stages of upheaval, dictatorship, and terror until at last implementing bureaucratic repression, the final phase of Soviet development before its demise.[51]

No doubt an objection can be raised against Solzhenitsyn's position. For example, it is inaccurate to say that the government in China was the same as that in North Korea, or that Hungary did not grant its citizens more freedom than did Albania. An objective appraisal of Communist nations uncovers a great many differences among them. Yet all shared common traits: They repressed their citizens and they pursued the destruction of the West.

What worried Solzhenitsyn most about Communist nations was that they were united on the basis of their governing principles. They were all joined in the common goal of instituting Marxian principles in practice. But, as we have seen, Marx's ideas cannot be implemented without tragic consequences; hence, all Marxist governments had to oppress their own people. Communists were constrained in their ability to pursue Marxist goals not by any limitation that the doctrine placed on them but either by the resistance of indigenous national cultures or by the limits nature itself places on human activities. In the former case, for example, Communist leaders in Poland found themselves faced with an enormously popular Catholic church, while in Yugoslavia the various nationalities resisted subjugation by the party. Thus the party's appetite for complete domination was everywhere the same, but in some places it found itself checked by vestiges of former cultures. In the latter case, the Chinese are perhaps the best example. During the Cultural Revolution, the party attempted to create the new socialist man, a deed to be accomplished by equalizing all of Chinese society. The resultant confusion, lack of order, and loss of incentive caused a famine of vast proportions. When the party cadre itself began to feel the shortages, enough momentum gathered to reform the system.

COMMUNISM IN THE WEST

What of Communists in the West? Have they not shown themselves to be militantly opposed to oppression, especially against the poor, and in favor of liberation, especially for the downtrodden? Solzhenitsyn acknowledges that Communism "disguises itself as humanitarianism," but he contends that the ideology somehow narrows and hardens people's souls so that they fail to recognize the suffering that they themselves inflict. As is his way, he tells a story to make his point.

While he was still living in his native land, the Soviet media buzzed for almost a year with stories of the arrest and incarceration of the radical American college professor Angela Davis. The Soviet Union was inundated with news of the injustice done to her and of the suffering she experienced in prison. Soviet schoolchildren were asked to sign petitions for her release.

As we know, Angela Davis was released. Although American prisons are far from perfect, her discomfort had been minimal as compared to that of the inhabitants of the Gulag. Still, she was invited to recuperate at a Soviet resort. While she was there, some Soviet and Czech dissidents addressed an appeal to her in the hope that she might intercede on behalf of a number of people thrown into prison as the result of their protests against the 1968 Soviet invasion of Czechoslovakia. "Comrade Davis," they wrote, "you were in prison. You know how unpleasant it is to sit in prison, especially when you consider yourself innocent. You have such great authority now. Could you stand up for those people in Czechoslovakia who are being persecuted by the state?" Comrade Davis responded, "They deserve what they get. Let them remain in prison." To which Solzhenitsyn comments: "That is the face of Communism. That is the heart of Communism for you."[52]

Obviously, this one story does not prove that all Communists become hardened to the misery of others. Yet Solzhenitsyn maintains that it is indicative of the tendency among dedicated Marxists to become cruel in pursuit of their goals. Not every follower of Marx became ruthless, yet, Solzhenitsyn points out, far more than can safely be ignored became so. All doctrines produce narrowminded, self-righteous fanatics, but Marxism spawned more of them, perhaps because they believed that history would justify all that they did.

If Communism was such a vile and degrading doctrine, how did it continue to exist? Why did people put up with it? Solzhenitsyn offers a number of suggestions. First, as we have seen, it has "inhuman strength." Second, it is philosophically and rhetorically allied with the three most popular currents in the twentieth century—the quests for material well-being, equality, and liberation. Finally, as we shall see in what follows, it had support in the West.

Notes

1. *Gulag I*, 332; *Gulag II*, 348; *Gulag III*, 22.
2. *Gulag II*, 347.
3. Ibid., 335; *First Circle*, 41, 481; Allaback, *Aleksandr Solzhenitsyn*, 78; Dunlop, *Critical Essays*, 142-43. Solzhenitsyn estimates that while only a small percentage of Russia's land was held privately, it produced almost half of the U.S.S.R.'s foodstuffs. Despite this seeming success, the state officially continued to discourage private farming and to support the inefficient collective-farm system. Once again, ideology won out over practicality. "Communism at the End of the Brezhnev Era," 29. See also, Scammell, *Solzhenitsyn*, 96.
4. *Warning*, 56-58; *Gulag III*, 224.
5. *East*, 23.
6. *Gulag I*, 168. Despite the evil within the human soul, Solzhenitsyn rejects the notion that it is impossible to judge between right and wrong or that people should not be held responsible for their actions.
7. Ibid., 173, 174.
8. Ibid., 172-75.
9. *Gulag II*, 615.
10. Ibid., 615-16.
11. Jerry F. Hough, *Soviet Leadership in Transition* (Washington, D.C.: Brookings Institution, 1980), 4.
12. Ibid., 37-77.

13. Compare the classic study of totalitarianism by Friedrich and Brzezinski. They offer six fundamental attributes of totalitarian societies that, taken together, differentiate them from autocracies and tyrannies. The criteria are: (1) an official ideology or doctrine that claims to cover all vital aspects of human existence; (2) a single mass party, usually headed by one person; (3) a system of police control that terrorizes the population; (4) monopoly control of all means of communication; (5) monopoly control of all means of effective armed combat; (6) a centrally managed and directed economy. The authors acknowledge that this list may not be complete. In fact, they also seem to suggest that totalitarian governments keep their citizens stirred up and ready for action, "continually on the march," as it were. Carl Friedrich and Zbigniew Brzezinski, *Totalitarian Dictatorship and Democracy* (Cambridge, Mass.: Harvard University Press, 1956), 11-12, 40.

14. Hannah Arendt, *The Origins of Totalitarianism* (New York: Harcourt, Brace & World, 1951), 378.

15. *Warning*, 62-64; *Gulag I*, 68n.

16. "Communism at the End of the Brezhnev Era," 33. *East*, 526.

17. Aleksandr Solzhenitsyn, "Sakharov i kritika 'Pisma vozhdyam," *Kontinent* 2. (1975): 352-53, quoted in John Dunlop, "Solzhenitsyn in Exile," *Survey* 21 (Summer 1975): 135-36 (hereafter cited as Dunlop, "Exile").

18. Aleksandr Solzhenitsyn, "Live Not by Lies," *Washington Post*, 18 February 1974, A26 (hereafter cited as "Live Not by Lies").

19. Ibid.

20. "Solzhenitsyn Speaks Out," 609; *Rubble*, 23, 117, 275, 278; *East*, 34, 129; *Warning*, 7.

21. *Mortal*, 22. See also *Warning*, 36-37; *Gulag III*, 477, 518, 525; *First Circle*, 84.

22. *Warning*, 36.

23. *Mortal*, 32-33.

24. See especially, "The Easter Procession" in *Stories*, 102-6; See also *Oak*, 209; *East*, 117, 223; Carter, *Politics of Solzhenitsyn*, 53; Kodjak, *Aleksandr Solzhenitsyn*, 121-22.

25. *Gulag III*, 494.

26. Ibid, 492; *Oak*, 42; *East*, 76-77.

27. Richard Truehart, "Solzhenitsyn and His Message of Silence," *Washington Post*, 24 November 1987, D1, D4 ; Paul Grey, "Russia's Prophet in Exile," *Time*, 24 July 1989, 56-60; David Remnick, "Solzhenitsyn—A New Day in the Life," *Washington Post*, 7 January 1990, B3.

28. David Remnick, "Solzhenitsyn Denies Talking with Soviets," *Washington Post*, 28 June 1988, A10; Associated Press, "Solzhenitsyn Rejects Invitation," *Washington Post*, 9 September 1988, B4; David Remnick, "Soviet Journal to Publish Solzhenitsyn," *Washington Post*, 21 April 1989, C1, C9; David Remnick, "Witness to the Gulag," *Washington Post*, 9 July 1989, B7; David Remnick, "Ivan Denisovich' Returns," *Washington Post*, 21 November 1989, D1. My thanks to John B. Dunlop who graciously shared "The Almost Rehabilitation and Re-anathematization of Aleksandr Solzhenitsyn," working paper, Hoover Institution, Stanford University, February 1989.

29. The enormous difficulty of transforming Communist governments was visible in the crackdown on student protesters in China in June 1989. It must be recalled that prior to this upheaval, China was thought to be more advanced along the road to reform than the Soviet Union.

30. Robert Kaiser, "'Dribs and Drabs' of Information Keep Turkmen Plot in Shadows," *Washington Post*, 13 January 2003, A16; Jackson Diehl, "Solidarity, Cuban Style," *Washington Post*, 13 January 2003, A21.

31. *Rubble*, 3; *Mortal*, 31-32; "Communism at the End of the Brezhnev Era," 28-34.

32. *Gulag III*, 350-55; *East*, 110.

33. *Warning*, 11-12; *East*, 122-23; *Gulag II*, 165-67.

34. *Gulag II*, 95, 101, 160-61, 577-78, 583-84; *First Circle*, 97, 151, 521-22.

35. *East*, 97-101, 118-19; Dunlop, "Exile," 542.

36. Carter, *Politics of Solzhenitsyn*, 50.

37. "Will Never Die" in *Stories*, 217-18; *Mortal*, 32-33.

38. *East*, 84, 91, 113, 119-25.

39. *Warning*, 85, 114.

40. Ibid., 88.

41. Dunlop, "Exile," 146.

42. *Gulag I*, 533, 145n, 247; *Gulag III*, 359, 386; *Oak*, 389.

43. *Gulag I*, 290. See also *Gulag III*, xi, 288n, 373, 385, 516; *Oak*, 112, 149, 332.

44. Robert Conquest, "Education of an Exile: Gulag Archipelago," in Feuer, *Critical Essays*, 94. See also *Gulag III*, 373, 385, in which Solzhenitsyn acknowledges the great suffering of black slavery in America. He maintains, however, that because it was not organized by the state, it was milder than the imprisonment of millions of zeks or the deportations of whole nations within the Soviet Union. Still, one could object, slavery lasted longer.

45. Carter, *Politics of Solzhenitsyn*, 536; Scammell, *Solzhenitsyn*, 946.

46. *Mortal*, 1-2.

47. *Warning*, 64.

48. Ibid., 63-67.

49. Ibid., 64.

50. *Mortal*, 37.

51. *Gulag I*, 68n, 398n; *Warning*, 63-64; *East*, 24, 83-84.

52. *Warning*, 60-61.

CHAPTER 6

SOLZHENITSYN ON THE WEST

While Solzhenitsyn's analysis of Marxism's influence on the politics of the East is certainly controversial, his analysis of the West has stirred an even greater debate. He has been called "confused" and "uninformed." His views have been likened to those of a "religious fanatic." After his commencement address at Harvard in 1978, he was told to "get out of the country."[1]

Despite the storm of protest that his remarks have raised, Solzhenitsyn claims to be a "friend" of the West. However, he is not—as he says he once was—a worshiper of the West. A friend, it can be inferred, is likely to be more objective in his appraisal than a worshiper. He is not willing, as a worshiper might be, to ignore his friend's faults. In this regard, a friend of the West might acknowledge its strengths while also drawing attention to its weaknesses in the hope of correcting them. A true friend might be compared to a doctor. The medicine he prescribes may be bitter, but it is given with the goal of doing the patient some good. Solzhenitsyn understands his criticism of the West in precisely this way. His message is, in effect, "I am not a critic of the West. I am a critic of the weaknesses of the West. I am a critic of a fact we can't comprehend: how one can lose one's spiritual strength, one's will power, and possessing freedom, not value it, not be willing to make sacrifices for it."[2]

This chapter will begin with a practical discussion of Solzhenitsyn's arguments against policies the West adopted toward the Soviet Union during the Cold War. It will then investigate his views on the sources of the "misunderstanding" that led Western scholars and political leaders to make disastrous decisions concerning the East. In particular, it will focus on the theoretical problem that Solzhenitsyn sees as the root cause of the West's shortcomings. Finally, it will examine some of the major criticisms that have been leveled against Solzhenitsyn's ideas and will speculate on how he might respond to these attacks.

WHY AID TOTALITARIANISM?

While he lived in America during the 1970s and 1980s, Solzhenitsyn claimed that the West had aided the totalitarian government of the Soviet Union almost from its very beginning. Beginning with the first exploratory trips of Armand Hammer during the Bolshevik Revolution of the 1920s, Western capitalists provided material assistance to a government incapable of furnishing even the bare necessities of life to its citizens. Without foodstuffs and technological expertise from the West, Solzhenitsyn said, "The clumsy and awkward Soviet economy could never cope with its difficulties."[3]

Western capital restored Soviet industry after the revolution, helped with construction projects, built automotive and tractor factories, and provided foreign aid in the form of low-interest loans. This assistance was "economically indispensable," he maintained because "the Soviet economy has an extremely low level of efficiency. What is done" in the West "by a few people and a few machines . . . takes tremendous crowds of workers and enormous amounts of material" in the Soviet Union. The system was so inept that it could not deal with such a large number of problems on multiple fronts. "War, space (which is a part of the war effort), heavy industry, light industry, and the need to feed and clothe its people," pulled the economy in different directions. The gaps, those things that were lacking, were supplied by the West.

What sort of country is it, he asked, that has nothing to sell? Except for military equipment, the Soviet economy had nothing to sell except oil and gas, "that which God put in the Russian ground at the very beginning." The Soviets produced so poorly that heavy equipment, complex technology, and even agricultural products had to be purchased abroad.[4]

Solzhenitsyn argued that the technology and goods from the West often were used to support agents of the secret police in its never-ending crusade to control Russian citizens.[5] Western aid was also turned into weapons of war, which were to be used to carry out the regime's long-term goals, the primary one of which was to destroy capitalism. Solzhenitsyn claimed that a "burning greed for profit that goes beyond all reason" is what led Western business leaders to overlook the fact that they were potentially supplying the tools of their own destruction. They seemed destined to fulfill Lenin's prophecy that capitalists would hang by the rope they once sold to socialists.[6]

Business was not the only culprit, according to Solzhenitsyn. The governments of the West also provided substantial support to the Soviet Union. In World War II, for example, the democracies, including the United States and Britain, sent Stalin vast supplies. They raised up one dictator to defeat another. If the West had been truly steadfast, Solzhenitsyn argued, it could have conquered Hitler without having to build up the Soviet economy and bring Stalin to world prominence in the process. After all, what did the West gain by its alliance with Stalin? Germany was defeated, but, as a consequence, Europe was divided, its eastern half under totalitarian rule, and Poland—for whose freedom the war was begun and so many lives were sacrificed—was reduced to virtual slavery. In their own countries, he explained, Winston Churchill and Franklin Roosevelt may have been honored as statesmen, but in Eastern Europe they were considered "shortsighted" and "stupid" for having bartered the freedom of so many people whose destiny had been in their hands.[7]

It was "incomprehensible to the ordinary human mind," he reasoned, that the Western powers should have ceded so much to the forces of totalitarianism at the conclusion of World War II. He wrote:

Victorious states always dictate peace: they create the sort of situation which conforms to their philosophy. Instead . . . President Roosevelt . . . gave unlimited aid, and then unlimited concessions. Without any necessity whatever the occupation of Mongolia, Moldavia, Estonia, Latvia, Lithuania were silently recognized at Yalta. After that, almost nothing was done to protect Eastern Europe, [thus] seven or eight more countries were surrendered.[8]

The West's situation after World War II deteriorated even further, he argued, during the 1970s and early 1980s. "Country after country" was sacrificed by the Western powers so as not to disrupt "their agreeable state of general tranquility."

Solzhenitsyn was particularly horrified by the debacle in Vietnam, where "Two of the great powers of the West—France and America—tried their strength" against the forces of Communism "and both in turn [have] quit the field." Such wars of "national liberation" were particularly dangerous to the West, he warned at that time, for they led Western public opinion to abandon the impulse to resist Communism in the Third World, thereby giving Communist leaders an open road to global domination.

A "calm and impartial comparison" between the West's strength in the 1970s and in 1945 showed that the West's power had slipped while the East's had increased. The West's "spirit of resistance," its "position throughout the world," and "the confidence" that "the neutral 'Third World'" had in it were "weakened." On the other hand, "The communist system . . . spread over huge areas" and "its powerful enemies" were "destroyed."[9] While some argued that Communism was "ready to collapse," he proposed that it needed to be boldly confronted because it "always managed to keep its balance."[10]

Solzhenitsyn contended that détente, the policy of compromise between East and West supported by Henry Kissinger, was an example of the West's lack of prudence. He agreed that détente was as necessary "as air," since nuclear war is a horrible prospect, but he found that East-West relations, particularly during the 1970s, "fell far short of détente."[11]

The West's shortsightedness was best epitomized by the SALT (Strategic Arms Limitation Treaty) accords that put a ceiling on the number of certain kinds of nuclear weapons that each side could deploy. These treaties also had the effect of maintaining the status quo in the division of Europe. In an effort to secure peace for themselves, Western powers entered into agreements that accepted Soviet domination of Eastern and Central Europe, effectively legitimizing the enslavement of half a continent. Solzhenitsyn questioned the signal such acquiescence sent to totalitarian rulers. If Europeans were unwilling to resist, even symbolically, the encroachments of a tyrannical force of occupation enslaving their fellow Europeans, one was led to wonder if they would in fact be prepared to defend their own freedom.

Solzhenitsyn found even more serious problems with the concept of détente. First, he argued that the policy did little to moderate the war that Communism was waging against its own people. What sort of détente was it, he asked, that allowed the Gulag to exist, doctors to destroy dissidents' brains with injections of drugs, and the entire Helsinki human-rights watch group in the Soviet Union to disappear?[12]

Second, détente, as it came to be practiced in the West, depended on the Soviet leaders keeping their word. However, according to Solzhenitsyn, Soviet leaders never kept their word—or they did so only when it suited them or when they had to. Real détente was impossible unless the power of the Soviet rulers could be checked. Who could guarantee, he asked, that détente would "not be violated overnight"? Soviet leaders were not controlled by public opinion. There was no adversary press and no freely elected parliament to insure that agreements would not be broken on a whim. Thus, there was "no way to insure compliance." Solzhenitsyn's own experiences with the authorities during the labor camp revolts at Ekibastuz and later when he became world famous convinced him that Soviet officials were never to be taken at their word. There was always an intrigue. Every action, every position, was taken for the sake of some political advantage or for propaganda purposes. Nothing was ever done for pure and selfless reasons. The goal was always to gain favorable publicity at home and abroad.[13] He warned:

> Khrushchev came and said, "We will bury you!" Now, of course, they have become more clever. . . . Today they don't say "We are going to bury you," now they say "Détente" Nothing has changed in Communist ideology. The goals are the same as they were, but instead of the artless Khrushchev, who couldn't hold his tongue, now they say "Détente."[14]

Third, he argued, real détente was possible only if some provision were made to reduce the ideological struggle against the West conducted in the Soviet Union. Peace would be unachievable, Solzhenitsyn claimed, if each day the state-run media decried Western nations as aggressors and imperialists. Such propaganda created an asymmetry of forces. In the West, the hope for a peaceful reduction of tensions tended to soften public opinion toward the Soviets. The need to stand firm was undermined, and the need to support military preparedness was questioned; hence, the West was often "outplayed" at the bargaining table. The "ideological warfare" of the Soviet Union was intended to incite hatred and fear of the West and thereby justify further sacrifices for military expenditures. An end to the ideological war was, therefore, the first step toward a lasting peace.[15]

During the Cold War, some policymakers and commentators on international relations, exemplified by such writers as Hans Morganthau and George Kennan, took the "realist" approach to the conduct of East-West relations. They argued that in foreign affairs it is not important to consider a nation's ideology, for all nations have the same goal: to further their own interests. Proponents of this view agreed with Solzhenitsyn that it was foolhardy to depend on the good intentions of Soviet leaders. Instead, they contended, Western policy should have been based on the common interests of East and West. Accordingly, this group sought to reduce tensions, slow the arms race, and divert resources into domestic programs. Since both sides should see the advantage in pursuing such goals, it was reasoned, both would have had an equal interest in détente.

The disintegration of Communism shows that Solzhenitsyn's analysis was more accurate than the "realist" approach. In challenging the realist school, Solzhenitsyn insisted that the interests and actions of Communist rulers depended on the principles they espoused and on the character of the individuals involved. In both cases, as has been pointed out, the interests of Marxist leaders seemed to be at odds with the ideals cherished in the West. For example, he agreed that both the Soviets and the West accept economic prosperity as an important goal. This seeming agreement, however, disguised the reality that Soviet rulers pursued their goals ideologically. For instance, they followed a policy of central planning for seventy years, despite impoverishing the nation in the process. Surely, he argued, it was in the interest of party officials to abandon an economic program that had had an unbroken history of failure and to adopt a system—private ownership—that has had a phenomenal record of success. Solzhenitsyn concluded that they did not change to the more efficient model because their actions were dictated by ideology. The fact that their own people suffered in deprivation and want did not have any bearing on their actions.[16]

Moreover, Marxist ideology spread its influence far beyond the borders of the Soviet Union. It was not the Soviets but indigenous Communists who were responsible for the Cultural Revolution in China, the genocide in Cambodia, the repression in Vietnam, and the suppression of Solidarity in Poland. The same sorts of events occurred with frightening regularity in lands separated both geographically and culturally. Thus, there can be nothing else to blame but the ideology.[17]

Solzhenitsyn argued that leaders who orchestrated such incidents could not themselves remain free from the poisonous effects of their actions. For the most part, the life experiences of Communist rulers consisted either of bloody revolutionary struggles or of vicious and occasionally deadly bureaucratic intrigues for dominance. Once in power, Communists routinely sought to oppress their own people. Solzhenitsyn made many people who read his work wonder whether the word of such demagogues should be respected. Would not the same mentality that fostered oppression at home necessarily influence their attitude in international affairs? Was the interest of people who proclaimed themselves to be the salvation of humankind, yet who cynically presided over a totalitarian system intent on stripping every vestige of freedom from the populace, truly to be measured by the same standards as applied to the West?

For Solzhenitsyn the answer to these questions was clear. He declared that it was folly to attribute a rational, Western calculation of interest to Communist rulers since they were dedicated to a program of internal oppression and external expansion. "The main goal of Communism," he wrote, was "an irrational and

fanatical urge to swallow the maximum amount of external territory and population, with the ideal limit being the entire planet." It was "symptomatic that
Communist imperialism (in contrast to the earlier colonial variety) did not benefit or enrich the nations that it [conquered]."[18]

Unlike tyrants of old, who were restrained in their designs by practical
boundaries, Communist leaders were motivated by an ideology that justified
global conquest as a means of fulfilling Marx's historical promise. Solzhenitsyn
explained, "No personal tyranny" could "compare with ideological Communism, since every personal tyrant attains a limit of power that satisfies him." For
Communism, however, "no single country" was enough. In fact, Communism
was "a type of virtually incomprehensible regime" because it was "not interested
in the flourishing of a country, or in the welfare of its people. On the contrary,
Communism sacrificed both people and country to achieve its external goals."[19]

The true interests of the West could be served, he insisted, only when Western policymakers acted on the supposition that "Marxism is hostile to the physical existence and the spiritual essence of every nation. It is futile to hope that a
compromise with Communism will be found, or that relations will be improved
by concessions and trade."[20]

Solzhenitsyn offered a number of policies that the West could pursue to
forward its long-term interests. First, he warned that diplomacy, no matter how
clever, and concessions, no matter how broad, could never serve fully to civilize
the Soviet leadership.[21] He attacked the carrot-and-stick approach formulated by
Henry Kissinger. Of course, Kissinger did not suppose that the United States
could influence the internal practices of the Soviet Union. But he did argue that
the Soviet leaders' conduct of foreign affairs could be altered, their aggressive
impulses blunted, and their actions toward other nations made to conform to the
standards of the world diplomatic community. When they acted civilly and kept
their word, Kissinger proposed, they would be rewarded with trade, loans, and
technology. When they acted badly, they would be punished by having the flow
of these essentials cut off. Kissinger realized that in the short run Western assistance might be used to build up the Soviet military, but he calculated that in the
end the leadership would be taught to keep their word and to become a partner
in the diplomatic community—playing by the rules. In sum, the advantage
gained by aiding the Soviets could be used to humanize their conduct in international affairs.[22]

Solzhenitsyn argued that while diplomacy alone could not tame the grand
designs of Soviet rulers, necessity might. If only the West had stopped helping
the Soviet government and refused to sell it the things it needed, it would have
been forced to loosen its grip. It would have had to make real concessions or
face total collapse. It would have become part of the world diplomatic community, not on account of the skills of a single political leader but because objective
conditions would have compelled it to moderate its behavior. In that regard,
Solzhenitsyn presented one of his ironic challenges to the East by asking the
West to

at least permit this socialist economy to prove its superiority . . . allow it to show that it is advanced, that it is omnipotent, that it has defeated you . . . stop selling to it . . . for ten or fifteen years . . . then see what it looks like. When the Soviet economy is no longer able to deal with everything, it will have to reduce its military preparations . . . the system will be forced to relax . . . stop helping it. When has a cripple ever helped along an athlete?[23]

Along with an economic boycott, Solzhenitsyn suggested that the West use its "mightiest weapon," radio broadcasts to the East, to engage in a war of ideas. He hoped that the West would drive a wedge between Communist governments and their people by encouraging feelings of nationalism. He deduced from past experience that strong feelings of nationalism would undermine the stability of every Communist state, forcing the leaders to moderate their actions both at home and abroad. One need only look to the antipathy toward the Soviet army stationed in Central Europe and how quickly countries freed from the Communist grip demanded the withdrawal of Soviet troops from their homelands to understand how prophetic Solzhenitsyn's statements were.[24]

There were many critics of Solzhenitsyn's views who did not doubt that the West could stir up turmoil in the Soviet Union—and even more in Central and Eastern Europe—but they worried that social unrest would drive Soviet rulers to take desperate measures. Rather than lose their power and privilege, these critics predicted, party leaders would be willing to take reckless military actions against the West.

Solzhenitsyn understood that engaging the East in a conflict of ideas entailed some risks, but he claimed that the dynamics of Communism made the quest for expansion and global domination inevitable.[25] He considered some sort of confrontation between East and West inevitable. The West could be victorious in that struggle only if it enlisted the support of the enslaved peoples of the Communist world, who far outnumbered those in the Western alliance.[26] The West could not avoid a confrontation with the East, Solzhenitsyn believed; it could only choose when and with what weapons—ideas now, military force later—the battle would be conducted. With a certain rhetorical flourish, Solzhenitsyn proclaimed:

Communism is a denial of life; it is a fatal disease of a nation and death of all humanity. And there is no nation on earth that has immunity against Communism. To improve or correct Communism is not feasible. Communism can only be done away with by the joint efforts of the many peoples oppressed by it.[27]

As a final practical suggestion, Solzhenitsyn argued that the West should deal with Communist nations from a position of strength and with a policy of firmness. Firmness, he claimed, was the one tactic that Communist rulers understood. The rough-and-tumble of bureaucratic politics and the harsh necessities of keeping a totalitarian government in power had taught them to take advantage of any weakness and to respect only strength. When confronted with resoluteness and determination, Solzhenitsyn extrapolated from his own tumultuous experience, they retreat.[28]

On the other hand, practical calculations of interest were not sufficient to forestall an advance by the East or to avoid catastrophe for the West. Behind any successful policy, he maintained, there had to be a purpose that made that policy worth defending. Hence, the West had to realize that by opposing Communism it was not merely promoting its own way but was protecting morality. If the West refused to take a moral stance, it would undermine its capacity to defend itself. (We employ arms, they employ arms; thus both sides are equally evil or, more accurately, foolish.)

We might infer, then, that for Solzhenitsyn the "realist" school of international relations was not realistic. By focusing exclusively on power relationships between states, realists failed to recognize the true nature of Communism, and, therefore, they were incapable of maintaining a steadfast resistance to that movement. After all, if one teaches that all states pursue essentially the same goals, and that the character of states must be discounted when considering foreign affairs (our side is not much different from their side), it is natural that people should become bewildered about the need for sacrifice. Without a moral perspective from which to judge, the global conflict waged for the souls and minds of the human race resembled a self-centered game played to gratify the egos of the superpowers. Therefore, Solzhenitsyn recommended that in the conduct of external affairs, "One cannot think only on the low level of political calculation. It is also necessary to think of what is noble, and what is honorable."[29]

Decisions that take their bearing from moral principles actually would serve the interests of the West better, Solzhenitsyn counseled, than those based solely on practical considerations. Only if the West cast its struggle against Communism in terms of good and evil, he argued, would it be able to muster sufficient will to withstand the "inhuman strength" which threatened to extinguish its way of life. Solzhenitsyn criticizes the realism of George Kennan. According to Solzhenitsyn, Kennan's position—that one "should not apply moral criteria to politics"— results in the mixing of

> good and evil, right and wrong, and make room for the absolute triumph of absolute evil. . . . Only moral criteria can help the West against communism's well planned strategy. . . . Practical and/or occasional considerations . . . will inevitably be swept aside by strategy. After a certain level is reached, [realism] induces paralysis; it prevents one from seeing the scale and meaning of events.

Although it may be "surprising" to some, Solzhenitsyn concludes, "a practical policy computed on the basis of moral considerations [turns] out to be the most far-sighted, the most salutary."[30]

Solzhenitsyn did not disagree with Kissinger's goals, but he reasoned that they were impossible to achieve unless a crisis of the severest form challenged the security of the Soviet leaders. Happily for the West, Ronald Reagan took Solzhenitsyn's advice. He called the Soviet Union exactly what it was, an "evil empire," declared that Marxism was a failure that needed to be discarded on the "trash-heap of history," and challenged Soviet leaders to tear down the Berlin Wall. Events in the Soviet Union proved Solzhenitsyn correct. It was Reagan's military buildup, tough rhetoric, and threat of a "star wars" defense system, along with the renewed economic strength of the United States during the 1980s, that produced the Soviet Union's fatal crisis.

SOURCES OF WESTERN MISUNDERSTANDING

We now know that Solzhenitsyn's analysis of the evils of Communism was correct. But why did so many in the West seriously misjudged their adversary? How could this have happened? Solzhenitsyn argued that a major triumph of Communism was to gain a foothold in the West through misunderstanding and deceit.

An important component in Communist strategy was to control the flow of information to the West.[31] For most of its history, little reliable information was actually available about what went on in Communist countries. Westerners were not allowed to travel freely and were not given access to areas outside the major cities. When seemingly impromptu meetings did occur between Western journalists and the average citizen in a Communist country either the encounters were staged by the secret police or an agent was nearby to insure that nothing derogatory about Communism was said. Indeed, reporters were consistently fooled into believing that conditions were better than they actually were. Real poverty and oppression existed in the countryside, but outsiders were prohibited from traveling to these areas.[32] Even clandestine discussions with dissidents were an insufficient means of collecting unbiased information, since most dissidents were urban dwellers who were themselves uninformed about what went on elsewhere. To support his point, Solzhenitsyn explained that the full extent of Stalin's fanaticism was not recognized in the West for many years, the 1962 Tambov peasant revolt was never reported to the outside world, and the vast majority of dissidents were never sought out by Western media.[33]

Solzhenitsyn also maintained that there is a tradition in the West of speaking ill of Russia. The faults of the Soviet system were blamed on the Russian character and the Russian people's willingness to endure tyrants. Soviet expansionism was blamed on the traditional geopolitical interests of the nation—the desire for warm water ports, for example—or on the legacy of oppression and imperial adventure held over from the tsars.

Perhaps these factors did play a role in forming Soviet behavior, but Solzhenitsyn asked why the analogy to the past was made only in the case of Russia. Did not all the nations of Europe—indeed, virtually every nation on earth—have a tyrant in their past? Why did Russia's despotic tsars explain and exculpate Soviet dictators? France had Napoleon, Italy the Caesars of ancient Rome, but no one suggests that such examples would provide a satisfactory explanation for present-day tyrants in those countries. Moreover, blaming the Soviet desire for expansion on the past misrepresents European history. When tsarist Russia was at its height, every other European power also was engaged in empire building. If the logic by which Soviet expansionism was explained were applied universally, then the sun would still be refusing to set on the British Empire. In fact, Soviet designs were far greater than those of any tsar, Solzhenitsyn argued. The Soviet Union endeavored to extend its influence and domain throughout every continent on earth.

Solzhenitsyn is particularly critical of Richard Pipes's attempt to demonstrate the defective character of Russian peasants under the old regime by singling out a few particularly cruel and cynical folk proverbs. He wrote that

> Pipes wrests those half dozen . . . that suit his needs . . . from among some forty thousand proverbs, which in their unity and their inner contradiction make up a dazzling literary and philosophic edifice. . . . This method affects me in much the same way as I imagine Rostropovich would feel if he had to listen to a wolf playing the cello.[34]

Blaming Russia for the faults of Communism comforted "the entire West," Solzhenitsyn reasoned, "If the horrors of the U.S.S.R." stemmed "not from Communism, but from the unfortunate Russian tradition," then the West had "nothing to fear." For Westerners could believe that "nothing bad will happen. If socialism does overtake them, then [it will be] a virtuous socialism."[35] However, he reminded the West that the atrocities of the Soviet Union were not unique in the Communist world, and it was impossible that Russian national flaws could be responsible for the horrific Communist governments in Albania, China, North Korea, Cuba, or Cambodia, to name just a few.

Solzhenitsyn argued that it was difficult for anyone to understand the suffering of another across national and cultural barriers. This is particularly true when one's own situation is safe and prosperous. He explained that it was not easy for the affluent to comprehend the suffering of others because they were too intent on maintaining their "well-being for as long as possible at any price." In this regard, the West was not alone. Self-interest is simply an "appalling human characteristic" that often makes people indifferent to the plight of others. This trait—to be caught up entirely in one's own concerns—is an aspect of human nature "against which religious books and many works of literature warn us."[36]

How many witnesses from Communist countries would it take, Solzhenitsyn wondered during the Brezhnev era, before the West was shaken from its easygoing attitude. How many stories of camps, murder, and repression did the West have to hear to comprehend the nature of Marxism and to understand the character of its proponents? He asked whether it was necessary that another Berlin Wall be built before the West saw the true nature of Communism. At some point, he argued, it had to be admitted that Western indifference and naïveté toward Marxism's vices were merely self-deceit.[37]

Finally, and most important, he argued that a true awareness of the nature of Marxism had been clouded by the sympathy that many intellectuals in the West felt for the ideals of Marx's philosophy. The principles that once had been the hallmarks of Western culture—its metaphysical openness to the spiritual nature of being—he maintained, had come under attack. As a result intellectuals moved in a particular direction—a direction that made Marx's principles of liberation, equality, and material well-being more and more acceptable as the sole criterion for judging the worth of human life. In order to comprehend fully the reasons for this acceptance, it is necessary to investigate Solzhenitsyn's analysis of Western philosophy and ideals.

CRISIS OF THE WEST

According to Solzhenitsyn, "today's world" is facing a crisis of momentous proportions. The clearest manifestation of that crisis was the rift between East and West. Yet there is a fissure, he says, which "is both more profound and more alienating" than any "political conception." It is doubtful that this danger can "be eliminated through successful diplomatic negotiations or by achieving a military balance." Moreover, the rift threatens to swallow up both East and West in its ever-widening maw. For Solzhenitsyn, the problems that the East and the West shared were more dangerous than the political differences that divided them. He writes, "This deep and multiform split threatens us all with an equally manifold disaster, in accordance with the ancient truth that a kingdom—in this case, our earth—divided against itself cannot stand."[38]

But what crisis could be worse than the antagonism between Cold War superpowers? What was the source of the crisis? How did it originate? What are its possible effects?

The source of our plight, Solzhenitsyn maintains, is modern man's having "lost the concept of a Supreme Complete Entity."[39] At one time this concept served "to restrain our passions and our irresponsibilities." It gave us the courage to resist evil, supplied a criterion by which to judge actions right or wrong, made us aware that there were more important things in life than the satisfaction of physical desires, and, not least significant, endowed our lives with meaning and purpose. One is led to wonder why a concept so beneficial to human life fell into disrepute.

Solzhenitsyn maintains that the spiritual aspect of human existence had not been overwhelmed all in one stroke—in fact, there are remnants of the spirit existing within Western culture today. However, belief in the spirit was challenged and finally undermined by ideas that came to be the fundamental premises of modern culture.

There are, he explains, certain pivotal points in human history when people reassess their way of thinking and acting, and set a new course for the future. One such shift came at the end of the Middle Ages when there was a reaction against an "intolerable despotic repression of man's physical nature in favor of the spiritual one."[40] Philosophies of the Renaissance and Enlightenment recoiled from the "excesses of Catholicism"[41] and proposed that, instead of God or na-

ture, man himself should stand as the center of the universe.[42] The medieval
ideals, he writes,

> pulled us, drove us toward Spirit, by force, and we naturally rejected this,
> jerked free, plunged into Matter. Thus began a long epoch of humanistic indi-
> vidualism. Thus did civilization begin to be constructed on the principle: man is
> the measure of all things. The whole inevitable path enriched the experience of
> mankind immensely.[43]

The ascendancy of the human species would be possible, Enlightenment
philosophers reasoned, if that which is said to be higher than human, and thus
beyond human control, were rejected in favor of that which humans could sense
—the material world that could be brought under human command. This feat
was to be accomplished in a number of ways.

First, humanity had to be released from the bonds of ecclesiastical servitude. During the centuries of Christian rule, church leaders had done little to
combat superstition, prejudice, and ignorance. Quite the contrary: The clergy
retained its influence by keeping the flock in a state of ignorance and innocence.
In a deeper sense, the position of the clergy rested on the belief that existence
was governed by immutable edicts issuing from God. For the religious person,
human beings were only one part of His creation, and their duty was to accept
life as it had been given to them.

The Enlightenment philosophers revolted against this supine acceptance of
human fate. They believed that the squalid conditions in which most of the race
lived could be conquered once the power of the clergy was broken and people
learned to think for themselves. Furthermore, the belief that human beings
should blindly submit to divine laws had to be destroyed. Rather than understanding themselves to be God's creations, people would see themselves as the
lords of nature. Humans could have dominion over nature if the laws of nature
were studied, understood, and put to use satisfying people's physical needs.
With nature mastered, people would be relieved of the constant struggle to obtain the necessities of life. Degradation, poverty, and ignorance would come to
an end.

Second, the human race as a whole was to be taught the benefits of intellectual endeavors. No longer would the incessant questions and inevitable skepticism of the philosophic enterprise undermine belief in and commitment to the
established political order. The struggle between philosophy and the practical
life, best exemplified by the trial and execution of Socrates in Athens, would be
settled by stripping intellectual pursuits of their normative content and using the
discoveries of the mind to increase material bounty. These twin goals could be
achieved if philosophers did not take part in the controversy over the best form
of political association. By abandoning the question that had so intrigued philosophers of antiquity, "modern" philosophers would seem less threatening to
the political community because they would no longer present themselves as one
of the many groups contending for power. Indeed, their primary concern would

be to assist their fellow men by making the scientific discoveries that would bring material benefits to all.

However, this seeming lack of political ambition on the part of philosophy was more apparent than real. The Enlightenment philosophers reasoned that they could conceal their true influence over people's thoughts and actions if the political and ethical horizons they established were popular with most people. Although in practice this turned out to be no mean feat, in theory it was quite simple: Give people what they want, peace and material comforts. Science was to turn its energies to technological inventions that would lighten man's burden. At the same time, a stable political foundation was to be constructed by turning people's attention away from matters that were likely to make them combative (for instance, theological disputes) and toward those things that would make them peaceful (for example, commerce). Dedication to religion and morality was to be replaced by a rational calculation of self-interest, and concern over spiritual matters was to be kept a strictly private matter.[44]

Commenting on the optimism that many felt would be achieved if people were liberated from spiritual considerations, Solzhenitsyn writes,

> Once it was proclaimed and accepted that above man there was no supreme being, but instead that man was the crowning glory of the universe and the measure of all things, man's needs, desires, and indeed weaknesses were taken to be the supreme imperatives of the universe . . . in the course of several centuries this philosophy inexorably flooded the entire Western world, and gave it confidence for its colonial conquests.[45]

The early twentieth century marked the high point of Western idealism. Since that time, however, one catastrophe has followed another, until it seems that living on the brink of destruction is the curse of our age. Two world wars, the Bolshevik Revolution of 1917 that initiated the struggle between East and West, the threat of nuclear annihilation, widespread crime in the midst of plenty, pollution, materialism, and alienation have all served to undermine the optimism that was so common when, at the beginning of the twentieth century, realization of the Enlightenment promises seemed to be at hand.

What caused this rapid—one might even say breathtaking—decline? For Solzhenitsyn, the reverses are a consequence of the Enlightenment's principles having reached their natural limits. He writes, "The West kept advancing steadily in accordance with its proclaimed social intentions, hand in hand with dazzling progress in technology. And suddenly found itself in its present state of weakness. This means that the mistake must be at the root, at the very foundation of thought in modern times."[46]

Solzhenitsyn's account of the process of Western decay can be explained as follows: A fundamental tenet of liberalism, the original political philosophy to emerge from the Enlightenment, held that human beings cannot, thus should not, be trained in virtue. It is not that liberalism failed to comprehend the need for self-restraint of a certain kind, but that it considered the traditional understanding of virtue impractical. Virtue demanded that people not be guided by their passions and desires but conform instead to higher moral principles. But, because passions and interests have their origin in people's physiological makeup, they are strong motivators. Moral principles, being cerebral rather than physical, are felt less urgently. According to liberalism, virtue, an enduring ideal since the Middle Ages, was little more than high-toned hypocrisy. The truth about human life is that while everyone pays lip service to the commandments of morality and religion, most obey the stronger urges of their bodies.

Moreover, the kind of virtue that liberalism criticized was not the somewhat narrow concept of restrictions on bad behavior (e.g., do not steal, do not murder). Virtue had a broader meaning, which, while it included those universal "do nots," also promoted positive actions. Thus, the virtue of a thing was its particular faculty and its highest form or excellence. We sometimes use the concept in its traditional way when we say, for example, "The virtue of a racehorse is to run fast." This statement connotes an ability on the part of racehorses to run fast and a notion that when they are acting as they should (excellently) they can run faster than any other horse.

When the concept of virtue is applied to human beings, crucial difficulties arise. What is the virtue of a human being? What are the particular faculties of the human species? What is human excellence? The answers to these questions are inevitably controversial. Indeed, liberalism maintained that in the previous two thousand years no moral philosopher had supplied a fully adequate explanation of virtue. The result was that there were multiple conceptions of virtue, all claiming to understand human nature, and all wishing to train people to a certain kind of excellence. These theoretical differences spilled over into political life, most visibly during the religious wars of Europe. In other words, the very concept of virtue precipitated theological struggles and political upheavals, which, as mentioned previously, the Enlightenment wished to put to rest.

As a replacement for virtue, liberalism proposed that people be taught to be law abiding. This was to be achieved in two ways. First, institutions would be constructed that would channel people's desires in ways conducive to public peace. Second, an environment favorable to material acquisition would be created. Citizens would learn that their interest lay in the continued existence of the state. It was reasoned that people who enjoyed prosperity would be unlikely to engage in subversion or revolt.

The Enlightenment's principles found their political expression in the doctrines of liberalism. The satisfaction of human desires could best be accomplished, according to liberalism, if people were left alone to pursue their own interests in their own way. All unnecessary hindrances standing as barriers to people's ambition were to be removed. The government's major functions were to enforce contracts and to insure that the contest for economic gain did not disturb the peace. The fundamental goal of the state was to secure liberty so that people could live as they chose—hence the name liberalism.

Despite the dazzling success that Enlightenment philosophy has achieved in inspiring human ingenuity, Solzhenitsyn maintains that it has also created some unsavory human traits. The freedom that liberalism so cherishes has given free reign to "pride, self-interest, envy, vanity, and a dozen other defects," which, along with our positive attributes, are also part of human nature. This tilt toward evil seems to be at odds with what the original proponents of liberalism had expected. They reasoned that once people overcame prejudice, superstition, and scarcity, they would use their newly won freedom to aid in the progressive betterment of the human condition. Advocates of liberalism held this belief, infers Solzhenitsyn, because their "anthropocentric" and "humanistic way of thinking . . . did not admit the intrinsic evil in man." Thus societies founded on liberal principles left

> [E]verything beyond physical well-being and the accumulation of material goods, all other human requirements and characteristics of a subtler and higher nature . . . outside the areas of attention of state and social systems, as if human life did not have any higher meaning. Thus gaps were left open for evil, and its drafts blow freely today.[47]

To support this proposition, Solzhenitsyn points out that despite unprecedented wealth, every Western nation seems to face an obstinate problem with crime. This unexpected phenomenon has occurred, he explains, because freedom is more easily abused in the service of our lower passions than exercised wisely for the cultivation of our higher faculties. Without principles to limit and guide our ideas and actions, decadence easily overtakes virtue because good must be nurtured, while evil flourishes all on its own.

Enlightenment philosophy has given rise to materialism, what Solzhenitsyn calls "the cult of well-being." It is fair to say that the original premise of liberalism did not necessarily sanction rampant acquisition. Liberalism left open the question about the proper ends of human life. Whether individuals sought to become wealthy or sought some other goal—for example, artistic creation or the life of the mind—was a matter of personal choice. Yet, given the reality of what interests most people most of the time, it was likely that liberty would be used for personal gain. Solzhenitsyn believed that material goods, alone, cannot make people happy. Rather than satisfying people's needs, a surfeit of goods tends to sharpen the appetites. People lose sight of the proper limits of consumption. They dash madly about, competing with one another to acquire more, always more. "This active and tense competition," Solzhenitsyn explains, "comes to dominate all human thought and does not in the least give rise to spiritual development." Indeed, the quest to achieve happiness through material gain is futile, for human desires are limitless. There is always a better sound system, a bigger house, or a faster car.[48]

The "humanism" of the modern world has done little to humanize human beings, Solzhenitsyn argues. The unlimited freedom humanism bestows has come to undermine people's ability to make moral judgments. Those who argue for limits on human desires and passions are branded fanatics, intent on imposing their narrow-minded beliefs on their unreceptive fellow citizens. With few moral grounds for restraint, natural human desires (especially avarice) and passions (especially envy) are rampant. Solzhenitsyn argues that the extent of industrialization since World War II alone has surpassed the production of all previous ages. Humanity is awash in a sea of commercial goods while corporations compete to introduce new products catering to virtually every desire—and creating new ones. The world's natural resources are squandered in an attempt to satisfy fickle and limitless appetites. Solzhenitsyn complains:

> Having placed man as the highest measure—imperfect man, never free from self-interest, self-love, envy, and vanity, man has given himself up without measure or restraint to Matter—we have arrived at a littering, a surfeit of garbage. We are drowning in terrestrial garbage. This refuse fills and obstructs all spheres of our existence.[49]

Although humankind gained much from the Enlightenment, Solzhenitsyn argues, it also lost something. There is little at the core of Enlightenment philosophy to encourage people to aspire to more than meeting their physical needs. Human beings could be conceived of as very smart animals who create an environment conducive to their well-being. Like other animals, however, many people have no purpose in life beyond staying alive, commodiously if possible. Solzhenitsyn laments,

> We have become hopelessly enmeshed in our slavish worship of all that is pleasant, all that is comfortable, all that is material—we worship things, we worship products. Will we ever succeed in shaking off this burden, in giving free reign to the spirit that was breathed into us at birth, that spirit which distinguishes us from the animal world?[50]

Solzhenitsyn acknowledges that the Enlightenment did not transform people into materialists all at once. He seems to agree with Tocqueville's assessment that the morals of an earlier age continued to hold great sway over the human conscience. In fact, the freedom created by the Enlightenment's political philosophy allowed religion to flourish as a private pursuit, acting as it always had to form people's characters and to restrain their desires. The vast edifice of the Judeo-Christian heritage continued to teach people the proper limits of their freedom and to preach the responsibilities they owed to each other and to the community.

Slowly but inexorably, however, the West's spiritual reserves eroded. Concern for material prosperity, so much a part of Enlightenment philosophy, began to overwhelm people's regard for the spiritual. Easygoing morality, quick profit, and unlimited freedom supplanted people's private religious beliefs. More and more, the premises of the Enlightenment sowed the belief that "politics and social reform" could bring about human happiness. Indeed, since the Enlightenment's ideals "did not admit the existence of intrinsic evil in man," many people came to believe that religious restrictions were an unnecessary nuisance. They reasoned that religion could be discarded altogether and that human beings could create morality for themselves.

The emancipation of the human race from moral constraints has proceeded apace with an ever-higher standard of living and ever-newer and better technological marvels. But despite the increase in wealth and the widespread enjoyment of "the rights of man," the last few generations have discovered that the price of freedom from religious restraint is very high. Every age has cruelty and injustice—such is the nature of the race—but in the twentieth century people inflicted indescribable harm on their fellow human beings. No other era reached the momentous scale of suffering as hundreds of millions of people were killed by their fellow human beings in the twentieth century. No other period succumbed to so many totalitarian movements. All this, Solzhenitsyn maintains, is the result of the diminution of religious belief.[51]

The decline of Western culture's belief in a "Supreme Complete Entity"— Solzhenitsyn's term for the Divine—has also driven the progressive elements of society to adopt more and more extreme positions on the public issues of the day. Ideas such as liberation, equality, and the possession of material well-being (often labeled "development" when applied to the Third World) have come to dominate the modern consciousness, and in turn have become the basis for social movements. Not only have these ideas served as rallying points for the overthrow of the hierarchical traditions of the aristocratic age, but they have undergone transformation and radicalization themselves. Some social critics have come to believe that absolute freedom, full equality, and uninterrupted abundance are not only the birthright of humanity but are possible to achieve in practice. Without higher moral standards to serve as the ordering principles of human life, all restrictions on personal freedom seem illegitimate, every distinction between higher and lower desires is thrown into doubt, and a dedication to anything other than physical well-being is considered unnecessary.

At one time, moral considerations provided the demarcation between liberty and license. Those who persisted in abusing their freedom rightly had it taken away. Today those strictures have been loosened. Everything not proscribed by law is permitted. But the law, even when supported by sufficient force, has been shown to be an inadequate means of controlling human behavior. Without some notion of morality to give them guidance, even those who make the laws have difficulty deciding right from wrong. Furthermore, as Solzhenitsyn points out, the law provides little motivation for the internal check on citizen behavior that is the hallmark of a civilized society.[52] He states that

> in early democracies, as in the American democracy at the time of its birth, all individual human rights were granted on the grounds that man is God's creature . . . freedom was given to the individual conditionally, in the assumption of his constant religious responsibility. Such was the heritage of the preceding one thousand years . . . even fifty years ago, it would have seemed quite impossible . . . that an individual be granted boundless freedom with no purpose, simply for the satisfaction of his whims.[53]

Once standards existed by which to assess and to emulate models of great character and noble deeds. Today, Solzhenitsyn alleges, those standards have been eroded by the demands for equality. This tendency toward leveling has occurred to the point that "an outstanding, truly great person who has unusual and unexpected initiatives in mind does not get any chance to assert himself; dozens of traps will be set for him from the beginning. Thus mediocrity triumphs under the guise of democratic restraints."[54]

Once people had faith that there were purposes in life higher than the gratification of physical desires. Solzhenitsyn argues that belief in those metaphysical goals has been weakened. Replacing the "higher view of life" is a hedonistic perspective based on the oft-quoted cliché that "you only live once." However, the quest for physical pleasures can become a never-ending trap from which the human spirit finds it difficult to escape.[55]

As demands for greater freedom, equality, and abundance have increased, Solzhenitsyn argues, the political expression of those demands has become more radical. Thus, there has been "a general transition from liberalism to socialism."[56] Although Solzhenitsyn never spells out in detail how this transition occurred, or whether the term "socialism" refers to all of the varieties of socialism practiced in the East or in the West, it is possible to imagine his arguments on these two issues.

Obviously, liberalism's vision of the world was realistic, since people used their freedom to produce prosperity on a scale that has transformed the lives of almost everyone in the world. Yet liberalism triggered a reaction against itself. The continual pursuit of money and the constant jarring of interests caused some people to draw back in disgust.[57] They saw that while liberalism tended to make everyone materialistic, it succeeded in making only a few rich. Even more disturbing was the disparity in wealth endemic to a liberal society. Indeed, in its original and pure form, liberalism seemed incapable of fulfilling its promise to better humanity's lot. The rich few used all their resources to reduce the poor multitudes to a state of economic dependence, making them a cheap source of labor.

The appeal to socialism was a direct result of the failures of liberalism. Laissez-faire liberalism sought to make people happy by increasing the stock of goods available by providing material incentives to inventive geniuses. Socialism, on the other hand, sought to make people content by equitably distributing the fruits of human creativity. The essence of the dispute lay in this: Liberalism depended on material rewards to inspire people to produce greater abundance. Socialism surmised that differences in wealth would result in differences in opportunity, making it impossible for all people to share equally in the material bounty.

Liberalism set forth no moral criterion or standard by which to justify the social hierarchy that free acquisition created. Of course, liberalism did support the notion that the ingenious and diligent are entitled to the greater benefits. In other words, given equal opportunity—in the form of equal rights—natural talent and determination would provide a proper basis for distinction. While there is some truth to the assertion, socialism attacked liberalism by arguing that equal rights cannot insure equal opportunity, since some people have the greater advantage of being born into rich families. Hence, socialism concluded that all differences in rank were unjust.

The process of self-criticism within Western thought did not cease with socialism's assault on liberalism. Solzhenitsyn explains that the interrelationship among social philosophies is such that

> the current of materialism which is farthest to the left, and hence more consistent, always proves to be stronger, more attractive, and victorious. Humanism which has lost its Christian heritage cannot prevail in this competition. Thus during the past centuries and especially in recent decades, as the process became more acute, the alignment of forces was as follows: Liberalism was inevitably pushed aside by radicalism, radicalism had to surrender to socialism, and socialism could not stand up to communism.[58]

The absence of unifying moral principles has led to the progression from liberalism to socialism in another way. In former times, the inequalities that were a part of social life were accepted as ordained by God or nature. Putting aside for the moment the historical defense of social hierarchy, one can see that moral principles of whatever kind justify inequality, since some people live up to the moral standards while others do not. Without commonly held ideals, however, no basis exists for distinguishing between good and bad, better or best. All differences between people are illegitimate—because all are conventional. Socialism solves this dilemma by reducing questions of moral worth to issues of bodily need. That is, we all have bodies. Those bodies have needs that must be satisfied if life is to continue. Thus, satisfying those needs equitably is a moral imperative.

Finally, the very liberty from which liberalism derives its name has served to undermine the principles of that philosophy. If the belief that everyone is entitled to an opinion is taken seriously, then anyone's ideas are as good as any one else's. All opinions are of equal worth. The opinion that liberalism is the proper political order is thrown into doubt. If there is no ground from which to make authoritative judgments, all ideas of morality merit the same respect—equality reigns. With no principles to support authority, even the authority underlying liberalism, all forms of inequality are suspect. Here again socialism solves the problem by recourse to what is most common and visible in our lives—our physical being. While moral and ethical precepts have always been open to debate, it is difficult to deny the fact that all human beings are equally in need of providing for the necessities of life. Socialism is more consistent in recognizing this fact.

For Solzhenitsyn, dependence on political and social movements as a way of finding purpose in life, the transition of political ideals to more and more radical forms, and the hollow hope of finding happiness in material possessions are all natural outgrowths of the "autonomous, irreligious humanistic conscious-ness" first established in Enlightenment philosophy. Thus, there is an intimate connection between East and West. Both denigrated "our most precious posses-sion: our spiritual life. It is trampled by Party hucksters in the East, by commer-cial ones in the West. This is the essence of the crisis: the split in the world is less terrifying than the similarity of the disease afflicting its main sections."[59]

THE CONSEQUENCES OF THE CRISIS TO THE WEST

What problems face the West as a result of the spiritual crisis of modern culture? Solzhenitsyn, identifies a number of troublesome ones.

First, he claims that intellectuals in the West have shown a marked sympa-thy for the aims of socialism. The newest, boldest, and most progressive abstract notions of social justice appealed to intellectuals' ways of thinking. He writes that the "tendency of ideas to continue on their natural course made people ad-mire them."[60] The intelligentsia's infatuation with leftist causes, he alleges, led many of them to turn a blind eye to the faults of the Soviet Union and other Communist nations.

> The Communist regimes in the East could endure and grow due to the enthusi-astic support from a number of Western intellectuals who (feeling the kinship!) refused to see communism's crimes, and when they no longer could do so, they tried to justify these crimes. The problem persists: In our Eastern countries, communism has suffered a complete ideological defeat; it is zero and less than zero. And yet Western intellectuals still look at it with considerable interest and empathy, and this is precisely what makes it so immensely difficult for the West to withstand the East.[61]

It is an overstatement to say that Western intellectuals advocate the Soviet system—although during the 1920s and 1930s many certainly did. The vast ma-jority abhor the repression and injustice so characteristic of Soviet life. On the other hand, as Solzhenitsyn points out, many Western intellectuals have been more reticent about blaming the Soviet Union's crimes on its Marxist ideology. He explains:

> Since the unmasking of the Soviet system, Western concepts have retreated from trench to trench. First they abandoned Stalin and shifted all the blame into a mythical Stalinism which never existed. Then, with a heavy heart, they aban-doned even Lenin: if everything bad stemmed from Lenin, it was not, they ar-gue, because he was a Communist, but because he was Russian. Since these are all Russian perversions, what has the West to fear? The West's intellectual sympathy [Marxism] is also conditioned by the common source of their ideo-logical origins: materialism and atheism.[62]

Ideological affinity for progressive ideas led many Western intellectuals to support Marxist movements, such as wars of national liberation. The process was almost always the same. A Marxist revolution aroused great sympathy within the intellectual class. Its goals were defended and its excesses forgiven. Then, as the revolutionary fire cooled and the centralized bureaucratic state came to dominate all life in the nation, intellectuals lost faith and returned to theorizing—until the next revolution broke out. Since intellectuals are the opinion leaders of society, many people in the general population became confused and unable to foresee the relationship between Marxist principles and the creation of totalitarian regimes. Intellectuals backed Marxist uprisings not so much because they were Marxist themselves but because these movements took the "correct" stance on the issues of our time.[63] Intellectuals attacked existing societies from the left and spoke out in favor of greater freedom,[64] more equality,[65] and increased material well-being.[66]

Of course, few intellectuals truly desired to pursue social reform the way it was done in the Soviet Union or in China under Mao. Yet many agreed that socialism, purged of the excesses, was the true path to social justice. To which Solzhenitsyn reacts:

> The decline of contemporary thought has been hastened by the misty phantom of socialism. Socialism has created the illusion of quenching people's thirst for justice: Socialism has lulled their consciences into thinking that the steamroller which is about to flatten them is a blessing in disguise, a salvation. And socialism, more than anything else, has caused public hypocrisy to thrive; it has enabled Europe to ignore the annihilation of 66 million people on its very borders.[67]

Obviously, there is a difference between socialism of the Soviet variety and that practiced in the West. Solzhenitsyn recognizes the difference, but he maintains that Western socialists are guilty of not resisting Communism as vigorously as they might have, and certainly not as strongly as more conservative groups have. Moreover, since the ideas behind socialism rest on Enlightenment principles—indeed, represent their culmination—they incline people to adopt a materialistic attitude toward life. In doing so, they diminish people's spiritual strength and, as we shall see in what follows, make people less inclined to lay down their lives in defense of freedom or any other principles. Moreover, people lacking faith in a higher spiritual purpose may be tempted to reform the world to conform to some vision of earthly perfection—as did the most idealistic and ardent followers of Marx.[68]

A second serious problem facing the West, Solzhenitsyn warned during the 1970s, was loss of courage. "A loss of courage," he argued in the post-Vietnam era, "is the most striking feature that an outsider notices in the West today. . . . Political and intellectual functionaries . . . [offer] self-serving rationales as to how realistic, reasonable, and intellectually and even morally justified it is to base state policies on weakness and cowardice."[69]

Solzhenitsyn recognizes the problem of liberal societies first brought to light by the English philosopher Thomas Hobbes: A way of life that rests on the protection of physical well-being has difficulty inspiring people to exhibit military valor. People who believe that life entails little more than the gratification of desires question why they should endanger those pleasures by placing their lives in jeopardy. After all, it is most difficult to enjoy any of life's pleasures if one is dead. Yet, "to defend oneself," Solzhenitsyn writes, reminding us of the harsher side of life, "one must also be ready to die; there is little such readiness in a society raised in the cult of well-being."[70]

All too often, he complains, the West has backed down from the challenges of totalitarianism. The "spirit of Munich" infected the late twentieth century. The West's once high principles are mocked and labeled reactionary. Its once high purpose no longer serves to rally its citizens from their private concerns. In the face of an implacable foe, the West became increasingly confused and paralyzed. It has sought to gain a respite of peace and security by making concessions. According to Solzhenitsyn, it deluded itself into believing that compromises with evil are noble and attempts to avoid conflict are moral.[71] "Behind all this," he warns, "lies that sleek god of affluence, now proclaimed as the goal of life, replacing the high-minded view of the world which the West has lost."[72]

One of the most devastating effects of the West's loss of spiritual balance, Solzhenitsyn insists, is the ascendancy of moral relativism. He says that inhabitants of the present generation are left with only the small change from the gold coins of their parents and grandparents. For ages people lived together with the understanding that some things were good and others bad. True, different countries and cultures held different things dear, yet all shared the belief that moral judgments not only were plausible but also were the ground from which all other opinions sprang. In the modern age, the idea that moral standards exist has come into disrepute. Choices between good and bad, noble and base, even true and false are said to be culturally bound, historically determined, or a matter of personal preference. One could almost go so far as to say that what is called relativism that pervades contemporary thought is, in fact, nihilism, the doctrine that there is no truth and that existence has no meaning. Except for the fact that modern culture retains an unshakable faith in the capacity of science to cure all our social ills, nihilism would be an apt description of our intellectual horizon. However, since the debate is over which of the many competing "values" should determine how the discoveries of science should be used, the terms "relativism" and "moral relativism" are more accurate descriptions of the contemporary ethos.

But how did we reach such a state? How have the once so optimistic Enlightenment teachings turned into the disheartening notions of relativism? Solzhenitsyn once again seems to find the answer in the "transition of ideas." More specifically, his argument in *August 1914* against the Kantianism of Tolstoy suggests that he understands the philosophy of Kant to be a critical factor in the introduction and general acceptance of relativism into the mainstream of Western thought.

Stated briefly, Kant had been roused from his easy acceptance of liberal ideals by an attack on those principles by Jean-Jacques Rousseau. Kant objected

to the position, put forward most strongly by Hobbes, that unless otherwise restrained by the state, people will always seek to further their own interests. One
of the corollaries of such a view of human motivation is that moral behavior,
indeed the concept of morality itself, rests on the power of the state to compel
citizens to act in ways not destructive of the public good; peace is founded on
force, virtue on fear. Kant hoped to find a foundation for morality that did not
rest on some force external to the individual who was making a moral choice.
He claimed to have discovered that foundation in the categorical imperative.

The categorical imperative grows out of the constructs of human reason. It
exists in human beings a priori and therefore makes the individual agent, not
some external power, responsible for his moral choices,. The categorical imperative dictates actions by logic, not by divine command or natural law. Because it
is universal, any reasonable person can understand its characteristics. The categorical imperative tells us not to steal because if we universalized the act of
theft, our belongings would be stolen as quickly as we stole from others. Stealing is illogical, hence immoral—we cannot obtain the goals we desire, acquisition, by the means we pursue. Kant also argues that people acting under the provisions of the categorical imperative can have no thought of themselves or of the
consequences of their actions, for to do so would mean that self-interest or fear
of retribution was the true source of morality. Therefore, the categorical imperative must be "contentless." It completely excludes—so as not to introduce self-
interest based on personal or cultural bias—moral values growing out of the
experience of an individual or a particular culture. Facts can in no way affect
one's values. Put simply, it is each individual thinking and acting in terms of all.

In order to maintain the validity of moral judgments based on the categorical imperative, Kant had to show that human beings could not make evaluative
judgments based on empirical evidence (one could not infer the "ought" from
the "is"), for this would mean that one people's moral code could be superior to
another's, opening once again the wound that gave rise to the religious wars of
Europe. Most philosophy and theology prior to Kant had made ethical judgments on the facts, of course. Kant attempted to show that such reasoning was
nothing more than idle speculation. Taking the place of an ethic grounded in
practical experience and prudence was a universal moral code founded on the
capacity of human reasoning power to make impartial judgments.

Despite the high hopes and good intentions of Kant's philosophy, it was
quickly overwhelmed by the transition of ideas to a more radical form. Marx
attacked Kant's principles on at least two fronts. First, Marx turned Kant back
on himself by showing that even a priori judgments, which Kant considered
immune from bias, were actually determined by the economic structure of a particular historical epoch, capitalism. Hence there were no grounds on which human beings could justify making moral decisions—all such choices were culturally and historically determined. Second, insofar as the universalism of Kant
reflected the moral future of the race, it was naive because it provided no
mechanism or historical agent, such as the proletariat, for its coming into being.

Marx did not reject all of Kant's thought, however. He accepted the notion that each should think in terms of all, but radicalizes the doctrine by maintaining that the categorical imperative could be made to have a material manifestation. Put simply, he thought that each should work for the good of all. Indeed, Marx went so far as to say that human beings could be truly human only when they abandoned the pursuit of personal gain and labored to produce for the good of the community. To support this argument, Marx reasoned that animals strive to produce for their physical well-being, but humans have the capacity to work for the sake of the universal. Thus, people could make themselves free if they cast off the chains of self-interest and personal desire so prevalent in the rest of nature and thought more of others than themselves.

From Marx's perspective, human beings could become fully human only after the overthrow of capitalism. While capitalism could make a few individuals rich, it necessarily compelled them to pursue their own interests. Even the richest capitalist was engaged in an undertaking no different from that of the lowliest insect. To be human, one needed to transcend the merely animal in human nature. One could be sure that the merely animal was transcended when one thought, not of oneself, but of others. In capitalism, a person was forced to treat himself and others merely as a means—himself as a means to survival, and others as commodities of exchange or consumers of products from whom wealth would be derived. Such a person would be alienated from his truly human capacity in much the same way that a person who acts selfishly, and not according to the categorical imperative, is not wholly rational and thus not wholly human.

Solzhenitsyn's characterization of Tolstoy shows that his ideas were transcended in practice in exactly the same way Kant's were in theory. Tolstoy's universal "love commandment" helped undermine the traditional views of morality that grew out of Russia's cultural past. However, progressive intellectuals in Russia came to see Tolstoy's principles as antiquated and even dangerous because they inhibited the urge for social upheaval. Moreover, Tolstoy's ideas were ridiculed as naïve, for pursing goodwill toward others was an ineffective policy when measured against the armed might of the government. Finally, as we have seen, the Communist party of the Soviet Union attempted to implement the ideas of Marx by creating a universal state based on the material community of humanity.[73]

Three doctrines have sprung from the "transition of ideas." Marxism holds that all morality is illegitimate except that which brings the revolution. Social science positivism argues that values can never be inferred from facts. Rationalistic humanism posits that only universal values are legitimate. The practical result of these three teachings is to make moral valuations impossible, or, in the case of humanism, to make valuations so difficult—because they abstract completely from self-interest—that they are all but impossible. Thus, many of the limits that traditional morality placed on people have theoretically been undone. It is no coincidence that despite the avowed humanism of the twentieth century, it was an era of inhumanity and brutality of a scale unknown in all previous history. Not even value-free science has been a total success. Discoveries intended to alleviate human misery have burst through those limits and now threaten to extinguish the race that created them. Evidently, the gold coins of our forebears have not been spent wisely.[74]

Relativism has also undermined the West's much-cherished principles of tolerance. Without some notion of limiting morality, tolerance becomes indifference. If people deem themselves unable to make ethical judgments, or think that it is wrong to impose their values on others, in fact they are legitimizing the activities of those who, in Michael Novak's words, "prefer torture, rapine, systematic murder, authoritarianism, and slavery." Despite these dire consequences, Novak maintains in his defense of Solzhenitsyn's position that "there are millions of people . . . in the vast middle range of our society" who refuse to acknowledge any moral codes that are "universal and binding upon us all."[75]

Solzhenitsyn concludes that relativism is an ignominious end to the optimism of the Enlightenment. Not only does relativism undermine all yardsticks by which human beings judge their actions but it also raises doubts that human life has any meaning and purpose whatever. The triumphant march of technological progress seems to have been a hollow victory, and the human race is left with little but emptiness.

THE TURN UPWARD

Solzhenitsyn maintains that the concepts that began in the Enlightenment have run their course. While these ideas have "enriched" us along the way, they have outlived their usefulness. "Today it would be retrogressive," he writes, "to hold to the ossified formulas of the Enlightenment. Such social dogmatism leaves us helpless before the trials of our time."[76]

To Solzhenitsyn it seems that the world is at a decisive moment in history. If an ecological disaster does not destroy us, surely a spiritual one will. Enlightenment principles are not adequate to resist the evil that lies at the core of many human hearts. Human beings must know that there is something worth struggling for before they are willing to struggle in its defense.

A spiritual revival is necessary, he believes, if the West is to avoid repeating the mistakes of the East or to avert a gradual decline into decadence and despair. The rejuvenation of humanity can begin only when the central flaw of modernity's philosophy is exposed. Human beings cannot find meaning in existence or be made happy merely by acquiring material objects and by nurturing their physical beings. Solzhenitsyn postulates, "If, as claimed by humanism, man were born only to be happy, he would not be born to die. Since his body is doomed to death, his task on earth evidently must be more spiritual."[77]

Because the impermanence of existence is the ultimate and undeniable fact of life—the shortage of times, as Peter Lawler puts it—the age-old longing for a connection to something imperishable, Solzhenitsyn agues, will cause people to embrace anew the concept of a "Supreme Complete Entity." How exactly this process of spiritual recovery will occur, Solzhenitsyn does not explain. However, as we shall see in the next chapter, he claims that there are a number of sources of spiritual strength; included among them might be the reaction of the human race to the specter of universal tyranny. Whatever course is taken, a change in the direction of human history will not be a simple matter, for it will take great effort and much vision to plot a course that neither curses "our physical nature, as in the Middle Ages" nor tramples "our spiritual being . . . as in the Modern Era." He writes, "This ascension is similar to climbing onto the next anthropological stage. No one on earth has any way left but—upward."[78]

<h2>CRITICISMS OF SOLZHENITSYN</h2>

Solzhenitsyn's assessment of the West has drawn much negative commentary. These criticisms are presented here for two reasons. First, for purposes of even-handedness it is appropriate to examine some of the problems that Solzhenitsyn's ideas raise. Second, the arguments against Solzhenitsyn help us to better understand his position and to perceive some of the misunderstandings that have surrounded his pronouncements. Finally, this section will show that, in the final analysis, Solzhenitsyn's judgments about world politics were more astute than those of his critics.

Solzhenitsyn was vilified because critics believed that his ideas (1) would lead to a renewed Cold War; (2) called for the West to liberate Russia; (3) may have initiated a nuclear holocaust; (4) did not accurately reflect the world situation because they overlooked the Third World; (5) left no room for diplomacy, compromise, and conciliation; (6) misrepresented America's so-called moral retreat from Vietnam; (7) were not sufficiently informed about the West; (8) were influenced by a particular strain of Russian nationalism that refused to see any virtues in the West's way of life; (9) painted America in too admirable a light and thereby discounted the role America played in beginning and sustaining Cold War tensions; (10) would cause a resurgence of anti-Communist hysteria because they were a simplistic characterization of the world situation; and (11) were too expansive and thereby overstated his case.[79]

1. Solzhenitsyn rebutted the first criticism directly. He argued that the Cold War had not ended in the Soviet Union and to revive it in the West was only to reflect a continuing political reality. The Cold War was a fact of life in the Communist media, and tensions between East and West originated in Moscow.[80]

2. Those who maintained that Solzhenitsyn advocated that the West liberate Russia are inaccurate. Quite the contrary, he insisted that the East had to free itself. He merely asked the West to cease abetting Communist governments' oppression of their citizens.[81]

3. The threat of nuclear war, everyone can agree, is a terrifying peril. All are united in opposing a nuclear holocaust. The real debate during the Cold War was over how much the West was willing to pay to avoid a nuclear confrontation. Solzhenitsyn argued that one course, capitulation, was actually not a choice. Given the history of the Gulag and the likelihood of what would happen if the West were conquered, he led his readers to wonder whether a quick death was not preferable to slow and agonizing enslavement. Moreover, he warned that too

many in the antinuclear movement were willing to sacrifice moral p. the sake of peace. For instance, he was particularly critical of the founde. antinuclear movement, Bertrand Russell. His slogan, "Better red than dea.., Solzhenitsyn asserted, lacks all ethical content. Russell's principle reduces life to mere survival and counsels people to submit even if it means losing their human dignity. Such a doctrine may even be riskier in the long run for staying alive.[82]

While Solzhenitsyn accepts the yearning for peace as a noble intention, he would not pursue peace at any price. For him, some things in life—integrity of the soul, for example—makes life worth living. Without these things, life would become intolerable. The things in life that make it worthwhile are, in a sense, more important than life itself and may very well be worth dying for.[83]

In addition, it is important to note that Solzhenitsyn doubted that a nuclear war was actually a real possibility. He reasoned that Soviet rulers had gained too much power and prestige in the international arena to risk it all in a nuclear exchange. Moreover, he reminded Westerners that Soviet leaders were materialists, and to them life was all that mattered.[84]

He also insisted that the human species has a marked instinct for survival. As proof he cited the case of the Nazis, who, despite their extreme wickedness, never used their stockpiles of nerve gas for fear of Allied retaliation. Rather than direct confrontation, Solzhenitsyn postulated that East and West would fight proxy wars like the Vietnam conflict and regional and local struggles in the Third World. He reasoned that wars of "national liberation," such as those fought in El Salvador and Nicaragua in the 1970s and 1980s, would be a means for the East to gain ground on the West without provoking a direct military confrontation between the superpowers.

4. Solzhenitsyn was acutely aware that a contest was being waged in the Third World between the ideals of East and West. He recognized, too, that the nations of the Third World would prefer to be left alone to settle their own problems. However, he claimed that the dynamics of Communism made expansion inevitable, and that many Communist states, particularly the Soviet Union, sought to exacerbate local and regional problems in order to use the resulting confusion for their benefit. He also recognized that Marxism has been an attractive doctrine to many in places with rampant poverty and class distinctions. Yet he questioned whether a system of government—Communism—should be adopted that would make conditions worse for most people.

5. The criticism that Solzhenitsyn's proposals left many diplomatic and practical matters unresolved had much truth to it. For example, Solzhenitsyn did not explain how a tough policy toward the Soviet Union and other Communist countries should be carried out. Was the West to have no dealings at all with Communist rulers? Were we to show our utter contempt by ignoring them? If a policy of neglect were adopted, how was the West to express its firmness? Unless we were willing to start a war each time the Soviets acted precipitously, was not some form of diplomatic leverage—in which both sides had an interest in accommodation—necessary to show our displeasure? Finally, was single-

minded firmness always the best course? For example, it was not simply Solzhenitsyn's strength of will that allowed him to "butt the oak" (the actual title of his autobiography, *The Oak and the Calf*, might be translated "the calf that butted the oak") and remain alive but also Kissinger's formidable negotiating skills and, one can surmise, an agreement not to use Solzhenitsyn's works on the broadcasts into the East that secured his release.[85]

To balance these practical considerations, it must be added that Solzhenitsyn was less interested in prescribing actual policy than in stiffening the resolve of policymakers. Of course, he succeeded, and the 1980s showed a change in Western leaders' attitudes toward the Soviet Union. In particular, under Ronald Reagan, a renewed and strengthened military capability backed American diplomacy toward the Soviet Union.

6. Solzhenitsyn was very critical of those who believed that America's defeat in Vietnam was nevertheless a moral victory. He warned early during the Paris peace negotiations that if the United States capitulated, a tyrannical government from the North would come to dominate Vietnam and help it extend its power over neighboring states. He predicted that the scale of human suffering inflicted by the newly installed Communist government would far outweigh the misery caused by the old regime or even by the war. Sadly, atrocities committed by the Communist governments of Vietnam and Cambodia have once again borne out his warnings.[86]

7. Solzhenitsyn responded directly to the charge that he did not know the West. He claimed that the West is easy to know, even for an outsider, because it is so open. One need only read a newspaper, listen to the radio, or watch television to gather all the information one needs. But he believed that it is virtually impossible for Westerners to understand the East. The East is cloaked in secrecy and very little news escapes.[87]

8. As if to prove the point that the West has lost its intellectual bearings, some commentators rejected Solzhenitsyn's arguments, based not on their substance, but rather on the claim that they were culturally determined. Tracing Solzhenitsyn's position to a particular strain of Russian thought, these scholars claimed to understand Solzhenitsyn better than he knows himself.

Putting aside the issue of whether cultural determinism can be reduced to nonsense (Is everything culturally determined except the idea that things are culturally determined?), there are serious flaws in the "Solzhenitsyn is part of the Russian tradition" argument. To assert that Solzhenitsyn could not understand the West because he came from an alien culture would also mean that Westerners cannot fathom Russia, since its ideas are foreign to them. To be consistent, cultural determinists would have to admit that even recognizing the tradition of another culture (never mind placing someone within it) is next to impossible.

Of course, this is not at all what these critics wished to say. They really wanted to argue that Solzhenitsyn did not understand the West because he was culturally biased and because he had few contacts with the Western way of life. Perhaps these commentators evidenced more than they realized by their assertion. Despite the isolated way in which he chose to live at his home in Vermont, he experienced far more of the West than any Westerner had of the Gulag or of Soviet life in general. Solzhenitsyn once took an unaccompanied auto tour of the United States and even was ticketed for speeding. Moreover, he can read. Since Solzhenitsyn actually lived in the West was it not prudent to listen to him about the dangers of Communism? However, cultural determinists really wished to have it both ways. They claimed to have not only a greater knowledge and appreciation of the West than does Solzhenitsyn, but also a fuller understanding of the Russian tradition and of who belongs to it.[88]

It could be that the determinists did not wish to extend their determinism generally but meant it to apply to Solzhenitsyn only. In that case, as Delba Winthrop points out, it does not matter where his ideas come from. The real test is how well his arguments reflect the truth.[89]

Solzhenitsyn claimed not to have been influenced by either the tradition of Russian nationalism that developed in the eighteenth and nineteenth centuries or by the Russian messianism that became intertwined with devotion to the Russian Orthodox church. He explains:

As for, "historical Russian messianism," this is contrived nonsense: it has been several centuries since any section of the government or intelligentsia influential in the spiritual life of the country has suffered from the disease of messianism. Indeed, it seems inconceivable to me that in our sordid age any people on earth would have the gall to deem itself "chosen."[90]

Solzhenitsyn's connection with the whole tradition of Russian nationalism seems even more remote if one considers his proposals for a post-Communist Russia. He favored freeing Eastern Europe and breaking the Soviet empire into its separate nationalities. He would have had Russia turn inward and concentrate on building a viable economy. He argues that Russia should remove itself from international affairs in order to recoup its spiritual strength and recover from the ravages of Communism, a task that would require "150 to 200 years of external peace."[91]

Solzhenitsyn's detractors do have a point when they argue that he lays all the blame for his nation's ills on Marx and Marxism and hardly any at all on old Russia's traditions or history. Yet a cursory reading of Solzhenitsyn's essay in *From under the Rubble* indicates that he was aware that his nation fell prey to flaws that affect every human creation. Communism merely exploited the inherent weaknesses in the Russian national character for its own advantage.

9. It should not escape notice that those who attacked Solzhenitsyn because he did not appreciate the West enough are contradicting those who criticized him for supporting America too much. This division of opinion would be more comprehensible but for the fact that the same people made both criticisms. Perhaps this problem of interpretation arises because Americans are accustomed to criticisms from the left, but they become confused when confronted by a powerful voice on the right.

In response to critics of the U.S. role in world affairs, Solzhenitsyn asserted that America is "most magnanimous, the most generous nation in the world." Of all the countries in the West, he claimed, the United States has done the most to preserve world order. Twice it helped European democracies win wars and twice it "raised Europe from postwar destruction." For "thirty years it has stood as a shield protecting Europe while European countries counted their nickels to avoid paying for their armies."[92] Yet despite America's obvious strength, he wondered whether it is suited for the role it has been forced to play in world affairs.

For centuries, Solzhenitsyn argued, the European continent ruled the world through a power generated by its ideas. That power has dissipated, partly as the result of two world wars, but, more important, because the ideas that thrust Europe to the forefront of world events have now run their course. Leadership has passed to the United States, itself a child of European thought. The United States has had to shoulder responsibilities for which it never asked, for which its principles make it unsuited, and for which its history has made it ill-prepared.

Solzhenitsyn seemed to have some doubts about whether America could bear up under the strain of its worldwide responsibilities. Of course, he lived in the U.S. after his forcible exile from the Soviet Union. He offered his views of America most clearly in a 1975 speech (poorly attended) before the U.S. Congress. The address skillfully endeavored to elevate the lawmakers above the parochial concerns of party and region by explaining to them that, although they were elected to represent their constituents, their decisions affected the whole world. Specifically, he reminded them that millions in the East had no voice in government, and all their hopes rested on policies that the United States adopted.[93]

Solzhenitsyn argued in favor of a truly farsighted policy that recognized freedom as indivisible. He maintained that the world could not exist half slave and half free. Such a state of affairs was too contradictory. He predicted that either the East would shake off its yoke of bondage or the West would be harnessed with chattels of its own. If the West lost sight of the difference between itself and the East, he warned, or if it began to doubt the superiority of its own way of life, then the West would not be able to defend its own highest principles.[94]

10. Because Solzhenitsyn is so adamantly opposed to Communism, many of his critics were fearful that if his sentiments spread to the U.S. populace at large they would rekindle the anti-Communist hysteria of the 1950s. What startled these critics about Solzhenitsyn's presentation of Communism was that even its strongest opponents during that era—for example, John Foster Dulles—actually may have underestimated its evil and the threat it posed to the West. Such an opinion is startling for two reasons. First, it throws a different light on U.S. foreign policy in the post-World War II era, especially the tragic events of Vietnam. Second, it conjures up memories of the red-baiting tactics of Senator Joseph McCarthy.

Many Americans feel revulsion toward the McCarthy era because they realize that anti-Communist hysteria posed a threat to civil liberties and destroyed

the careers of a number of innocent people. One is tempted to say that the dema-
goguery of Senator McCarthy established a prejudice against anti-Communism
in an important segment of the intellectual class of America. Indeed, almost all
those critical of Solzhenitsyn's views raise the specter of McCarthy. The ghost
of McCarthy has prevented a fair-minded consideration of Solzhenitsyn's ideas.

Solzhenitsyn never confronted this issue, perhaps because he knew little of
that period. It is more likely that he is disdainful of the whole topic. During the
time a few Hollywood writers and actors were losing their jobs in America,
Solzhenitsyn and most of his fellow Russian artists were helping to build socialism, against their wills, in the Gulag. The comparison speaks for itself. It is also
conceivable that he has ignored these criticisms because they are unfair to him.
Solzhenitsyn never adopted the tactics of McCarthy. He did not unscrupulously
implicate innocent people in an attempt to oppose Communism or enhance his
career. As Norman Podhoretz pointed out, the real crime of McCarthy was that
he wrongly accused people of being Communists. McCarthy's campaign against
Communism does not make Communism any less odious or guilty. It was not
hysteria on Solzhenitsyn's part to oppose a doctrine with a record of producing
such inhuman evil.[95] Solzhenitsyn explains: "That which is against Communism
is for humanity. Not to accept, but to reject this inhuman Communist ideology is
simply to be a human being. Such a rejection is more than a political act. It is a
protest of our souls against those who would have us forget the concepts of good
and evil."[96]

Solzhenitsyn's opponents accused him of drawing a simplistic division of
the political map into "evil" Communist governments and "good" non-
Communist ones. They argued that the Communist world was not unified but
had deep political divisions among its members. If Communist governments
were all alike, as Solzhenitsyn claimed, what could explain these political differences? If pure power politics were the source of these divisions, then the ideology could not be the only motivation behind the action of Communist states.
Critics also maintained that Communist governments were not all alike in their
internal policies. True, all were totalitarian, but some were more repressive than
others. If commitment to Marxism was the one common characteristic of these
states, again, how could one account for the differences among Communist nations?

For example, Solzhenitsyn's analysis did not fully explain Deng Xiaoping's
reforms in China. There, the Communist party led the way in introducing free-
market mechanisms into the economy. It loosened its political grip on the society and even allowed criticisms of Marxism to surface. Whether these free-market liberalizations will bring a true democratization China is still not clear—the
interest of the party cadre may yet put an end to the reforms, as occurred during
the crackdown on student demonstrations in 1989. What is clear, however, is
that China has undergone changes that run directly counter to the ideology of
Marx.[97]

According to Solzhenitsyn's analysis, changes within any Communist country were impossible. He warned that no Communist party would allow its posi-

tion to be questioned, and that any reforms that challenged the "leading role of the Communist party" would be brought to a halt.[98] Evidently, Solzhenitsyn was incorrect about the liberalization in China and to a lesser degree in Communist Vietnam. A number of factors might account for this misjudgment. First, commentators on political events cannot predict the course of future events with certainty. They can only make assessments based on trends evident in past performance. There is always a realm of existence that escapes prognostication. Thus, given Communism's history of cruelty and oppression, Solzhenitsyn could not anticipate a weakening of its resolve in some places. He did, of course, predict its actual collapse.

Solzhenitsyn counted on the resilience of human nature to thwart the power of Communism. As we have seen, Solzhenitsyn (perhaps more forcefully than any other contemporary commentator on human affairs) argues that many of Marxism's tenets run counter to the strongest longings of human beings and that people with an unwavering commitment to ideology ignore even the most commonsense truths about human motivations. Communist governments paid a heavy price for ignoring the aspirations of their people. Many Communist regimes virtually bankrupted themselves in an effort to implement the principles of Marx. At some point, even committed Marxists had to acknowledge the inadequacy of policies that were impoverishing the nation, as seems to have been the case in China.

Solzhenitsyn was correct that the Soviet economy was so backward that it could not compete with the West. A feeble economy undermined the Soviet Union's military strength. While most Western nations had moved to greater flexibility in their economies, the Soviet Union maintained unwieldy plants equipped to produce primarily manufactured goods needed for heavy industry. In the age of computers, when new designs and technologies are fabricated in cyberspace, the ability to retool quickly is essential.

Not only could the Soviet Union's centrally planned economy not cope with these rapid innovations, but its political system, which restrained the free exchange of information, stymied the introduction of computers into society. As the Soviet economy fell further and further behind its Western rivals, its military position became more and more tenuous. Perhaps this inability to compete with Western technology explains what can only be termed a Soviet obsession with halting "star wars," America's strategic defense initiative.

Solzhenitsyn's remarks may have actually influenced the course of events in his homeland. The publication of *The Gulag Archipelago* in the West discredited the Soviet system and Communism in general. Although the repercussions of *The Gulag Archipelago* were most strongly felt among French intellectuals, its publication also hardened anti-Communist attitudes among the general public. The fear and distrust that its accounts of atrocities engendered among Western public opinion played a role in bringing strongly anti-Communist governments to power in Germany, Great Britain, and the United States. A consensus formed to thwart the Soviet Union by building a vigorous military, nearly one trillion dollars was allocated for defense in the United States alone. Clearly, this heightened military competition overmatched the already overburdened Soviet economy. The result was, first, a new willingness on the part of the Soviet leadership to seek diplomatic accords that slowed the arms race, and then a dawning realization that, if the party abandoned its Marxist ideals of social and political equality in the name of the efficiency of free-market exchanges, it would also have to abandon any moral authority by which it could claim to rule. Why, after all, should citizens be willing to obey a ruling group whose legitimacy rests on a discarded doctrine? Hard-line Communists made a belated desperate effort to reverse Gorbachev's reforms by staging a coup against his leadership, but it failed and the Soviet Union was thrown on the trash heap of history, just as Solzhenitsyn had foreseen.

11. Occasionally, Solzhenitsyn falls into the disturbing habit of overstating (one word) his case. For example, at one point he claims that there has been "a total emancipation" from Christianity. Elsewhere he states that there is a "universal sympathy for revolutionary extremists." In neither instance does Solzhenitsyn's dramatic statements seem correct. There are many people who cherish their Christian beliefs and work hard to live by them. There are as many people who abhor extremism.

Perhaps Solzhenitsyn intended no more by these statements than to drive home his point with a rhetorical flourish. Whatever the case, these unqualified judgments tend to weaken his arguments and make him vulnerable to the charge that many make, namely, that he is a fanatic.[99] As a careful reading of *The Oak and the Calf* shows, Solzhenitsyn plans everything he does carefully, and it may be that he consciously intended to overstate the strength and ferocity of the Soviet Union and to underestimate the reserves of the West in order to galvanize Western public opinion.

Whatever his true intentions, Solzhenitsyn's assertions about the West's loss of will do not seem altogether accurate. It may be true that within the intellectual community a certain dislike for spirited actions holds sway, but among the citizen body as a whole there are great reserves of patriotic sentiment—duty, honor, and country are still held in high regard. Perhaps Solzhenitsyn recognizes this, for he qualifies his appraisal of the West by specifically naming "the ruling and intellectual elites" as those who have most lost their courage.[100]

There is a sense in which the dichotomy between intellectuals and average citizens reveals only too clearly the validity of Solzhenitsyn's analysis of the loss of will and its relationship to the movement of Western thought, detailed above. Intellectuals are exposed to the latest and most progressive ideas and traditionally have been the standard-bearers of Enlightenment aspirations. It should not be surprising, then, that from among this group have arisen those who consider patriotism and civic courage merely naive jingoism. In the contemporary era, they have been the leaders of virtually every peace movement. In spite of the massive Soviet arms buildup, such groups invariably counseled the disarmament of the West. Most disturbing, many intellectuals showed a marked sympathy for political and social movements of the left. Despite all the evidence of Communist atrocities that came to light from secret police files opened to the public in the post-Communist era, the fondness of many intellectuals for radical leftist ideas remains largely undiminished.

On the other hand, during the 1980s many citizens in Western nations showed that they were far from enthusiastic about disarming their own countries while aiding those who publicly decried their way of life as evil. Perhaps this is because such people are less affected by the latest wave of progressive idealism and base their judgments on common sense instead. Although such anti-Communist leaders as Ronald Reagan and Margaret Thatcher were not popular among the intelligentsia, they were elected by large popular majorities.

Finally, Solzhenitsyn's supposition that Western culture is about to collapse seems to fit into the category of doomsday prediction that originated with T. R. Malthus. Philosophers as diverse in views as Marx, Friedrich Nietzsche, and Martin Heidegger have proclaimed that the West was about to fall—yet it remains. Perhaps there is sufficient resolve within the West for it to last for some time yet. One source of that strength is religion, which remains a powerful influence on people's opinions; another is an attachment to the principle of freedom, which is most apparent when freedom is most in peril; and, yet a third might be a natural inertia, which makes human beings unwilling to change their way of life too radically.

Of course, Solzhenitsyn may be right. Intellectuals have used their formidable powers of persuasion with great success in spreading progressive principles. In the West, religion has become as much an engine for social change as a source of spiritual authority. The principle of freedom has been used to defend ideas antithetical to the concept of freedom. In addition, attachment to the way of life of the West based on an assertion of its superiority over others is considered narrow-minded and bigoted.

Still, even though Solzhenitsyn has exhibited an astonishing ability to predict the course of events, it is hard to conceive of the Western way of life collapsing. This may be due to my lack of imagination. The most difficult of all intellectual tasks is to look beyond the horizon of one's culture and project the outlines of a future civilization. My belief that the West will survive may be among those yearnings of the heart for one's own way of life that were also experienced by monks at the end of the sixteenth century as they contemplated the meaning of the Renaissance.

Notes

1. *Mortal*, 64.
2. *Warning*, 106. See also *East*, 39, and *Warning*, 22, in which he relates a Russian proverb: "The yes-man is your enemy but your friend will argue with you."
3. *Warning*, 11.
4. Ibid., 85-86.

5. Ibid., 12. He tells of the greed of Western businessmen who exhibited sophisticated security equipment at a trade fair in Moscow. The devices, used to catch criminals
in the West, became a means of spying on people in the hands of the KGB.

6. Ibid., 12-13.

7. Ibid., 20-25, 136; *East*, 197; *Gulag I*, 259-60n.

8. Ibid., 23.

9. "The Artist as Witness," 561.

10. "Communism at the End of the Brezhnev Era," 34.

11. *Warning*, 38.

12. Ibid., 39, 117-18, 137, 139; *East*, 63.

13. *Warning*, 38-40, 70-71; *Gulag II*, 320; *Gulag III*, 270-79.

14. *Warning*, 14.

15. Ibid., 39-40, 76-78.

16. "Communism at the End of the Brezhnev Era," 28- 33.

17. *Warning*, 33; Aleksandr Solzhenitsyn, "Solzhenitsyn Speaks Out on Poland,"
Cleveland Plain Dealer, 24 January 1981, 7AA.

18. See "Communism at the End of the Brezhnev Era," 34, in which Solzhenitsyn
warned that any Communist government is "restrained in its behavior . . . merely because
it has not yet gained military strength."

19. Ibid.

20. Ibid.

21. *Mortal*, 20-21.

22. Henry Kissinger, *The White House Years* (Boston: Little, Brown, 1979), 112-62,
215-16, 552-57. Compare Aleksandr I. Solzhenitsyn, "Schlesinger and Kissinger," trans.
Raymond H. Anderson, *New York Times*, 1 December 1975, 31. See also Scammell,
Solzhenitsyn, 857.

23. *Warning*, 87. The practical difficulties of implementing a unified trade embargo
were apparent in the Siberian natural gas pipeline negotiations during the mid-1980s.

24. *Mortal*, 20-21, 53, 71. Solzhenitsyn says that at the very least the West should be
able to distinguish "the enemies of humanity from its friends."

25. *Warning*, 111; *East*, 40. Solzhenitsyn's argument is similar to Lincoln's. The
world cannot exist half slave and half free. As long as one island of freedom is left in the
world from which the truth about Communist practices could be told, Communist leaders
would not be secure, hence the aspiration for global conquest.

26. *Warning*, 46-47. He explains: "under the cast-iron shell of Communism a liberation of the human spirit is occurring. New generations are growing up, steadfast in their
struggle with evil, unwilling to accept unprincipled compromises, preferring to lose
everything . . . so as not to sacrifice conscience."

27. "Communism at the End of the Brezhnev Era," 34.

28. *Warning*, 40-44.

29. Ibid., 45, 100.

30. Ibid., 80-81; *East*, 59.

31. *Mortal*, 7, in which Solzhenitsyn also argues that since certain "topics" are "hid-
den and carefully hushed-up" by the Soviet government, Western scholars have no choice
but to "unwittingly adopt the Procrustean framework provided by official Soviet histori-
ography."

Solzhenitsyn distills the ability of Communist governments to manage information
in a delightful chapter (54), entitled "Buddha's Smile," in *The First Circle*. He writes of a
visit to a Soviet prison by the activist wife of an American president during World War
II. Miraculously, before she arrives, the tattered clothes, bedbugs, slop buckets, and over-

crowding all disappear thanks to quick work by the prison. In their place is a clean, well-stocked cell inhabited, the Soviet translator explains, by unusually happy prisoners who are free to observe whatever religious practices they choose. The president's wife is astonished at the humane conditions and returns home believing the Soviet penal system is the most progressive in the world. After her departure, everything, except a forgotten statue of Buddha, reverts to its unsanitary norm.

32. *Warning*, 34-36; *Mortal*, 26-27.

33. "Artist as Witness," 561; "Solzhenitsyn Speaks Out," 604, 607.

34. *Mortal*, 11-12.

35. *East*, 171-72.

36. "Artist as Witness," 561. Solzhenitsyn quotes a Russian proverb: "The man with a full belly cannot understand the hungry man." See also *East*, 16-17; *Warning*, 81.

37. *Warning*, 133, in which Solzhenitsyn points out, for example, that George Bernard Shaw, who, while millions starved in Ukraine, commented from Moscow, "I never dined so well or so sumptuously as when I crossed the Soviet borders." See also *Warning*, 35; Dunlop, "Exile," 146, 152; Carter, *Politics of Solzhenitsyn*, 38; *East*, 172.

38. *East*, 40.

39. Ibid., 69. What precisely Solzhenitsyn means by "Supreme Complete Entity," he does not say. Perhaps he wishes to convey an idea that is not limited to the concept of the Judeo-Christian God. Solzhenitsyn seems almost more interested in the effects of Christianity than its verity. See also Scammell, *Solzhenitsyn*, 867.

40. *East*, 65; see also 66-71.

41. *Warning*, 129. Solzhenitsyn does not specify what the excesses were, but one supposes that they were the result of the Church's zealous attempt to enforce strict rules of natural law on all aspects of human life.

42. Machiavelli's advice that "imagined republics and principalities" are the source of our misunderstanding of politics and Hobbes's claim that there is no *summum bonum* come to mind. Machiavelli, *Prince*, chap. 15; Thomas Hobbes, *Leviathan* (Cleveland: Meridian Books, 1963), chap. 11.

43. Aleksandr Solzhenitsyn, *"Rech pri poluchenii 'Zolotoe klishe' soyuza italian-skikh zhurnalistov,"* in *Mir i Nasilie* (Frankfurt: Possev, 1974), 99-100, quoted in Dunlop, "Exile," 145.

44. *East*, 64-66, 69-71. See also Solzhenitsyn's comments on Descartes's method. *Gulag I*, 193.

45. *Warning*, 1

46. *East*, 64.

47. Ibid., 64-65, 69.

48. Ibid., 45-46, 64-71.

49. Solzhenitsyn, *"Rech pri poluchenii 'Zolotoe klishe' soyuza italianskikh zhurnalistov,"* 99-100, quoted in Dunlop, "Exile," 145.

50. *Warning*, 145-46.

51. *East*, 65-66, 69.

52. Ibid., 50-51. See also 58, in which Solzhenitsyn writes, "The center of your democracy and of your culture is left without electric power for a few hours only, and suddenly crowds of citizens start looting and creating havoc. The smooth surface film must be very thin, then, the social system quite unstable and unhealthy." He argues that without internal moral checks, only the law stands in people's way. They will be open to doing almost anything as long as they do not get caught. Unless a society is willing to employ sufficient force to continually frighten citizens into compliance—something unlikely under a liberal government—there must be reliance on self-restraint.

53. Ibid., 65-66.

54. Ibid., 49.

55. *First Circle*, 391-400. See also *Warning*, 145-46; *East*, 70-71.

56. *Warning*, 132, 141-42.

57. *East*, 55-56.

58. Ibid., 67-68. Lenin's strategy was always to attack from the left.

59. Ibid., 69-70.

60. *Warning*, 132.

61. *East*, 68.

62. Ibid., 172.

63. In his article comparing Sartre and Solzhenitsyn, Raymond Aron points out that Solzhenitsyn understands the crisis of the West to be intellectual and not political or military. Sartre, the "ruler of minds," immersed himself in leftist politics because he believed Marxism to be the "unsurpassable philosophy of our epoch" (Raymond Aron, "Aleksandr Solzhenitsyn and European 'Leftism,'" *Survey* 22 (Summer/Autumn 1976): 233-41. Evidently, Solzhenitsyn is less influenced by the fashions of thought in our epoch. See his remarks to Western intellectuals in *Warning*, 119; *Gulag II*, 51n, 57n; *Gulag III*, xi, 328n; *Oak*, 119n, 332; see also *Rubble*, 229-79.

64. For example, one Western intellectual, Melvin Gurtov, criticizes Solzhenitsyn by proclaiming that, "Liberation is the critical problem of our time." Melvin Gurtov, "Return to the Cold War," in *Aleksandr Solzhenitsyn, Détente: Prospects for Democracy and Dictatorship* (New Brunswick, N.J.: Transaction Books, 1976), 77 (hereafter cited as *Détente*).

65. For example, Francis Barker criticizes Solzhenitsyn for abandoning the "fierce egalitarianism" expressed in his early novels. Francis Barker, *Solzhenitsyn: Politics and Form* (London: Macmillan, 1977), 1.

66. For example, Lynn Turgeon held in 1977 that the Baltic areas were "flourishing" under Soviet rule and "never enjoyed comparable well-being." Lynn Turgeon, "In Defense of Détente" in *Détente*, 79.

67. *Warning*, 65, 141. "We in the East," Solzhenitsyn says, "never applauded the hangman who appeared in the West. But the Western intelligentsia for decades applauded our hangman." Aleksandr Solzhenitsyn, "Excerpts from a Press Conference," in *Posev* 12 (1974): 2-10, quoted in Dunlop, "Exile," 136.

68. *Warning*, 88. This trend does not include every intellectual in the West, of course. Solzhenitsyn claims to admire certain academics "who could do much for the renewal and salvation of [their] country." However, because of the "fashions of thinking" that sweep over Western democracies and because the ideas of such people tend to run against the "current" of thought, they are rarely given the opportunity to quietly, if persistently, evoke the light in people's minds. *East*, 54-55.

69. *East*, 44.

70. Ibid., 62. See also a somewhat fuller account in ibid., 46, and in *Warning*, 130-31.

71. *Warning*, 75-78, 85-84; *East*, 63.

72. *Mortal*, 70.

73. Immanuel Kant, *Critique of Pure Reason*, trans. F. Max Mueller (New York: Macmillan, 1957); Immanuel Kant, *Fundamental Principles of the Metaphysics of Morals*, trans. Thomas K. Abbott (New York: Liberal Arts Press, 1940). Compare Tucker, *Marx Reader*, 76-77, in which Marx writes:

Conscious life-activity directly distinguishes man from animal life-activity. . . . But an animal only produces what it immediately needs for itself or its young. It produces one-sidedly, whilst man produces universally. It produces only under the dominion of immediate physical need, whilst man produces even when he is free from physical need and only truly produces in freedom there from. . . . [I]n degrading spontaneous activity, free activity, to a means, estranged labor makes man's species life a means to his physical existence.

The consciousness which man has of his species is thus transformed by estrangement in such a way that the species life be comes for him a means.

For Solzhenitsyn's views compare *August 1914*, chaps. 1-3, 5, 33, 42, *Warning*, 140, 141; *Gulag I*, 161; *First Circle*, 396-98.

74. *Rubble*, 104-5.

75. Michael Novak, "On God and Man," in Berman, *Solzhenitsyn at Harvard*, 135.

76. *East*, 70.

77. Ibid.

78. Ibid., 71.

79. Melvin Gurtov, "Return to the Cold War," in *Détente*, 74-78; Richard Lowenthal, "The Prophet's Wrong Message," in *Détente*, 87-88, 93-94; Norman Birnbaum, "Solzhenitsyn as Pseudo-Moralist," in *Détente*, 101; Ronald Berman, Introduction, in Berman, *Solzhenitsyn at Harvard*, xii; James Reston, "A Russian at Harvard," in Berman, *Solzhenitsyn at Harvard*, 39; Joseph Kraft, "Solzhenitsyn's Message," *Washington Post*, 3 July 1975, A23; "The Obsession of Solzhenitsyn," *New York Times*, 13 June 1978, editorial, A18.

80. *Warning*, 87-89.

81. *Mortal*, 65.

82. *Warning*, 119.

83. *East*, 61-63. During the nuclear freeze movement of the 1980s there was a debate about whether the generation then living had a right to decide what principles were worth defending, if that defense entailed annihilating the race. Nuclear freeze advocates argued that future generations might not think those principles so important. Solzhenitsyn maintained that the living generation should not sacrifice the spiritual life of their "children" merely to preserve their bodies. See *Rubble*, 249.

84. *Warning*, 116; *East*, 79-82.

85. Henry Kissinger, *Years of Upheaval* (Boston: Little, Brown, 1982), 986-88.

86. See, for example, the statements of former Viet Cong leaders who claimed that teenage Vietnamese women were shipped to the Soviet Union to work at forced labor in repayment for Soviet arms, and that Vietnam had its own Gulag of about 500,000. Al Santoli, "Why the Viet Cong Flee," *Washington Post*, *Parade* magazine, 11 July 1982, 1-6. See also *Warning*, 25.

87. *Warning*, 28-29; "Artist as Witness," 558, 561.

88. *Warning*, 35.

89. Delba Winthrop, "Solzhenitsyn Reconsidered II," *American Spectator* 13 (December 1980): 15.

90. *Mortal*, 33-34.

91. Ibid., 39, 58.

92. *Warning*, 26-27.

93. Ibid., 27, 91-96, 144.

94. *East*, 40, 42-44.

95. "Norman Podhoretz, "Why Can't You Call a Communist a Communist?" *Washington Post*, 16 March 1986, D8.

96. *Warning*, 59.

97. During the Brezhnev era, the local party chief in Uzbekistan was reported to have extorted and stolen four billion dollars. David Remnik, "Corrupt Soviet Uzbekistan Learns about 'Our Rotten History,'" *Washington Post*, 7 October 1988, A1, A27. See also David Remnick, "Lenin's Errors Aired in Pages of *Pravda*," *Washington Post*, 30 December 1989, A12.

98. "Aleksandr Solzhenitsyn, "Three Key Moments in Modern Japanese History," trans. Michael Nicholson and Alexis Klimoff, *National Review* 81 (9 December 1983): 1536-37, 1540, 1544, 1546.

99. *Warning*, 103, 130. *National Review* editorial, in Berman, *Solzhenitsyn at Harvard*, 30-32. See also Scammell, *Solzhenitsyn*, 933.

100. *East*, 44.

CHAPTER 7

ON A REVIVAL OF THE SPIRIT

It is often said that Solzhenitsyn criticizes the policies and ideas of others but never proposes anything of his own. This claim misunderstands Solzhenitsyn's project. He holds the commonsense view that people's opinions lead them to act. The ideas that inform those opinions exert a crucial influence over human behavior. Solzhenitsyn does not overlook the other motivations in life, such as desire, passion, and the longing for love, beauty, and honor, but he maintains that ideas shape people's responses to these traits. Given this view, he attempts to change what he considers evil behavior by undermining the ideas that support it. The first step in such an enterprise is to shake people's confidence by jarring the contemporary wisdom. The more difficult next step is to supply a new basis for people's actions and a new goal for them to work toward. Solzhenitsyn admits that he is engaged in an effort to force a change in the way people act. Perhaps an artist can be a second government.

SPIRITEDNESS

The task of laying out a new path is particularly difficult in the modern world. Even a mind of the first order is faced with a Herculean task in trying to counter the contemporary ethos of moral relativism. People are skeptical, not just of new ideas but of any principles that claim to be universally true. Seeing that all the precepts of the past have been overturned, and that today's myriad belief systems often contradict one another, many have concluded that there are no grounds to trust in anything. The intellectual horizon of many people is nihilism—a conviction that holds nothing to be true or right.

Much has been written about Solzhenitsyn's effort to reawaken people to the spiritual side of life. It is even more true that he wants to invigorate the spirited element in human nature. Spiritedness is an aspect of the soul closely allied with anger. It causes people to strike out at anything that threatens what they hold dear, such as family, homeland, or principles. Spiritedness has another element that provokes people to seek honor for themselves in service to the community, even at the risk of their own lives.

To promote spiritedness, Solzhenitsyn relates stories, often in a bitterly satirical style, that are intended to outrage the reader. Not only are we led to doubt the ideas that he attacks—for example, those of Marx—but he also provokes our righteous anger against the evil deeds that those ideas have instigated. Solzhenitsyn appeals to people's reason, but he does so by summoning their passions. He aims above all at animating that passion which defends and nurtures justice and goodness. There are many instances in which Solzhenitsyn attempts to elicit righteous anger, but one, concerning the fate of the kulaks, best illuminates the point and merits quoting at length.

> This chapter will deal with a small matter. Fifteen million souls. Fifteen million lives. They weren't educated people, of course. They couldn't play the violin. They didn't know who Meyerhold was, or how interesting it is to be a nuclear physicist. In the First World War we lost in all three million killed. In the Second we lost twenty million (so Khrushchev said; according to Stalin it was only seven million. Was Nikita being too generous? Or couldn't Josif keep track of his capital?) All those odes! All those obelisks and eternal flames! Those novels and poems! For a quarter century all Soviet literature has been drunk on that blood! But about the silent, treacherous Plague which starved fifteen million of our peasants to death, choosing victims carefully and destroying the backbone and mainstay of the Russian people—about that Plague there are no books. No bugles bid our hearts beat faster for them. Not even the traditional three stones mark the crossroads where they went in creaking carts to their doom. Our finest humanists, so sensitive to today's injustices, in those years only nodded approvingly: Quite right, too! Just what they deserved![1]

Why does Solzhenitsyn want to anger people with such a story? Why does he want to provoke a sense of outrage or spiritedness? Is not spiritedness upsetting to public peace? Could people under its spell become so enamored of their own way of life and their own moral principles that they would be willing to strike out blindly and zealously at others? Is not spiritedness the root cause of war?

Solzhenitsyn inspires a sense of righteous indignation as a means of teaching his readers that there are such things as morality and justice. The pervasive spirit of relativism in contemporary life has led many to doubt that common human standards for judging ethical conduct exist. Yet somehow people can be persuaded to condemn certain acts as unjust. People may not be able to decide what justice is, but they can be made to feel the sting of injustice. It is almost as if there was a natural physiological response to experiencing the misery of others—which is why Solzhenitsyn counsels people to listen to their hearts and not just their heads. Indeed, empathy is exactly what his artistry hopes to educe. If Solzhenitsyn's readers respond with outrage and horror to the stories he presents, is this not a sign that they believe in justice? After all, can human beings understand injustice if they have no awareness of its opposite—justice? Do we not know what injustice is because we know that something is lacking? Must we not then have some idea of what justice is? It is by this reverse method that Solzhenitsyn seeks to accomplish his goal. A reaction against injustice and in-

humanity may be only a first step, but it is intended to show people that in practice they are not relativists, and thereby to move them toward acceptance of
moral criteria.[2]

Second, spiritedness is a passion that contributes to a sense of community.
Sometimes, no doubt, this sentiment can be turned to petty concerns, such as to
defense of party or faction. Yet more often, spiritedness breeds civic responsibility. It combats the all-too-human tendency of people to pursue nothing but their
own self-interest. Spiritedness is connected with love of one's country, way of
life, and people. Although it is a passion and not wholly rational, it gives rise to
high-minded, even noble, actions on behalf of others.[3]

Third, spiritedness is essential as an antidote to the crass materialism of the
modern age. It animates people, making them concerned with pursuits of a
higher and finer sort than the mere maintenance of their physical existence. If
not the highest of human virtues, spiritedness can induce that greatness of soul
from which heroism arises. Solzhenitsyn's tales of resistance to oppression and
escape from imprisonment, particularly in *Gulag Archipelago III*, portray people
fervently dedicated to their principles. They are resolved to risk hunger, deprivation, even death rather than allow their will to be crushed.[4] Their souls have an
inextinguishable fire that lights the way toward those aspirations that enrich humanity. For example, to understand what true love of freedom entails, one need
only turn to the deeds of Solzhenitsyn's indefatigable friend Georgi Tenno and
his perpetual attempts to escape from the camps, once almost succeeding after a
trek of nearly one thousand miles. Indeed, it is a testament to all that is finest in
the human spirit that Solzhenitsyn and the other survivors of what once was her-
alded as the "Marxist utopia" remained unbroken in the face of such fearsome
evil, holding aloft all the while the banner of freedom and justice.[5]

Despite all their difficulties, Solzhenitsyn's heroes are truly alive, while
those who sit on the sidelines, afraid to raise a finger for fear of losing their
lives, are spiritually dead. Without spiritedness, Solzhenitsyn warns, human beings can become a "herd"; they follow closely behind the pack so as not to be
singled out. If they become too cowardly to stand up even for the truth, they will
lose their humanity; thus it is that a "spiritual death" can overtake them. In an
open letter written to his fellow citizens in the 1970s, Solzhenitsyn attempted to
fortify their courage to resist their rulers. He entreated them to stop reciting the
party's lies and then challenged them to stand up for their rights as humans,
"And if we get cold feet even taking this step," he said, "then we are worthless,
and the scorn of Pushkin should be directed at us: 'Why should cattle have the
gift of freedom?' 'Their heritage from generation to generation is the belied
yoke and the lash.'"[6]

Spiritedness is also needed in the West, Solzhenitsyn argues, for the struggle to maintain human freedom and dignity is never easy. Yet the West considers itself too civilized and intelligent for this primitive passion. It prides itself on
its humanity toward others and its concern for the welfare of every individual.
No Western nation wants to inflict suffering, particularly in an age of instanta-
neous communication, when the anguish of the victims is plainly visible.[7]

The West's Enlightenment principles, which originally dictated that individuals protect their own lives, have now been extended to encompass everyone's survival. These codes of conduct have given rise to a strong sentiment of pacifism, for one way to protect one's life is to strive for a completely peaceful world. While Solzhenitsyn recognizes the noble instincts of true pacifists, he complains that many who extol these principles do so in order to hide a self-interested desire to survive at any price.[8] More important, the West's reluctance to commit itself to military action against inhuman regimes does not reduce the sum total of human suffering. Those people conquered and subjugated under tyrannical governments are forced to endure the worst forms of despotism and terror. How is tolerance for governments that oppress their own people a victory for morality? Solzhenitsyn argues that the morality born of Western pacifism takes no responsibility for what happens as a result of inaction. It is, to use Max Weber's term, the ethics of intention.

Solzhenitsyn's morality is grounded in the disquieting fact that some forms of government, especially Communist regimes, oppress their own people. Peaceful intentions do not always work, for abandoning the struggle against inhumanity allows, indeed encourages, oppression to occur. When we are making a decision about whether military force should be exerted, Solzhenitsyn would have us calculate the nature of the regime to be opposed (for example, taking into account the dismal history of Marxist rule). His are the ethics of responsibility.

No one can doubt that when we are directly responsible for inflicting pain and death on others the consequences rest heavily on our consciences. But this sense of inner self-restraint of which the West is rightly proud can easily become a source of irresoluteness. To infuse Western public opinion with the strength of will necessary to make the difficult choices of political life, Solzhenitsyn attempted to breed a spirited hatred of Marxism. Except by adopting some of Marxism's passion, he claimed, there is no way for the civilized world to resist the barbarism that confronts it.

Solzhenitsyn was particularly worried that the West had lost heart immediately after the U.S. defeat in Vietnam. In an attempt to inspire spiritedness in the West, he went on the road, so to speak, giving many public addresses intended to undermine the legitimacy of Marxist regimes and to bolster the Western powers' sagging morale. In those addresses he acknowledged that resistance to Communist uprisings and expansion was fraught with danger. But, Solzhenitsyn asserted repeatedly after his exile to the West, the high-minded road was safer in the end than the path of least resistance. Was it not better to stand fast in the present, he asked, than to face an invincible foe in the future? He argued that an impartial reading of history showed that Marxist leaders take any sign of weakness as a cue to advance. Continual vacillation would lead only to further encroachments, to further losses of power, to more concessions, and to final defeat. He reminded his audience of the atrocities that the Progressive Doctrine might commit if no one stood to oppose it.[9]

The world situation did not have to slide so far, he predicted. If the West remained firm, Communist rulers would back down. For example, Solzhenitsyn

pointed out that West Germany's prime minister Konrad Adenauer's tough political negotiations with Khrushchev "initiated a genuine détente."[10] Marxist
rulers fear spiritedness, Solzhenitsyn claimed, for the party can remain in power
only so long as people acquiesce to its commands. As with other forms of despotism, the party preys on people's weaknesses. However, once citizens refuse
to pay any price for survival, the party loses its strength and must retreat. Tyrants have the courage of bullies. When on top, they are relentless, but they
quickly lose heart when tested by a resolute foe. Solzhenitsyn offered no guaran-
tees, but he reasoned that the West could take some comfort in the examples of
Lenin, who caved in to German demands, and even of the mighty Stalin, who
could not conquer Finland and who panicked during the Nazi advance.[11] He
explained:

> You misunderstand the nature of communism. The very ideology of commu-
> nism—all Lenin's teachings—are that anyone is considered a fool who does
> not take what is lying in front of him. If you can take it, take it. If you can at-
> tack, attack. But if there is a wall, then go back. . . . You defended Berlin in
> 1948 only by your firmness of spirit, and there was no world conflict. In Korea
> in 1950 you stood up against the communists using only your firmness, and
> there was no world conflict. In 1962 you compelled the rockets to be removed
> from Cuba. Again it was only your firmness, and there was no world conflict.[12]

As suggested earlier, when *The Gulag Archipelago* was published Western
public opinion became more spirited in opposition to the Soviet Union, electing
the most strongly anti-Communist leaders in a generation. Initially, Soviet leaders belittled Ronald Reagan's rhetoric and his aggressive military buildup. They
labeled him a cowboy and a warmonger. They did everything in their power to
separate the United States from its European allies. Yet it is possible that the
Soviet leaders began to believe their own rhetoric. After years of vacillation in
the West, Soviet leaders faced a strong anti-Communist alliance and a popular
American president. The Soviet economy, overburdened with military expenditures, could not compete with the revitalized free-market system of the West. In
what must have been a moment of self-doubt, Soviet apparatchik turned to a
new leader who could both make a deal with the West and bring life to the
economy. In other words, the Soviets yielded.

This line of argument is difficult to prove, but it is supported by one undeniable fact. Communism collapsed not long after the term of Ronald Reagan, the
president least sympathetic to the Soviet regime. To state the proposition
plainly, if Solzhenitsyn's writings stiffened Western resolve and that firmness
helped bring about the end of Communism, then Solzhenitsyn had an important
hand in Communism's downfall.

SOURCES OF THE SPIRIT

Life is very dear, and few people are willing to risk danger in vain pursuits. It
takes strongly held principles and high purposes to induce people to put their

lives in jeopardy. But what gives rise to self-sacrifice? What are the sources of the spirit?

According to Solzhenitsyn, inner strength has many sources. One is attachment to family, country, or, more generally, an individual's wider community. Family ties evoke spiritedness by appealing to the natural desire to protect and nurture loved ones. Strong national ties are rooted in the mystic connection that human beings feel toward the place of their birth (or their adopted land) and the generations past, present, and future who inhabit it. The bond of community is nourished by traditions and customs that prepare citizens for the burden of civic responsibility. The greater that bond, the less people feel isolated and alone. Some may even consider it their duty, in order to protect the country's way of life, to sacrifice themselves for the good of the whole.

Another source of spirit seems to be a gift of nature. Some people are blessed with such tenacious character that they will not break even under the severest pressure. Solzhenitsyn tells of people who, rather than expiring in the confines of the Gulag, actually flourished there. The stiffer the test, the greater their resistance, and the more their inner strength grew.[13]

Since nature produces only a certain number of people with immovable wills, the rest of humanity must look elsewhere to find strength of character. The most common support of the soul is religion. It teaches that human life derives meaning and purpose from a divine plan. The rewards of this life—money, position, even happiness—are considered less important than abiding by God's will. Religion turns people away from the daily care of their bodies and toward the preservation of their souls. It makes people spirited, as well as spiritual, by teaching that a fate worse than death may befall those who sell their souls to save their bodies. Solzhenitsyn repeatedly extols the courage and determination of members of the various religious sects in the camps. Try as it might, the state could not break their spirit.[14]

Finally, there is a category of people who are animated by dedication to certain ideas. Indeed, it is the commitment to the various manifestations of Enlightenment ideas that has driven the modern world on its course. The enormous appeal of Marxism derives from its being the most progressive expression of the Enlightenment ideal. However, if this dedication becomes too extreme, one may become an ideologue. This is especially true when the doctrine counsels no self-restraint—as in the case of Marxism. Philosophy need not go that far. The classical philosophers could be distinguished from other human beings by their particular love of ideas, and they were hardly ideologues.[15]

SELF-RESTRAINT

While spiritedness is usually associated with an assertion of the will, it does have elements of self-sacrifice. Spirited people must keep their desires in check if they wish to accomplish something nobler. Rather than being pushed and pulled by their impulses, such people must practice self-control in order to set goals of their own choosing. If, as in the camps, they cannot control external events, at least they can govern those things within their power. The heroes of the camps refused to grovel before their captors, even when rations were short and death seemed near. Self-restraint actually affirms the more noble aspects of human life—hence its connection with spiritedness—for it is the root of people's freedom of will over the petty concerns of practical life and the deadening effects of materialism.[16] "The main thing," Solzhenitsyn "spells out" for us, is to "live with a steady superiority over life."[17] It should be noted that Solzhenitsyn uses the word spirit to express the concepts of both spiritedness and spiritual. In fact, the two are closely connected. For him, an acceptance of spiritual principles is almost an exertion of will. Those who believe in a spiritual realm are very likely to be spirited in its defense.

The road upward from matter to spirit is not without trials, however. Most people need to be compelled into restraining their physical appetites. A personal crisis is often the occasion for a thorough examination of conscience. For instance, Solzhenitsyn reports that when people came face to face with the grief of prison life, often they had to exert the "highest form of moral effort," one that "has always ennobled every human being."[18]

Solzhenitsyn agrees with Christian moralists that suffering can be a good thing. People who are riding high, basking in success, rarely feel the need to consider the needs and hopes of others. They can be deceived by their own pride into believing themselves infallible. They can easily become self-righteous and arrogant.[19] Solzhenitsyn does not discount the value of a comfortable life. He realizes that modest prosperity can lead many to acts of kindness and generosity, while deprivation can inspire great cruelty. Yet his own experience taught him that only after a fall do people engage in true soul searching and thus realize moral limitations. Their smugness and complacency shaken, they begin to open themselves to compassion and even wisdom.[20]

Since self-limitation is most often taught by circumstances, the most extreme deprivation can provide the most insightful lesson. It is not surprising, therefore, that the Gulag taught a number of its citizens how to be self-sufficient. Faced with meager rations, prisoners had to achieve mastery over their hunger. They did so "as far as possible" by "lifting" themselves "into higher spheres." Subordinating their physical needs, they retreated to the more sublime enjoyments of the mind. Solzhenitsyn writes of his experience in Lubyanka prison:

> A weightless body, just sufficiently satisfied with soup so that the soul did not feel oppressed by it. What light and free thoughts! It was as if we had been lifted up to the heights of Sinai, and there the truth manifested itself to us from out of the fire. . . . And there we suffered and we thought, and there was nothing else in our lives.[21]

In the camps, ascent was not easy. Prisoners found themselves at a crossroad. They owned nothing and had little hope of possessing anything in the future. They were utterly dependent, their fate in the hands of others. Thus their concerns could not be of normal preoccupations of everyday life. Their thoughts had to dwell on beautiful and eternal concepts, or they would be consumed by the gnawing desire for food.[22]

While most people were degraded by their term in the Gulag, some used it as an opportunity. It was perhaps the only time in history when much of the educated class of a nation suffered the sorrows of the underprivileged classes. Rather than imagining the pains and woes of others, they actually experienced them. Unlike the often semiliterate lower classes, who understand suffering but rarely find a spokesperson to write of their plight, the Russian intelligentsia was educated and could convey its miseries to others. Solzhenitsyn hoped that because Russia's educated classes possessed this unique experience, when Russia became free, that class would spark a literary and artistic movement unique in history. Sadly, no such literary flowering has happened in post-Communist Russia.[23]

There is an ironic justice to Solzhenitsyn's claim that the camps have raised up a class of people who are unmoved either by the materialistic appeals of Marxism or by its threats to their lives. Their self-control and fearsome spirit make them formidable enemies. He calls them *lichnost*, people with fully developed characters.[24]

SELF-LIMITATION IN THE MODERN WORLD

Sadly, Solzhenitsyn proclaims, it is not only Communist nations that need self-limitation. Much of modern political philosophy is premised on the idea that happiness can be attained by an ever-higher standard of living and the fulfillment of desire. New ways to produce more goods, so the theory went, could be a catalyst for infinite progress.[25]

Solzhenitsyn repeats the truth expressed most clearly in Aristotle's *Ethics*: It is not how much wealth one has, but to what end one puts it that is important. Because acquisitiveness too easily becomes unbridled avarice, human beings can never be fully satisfied by material possessions. While Enlightenment philosophy postulated that people could attain happiness by conquering the material world, Solzhenitsyn grounds his thinking on the more ancient teachings that guided people to turn inward and conquer themselves.

As Fernand Braudel's history of premodern societies points out, people of the ancient world were constrained to limit themselves because there were not enough material things to go around. Either they practiced self-control or they coveted others' share of the finite store of goods. The philosophy of the Enlightenment taught that mastery of nature could conquer want; by unlocking the mysteries of nature, science and technology could increase nature's bounty.[26]

To a great extent the experiment was a success, but, as with almost all other things in life, there was a price to be paid. Citing the evidence of many ecologists and scientists, Solzhenitsyn argues that the world may soon face an ecological disaster. The misguided optimism of the modern world, he asserts, has caused us to overpopulate, overproduce, and overindustrialize. We are polluting the world in a senseless effort to produce commodities we do not need.[27]

At some point, he suggests, the earth will reach its productive capacities. People will be forced once again to think in terms of limitation and not expansion. Their energies will have to be spent on the development of inner strength rather than competing and consuming. Solzhenitsyn asks if there is not a realignment of human culture in the offing. If productive limits are reached, the shortage of goods could precipitate a revolution against Enlightenment principles. A moral and spiritual revival would then occur, for people would be driven to despair, with no place to turn "except . . . upward."[28]

As with all predictions of impending doom, it is easy to criticize Solzhenitsyn's.[29] After all, Malthus, who might be called the theoretic progenitor of modern-day ecologists, has been discredited. He underestimated the capacity of technological innovation to solve the problem of overpopulation. For that matter, the suppositions of the de Chargin Society and the Club of Rome, on which Solzhenitsyn bases his dire forecasts, have proven inaccurate. The shortages of the 1970s did not lead to a reevaluation of Western thought. Quite the contrary, the free market adjusted in such a way as to efficiently produce more goods.

Yet these signs of strength in the West do not entirely refute Solzhenitsyn's position. What will happen, he asks, if, as forecast, the world's population doubles? Under such conditions, can our standards of living continue to improve? Are there no upper limits to expansion and progress? Can human ingenuity overcome the inevitable exhaustion of the world's natural resources?

Solzhenitsyn argues that some adjustments to the Western way of life may come, and that the anxiety resulting from a serious economic or ecological crisis could initiate a period of soul-searching. Thus, as Winthrop points out, Solzhenitsyn's argument in favor of self-limitation rests on "the nature of nature" as well as "the nature of man."[30]

Those who contend that Solzhenitsyn is conservative on every issue are wrong. In agreement with the ecological movement, Solzhenitsyn advocates a "small technology," which aims at a stable rather than an expanding economy and at cleaning up rather than polluting the environment.[31]

Solzhenitsyn argues that the Enlightenment's optimism is already beginning to wear thin. The more hopeful advocates of its ideas had promised that people and society would progress and improve once they were emancipated from natural necessity and allowed to develop freely. Yet many people feel uneasy and alienated even in a world of plenty. At the same time that unprecedented standards of living have been achieved, therapeutic drugs are widely prescribed to alleviate people's despair. Rather than making people better, affluence seems to have weakened their spirits and given them a vague feeling of gloom. Thus, the notion that people can be made whole merely by improving their material wealth is now seriously in doubt. The recognition that the sources of human motivation run deeper than people's material circumstances, Solzhenitsyn suspects, will lead to a reexamination of the very foundations of the modern edifice.[32]

Repentance

Spiritedness directs people to assert their will, defend their community, and oppose injustice. However, it can become a source of arrogance used to injure others. While Solzhenitsyn wants to animate people's spirit, he does not want to undermine their morals. In "Repentance and Self-Limitation," he reiterates his belief that there is a dividing line between good and evil in the heart of every person. No nation, class, or party is totally good or completely evil. Such a truth demands that we "search for our own errors and sins" rather than attributing every problem to others. Only when we acknowledge our own faults can "spiritual growth" begin. History shows that repentance is difficult. "All throughout the ages," Solzhenitsyn writes, people have "preferred to censure, denounce and hate others, instead of censuring, denouncing and hating" themselves. The hope for repentance is even dimmer today. Commercialism blinds people to the need for a repentant attitude, and relativism rejects the concept altogether. Moreover, for "all countries which previously suffered oppression and now fanatically aspire to physical might," it "is the very last feeling they are about to experience." Yet given "the white-hot tension between nations and races, we can say without suspicion of over statement that without repentance it is . . . doubtful we can survive."[33]

Repentance is difficult not only "because we must cross the threshold of self-love, but also because our own sins are not easily visible to us."[34] Overcoming our natural vanity requires courage, especially in a situation in which we are the first to repent.[35] The outward sign of repentance is forgiveness, and it may even induce generosity and magnanimity.[36]

An attitude of repentance is likely to produce moderate, self-sacrificing, even pacific behavior. Does this not mean that he counsels people to accept evil? Repentance seems at odds with Solzhenitsyn's earlier stated intention of making people spirited in defense of justice.

Repentance can become "counterproductive," he claims, if, as in the case of the prerevolutionary Russian intelligentsia, people acknowledge sins only within their own group or nation. This attitude may create an intellectual paralysis that results in people abdicating to others their responsibility for making choices. Thus, it is equally a mistake, although a less common one, to see only good in others and to overlook their evil. Solzhenitsyn reasons that full repentance is possible only when both sides in a conflict or confrontation limit themselves, when it is mutual. Obviously, this sort of an ideal is impractical, especially in the anarchy of the international arena.[37] the best one can hope for is a middle ground between the rigidity of arrogance and the frailty of surrender.[38]

In the West, most of the criticism of Solzhenitsyn has come from those who consider his strident opposition to Marxism a sign of fanaticism. In truth, he is strident, but, as his stance on repentance makes clear, it is unfair to label him a fanatic. He asks that we strike a balance between assertiveness and self-sacrifice; in other words, he calls on people to be prudent. Indeed, he calls for a "prudent self-restriction."[39]

He is no less aware than other moral teachers of complexity of ethical decisions. He understands that innocence and guilt are often difficult to sort out (as
his views on Russo-Polish relations and his attitude toward West Germany
show).[40] He presses his case against Marxism so strenuously, not because he is
blind to the faults of Communism's opponents or unaware of the dangers of
righteous indignation but because he has experienced, firsthand, the full fury
which that doctrine reserves for human beings of extraordinary character and
others who resist its commands. He appreciates that the calculation of a prudent
person must change from case to case, implying a knowledge of circumstances
and, perhaps, wisdom about ends. Yet even the most moderate people ought to
take heed if their adversary is unusually vicious. While most situations call for a
response somewhere between temerity and timidity, in extreme situations, only
audacity will do. The evidence presented throughout Solzhenitsyn's work, but
most clearly in *The Gulag Archipelago*, is meant to convince prudent people that
Marxism tramples all that is finest in the human spirit, and that if they wish to
protect human dignity, that doctrine must be defeated.

But how are people to decide when an action is appropriate? On what basis
should they make such judgments?

MORALITY

Moving against the tide of "social sciences . . . particularly the more modern of
them," Solzhenitsyn argues that it is possible for human beings to make correct
moral decisions.[41] For instance, he writes that the concept of justice is "inherent
in man," not relative to one's "own way." The "voice of justice" can be "recognized" by those who listen to "the voice of their own conscience." Furthermore,
"convictions based on conscience are as infallible as the internal rhythm of the
heart."[42]

Despite his reliance on conscience as the ground for morality, Solzhenitsyn
does not seem fully to endorse St. Thomas Aquinas's view that the capacity to
discern good from evil is imprinted on the soul. Rather, he observes that it is a
common human trait to evaluate things on the basis of whether they are "noble,
base, courageous, cowardly, hypocritical, false, cruel, magnanimous, just, unjust, and so on."[43] The argument against making such valuations holds that there
is no natural or divine support for these distinctions. But Solzhenitsyn contends
that human beings are also part of nature, and it is in their nature to make such
judgments—humans are the value-making species. Of course, people's mores
will differ from political community to political community. It could even be
argued that morality is a human creation acknowledged by one generation and
given to the next as tradition. In this view, morals are no more than customs—
invented to meet the needs of social interaction—whose origins have been lost
in the mists of time. But this argument merely pushes the questioning further
back. Why did all societies establish moral rules? Why were narrow self-
interest, dishonesty, theft, and, cruelty, especially to the innocent, proscribed in
every culture known to us? Why does every society celebrate honesty, courage,

and the other virtues? Perhaps because nature dictates these restrictions, and humans discovered, rather than invented, morality.

The argument that supports our ability to make moral judgments may never rest on apodictic demonstrations, but, Solzhenitsyn asserts, it is certainly no weaker than the argument put forward by those who claim such judgments are impossible. No one, in his or her private life, is a thoroughgoing skeptic. If one is human, one naturally holds some things to be better than others, and, in doing so, one shows that it is reasonable to assume that standards of judgment do in fact exist.[44]

Clearly, the natural argument in support of morality is far too subtle to hold great sway. Indeed, Solzhenitsyn is a staunch proponent of the religious way of thinking. For most people, religion is the ultimate source of moral truth. It reminds people to abandon their earthly cares, at least for a while, and give their thoughts over to "life eternal." It raises them above the level of beasts by making them aware that all who live are destined to die, and that the meaning of life must have more to do with the development of the soul than the care of the body.[45]

Solzhenitsyn is most often taken to be a spokesperson for Christian ideals. There is no doubt that he understands and even fosters religious sentiments. Whether he is himself a Christian writer is a deeper and perhaps unanswerable question. He joined the Orthodox church in 1970, rather late in life, and only after his character had been formed in the camps.[46] We have no reason to doubt his piety, but in his public works he rarely invokes the authority of revelation. He chooses instead to rely on appeals to unaided reason.[47]

It is important to note that Solzhenitsyn is less interested in stressing the differences between the religious and philosophic ways of thinking than he is in showing their similarities in comparison with the modern understanding of life. As Charles Kesler points out:

> He is, in many ways, the greatest living representative of the West, an avatar of the West's most ancient and honorable principles . . . having witnessed the diminution of man by modern science, and . . . having known that greatness of which the human soul is capable even in the most terrible circumstances, it's not surprising that he could reappraise, indeed resurrect, the almost forgotten alternative to modernity: classical and early Christian political philosophy.[48]

Solzhenitsyn reminds us of what is finest and noblest in the Western tradition. Contrary to the contemporary positivist belief that law is the only grounds for judging actions good or bad, he argues that morality is higher than law. Morality is not inchoate and amorphous, while the law is clear and complete. Law is the "human attempt to embody in rules a part of the moral sphere which is above us all."[49]

He makes us face the once widely held truth that people are responsible for their own souls and their own actions. No social construction, no matter how closely it approximates justice, can resolve every human dilemma. There can be little doubt of the importance of justice, yet there is a realm of human activity that transcends political life. Politics is secondary to the development of human character. The form of government that allows and encourages the fullest development of human potential is the best regime. Yet, no government can complete a task for which every individual is personally responsible. Politics is incomplete; it points beyond itself to the higher purposes of life. At best it can create an environment in which people can develop integrity, and in some instances it may even foster greatness of soul.[50]

Solzhenitsyn reminds us that no individual can be "the creator of an autonomous spiritual world." If a person accepts nothing "above himself," and instead "hoists upon his shoulders the act of creating this world and of populating it, together with total responsibility for it," he "collapses under the load." Not even a "mortal genius can bear up under it."[51]

Finally, Solzhenitsyn revives the idea that human beings are capable of using their intellect to discern good from evil. He attempts to show that we can make rational choices and can judge the relative worth of various forms of government. For example, we can perceive the difference between totalitarian, autocratic, and democratic regimes. We can then adjust our policy to aid the friends of freedom and dignity, while opposing their enemies.

Obviously, reason cannot fathom all of life's mysteries, but it can help guide people to choose the appropriate actions for any given situation. Perhaps more important, it can teach them the proper limits that life places on their expectations. In truth, the exercise of the mind is a purpose unto itself. Since humans are separated from other beasts by their capacity for speech and reason, it follows that those who develop those peculiarly human skills are the most fully human.[52]

THE FORM OF GOVERNMENT SOLZHENITSYN FAVORS

Solzhenitsyn's insistence that he is not a political scientist is persuasive. For example, he does not postulate an ideal or best form of government by which to judge the relative worth of existing states. He has not attempted to collect his thoughts on politics into a unified whole. But, despite his lack of organization, he does make some suggestions about the proper arrangement of political life.

He may have forsworn for practical reasons the opportunity to design the ideal regime. The philosophy of the Enlightenment has led many people to believe that an ideal political regime can exist, and that by reforming political institutions, we can resolve all human problems. This idea especially appeals to people who do not believe in God. They want to create an earthly substitute for heaven. But, as we have seen, this aspiration steers people down the wrong path. It omits spiritual improvement, which is a more important source of human motivation and for which every individual is personally responsible. In a sense, Solzhenitsyn wants to limit what people expect of politics while raising their expectations of themselves. With such a goal in mind, presenting an ideal form of government might serve only to lead people astray.

His moderation in this respect derives from an organic conception of the development of communities. In *August 1914* one of his characters asks: "Who is conceited enough to imagine that he can devise ideal institutions? The only people who think that are those who believe that nothing of significance was ever done before their own time."[53] It is arrogant, his character asserts, to imagine that a perfect social order can be instituted because "history is not governed by reason. History is irrational . . . history is a river, it has its own laws which govern its flow, its bends. . . . The bonds between generations, bonds of institutions, traditions, customs, are what hold the banks of the riverbed together and keep the stream flowing."[54]

The life of each nation, the argument continues, is somehow independent of those who wish to control it.[55] A country's culture consists of millions upon millions of decisions concerning the proper way of life, made by generation after generation of its inhabitants. Traditions limit what reformers can do to change the way of life of a people. Although Solzhenitsyn's *August 1914* makes the point that "one kind" of social order is "less evil than others," and "perhaps there may even be a perfect one," it warns that "the best social order is not susceptible to being arbitrarily constructed, or even to being scientifically constructed."[56] Those who wish to alter society radically, according to some abstract ideal, are naive about the possibilities of positive change and ignorant of the wisdom stored in the folkways of a nation.[57]

Solzhenitsyn is not, however, in total agreement with those, such as Edmund Burke, who look to the traditions of their community as the only source of moral standards. He rejects the absolute correctness of one's own way; he does not believe that prejudice is more valuable than reason; and he claims that a return to the past would be foolish.[58]

If a perfect form of government could exist, bringing it into being would be a matter of chance, he claims. In practice, the best one can hope for is to live in a decent society—one that foregoes the temptation to terrorize its citizens in order to perfect them. Such a regime strikes a compromise between the ideals one hopes to attain and the traditions and habits people are reluctant to surrender. Only the foolish or the ruthless, he reasons, would attempt to build the future without giving the past its due.[59] There are, furthermore, more important things than the right form of political association, such as the opportunity to make friends.[60] And "there is nothing more precious than the development of a man's soul."[61]

Although he is known as a conservative, Solzhenitsyn would not have us become slaves of the past. He ridicules the frequent criticism that his ideas propose a return to "a patriarchal way of life," or the foundation of "a theocratic state." He explains that a careful reading of his "Letter to the Soviet Leaders" would show, not that the state should give itself over to religion, but only that religion ought to make "an appropriate contribution to the spiritual life of the community."[62] In no instances should it be suppressed, as was the case in the Soviet Union and elsewhere in the Communist world.[63]

Solzhenitsyn rejects a return to the patriarchal way of life, although his attitude toward autocracy, the government that fostered patriarchy, is more complex. He argues that for centuries people lived tolerable, even fruitful, lives within hierarchical societies, free from the turmoil that has so marked the democratic twentieth century. Just as do other types of government, autocracy has both its strengths and its weaknesses. Its virtues of stability and continuity must be measured against its vices, which include "the danger of dishonest authorities, upheld by violence, the danger of arbitrary decisions and the difficulty of correcting them, the danger of sliding into tyranny."[64] But autocracy need not become despotic if its leaders are correctly restrained. He explains that "authoritarian regimes as such are not frightening—only those which are answerable to no one and nothing. The autocrats of earlier, religious ages, though their power was ostensibly unlimited, felt themselves responsible before God and their own consciences."[65]

Although autocracies have great power over the lives of their citizens, they rarely use that power to control people's souls. The fearsome dictatorships that Marxism spawned were not interested in gaining mere compliance from their citizens. Marxist states demanded that people make a positive commitment to the goals of Communism. Therefore, Marxist regimes endeavored to eradicate every shred of freedom and independent spirit from the populace. It forced people to concur in lies, thereby corrupting their personal integrity and leaving them little control over their individual wills.[66]

Solzhenitsyn's admiration for autocracy is partly a result of his uneasiness about democracy. In many nations with no tradition of self-rule, democracy has led first to anarchy and then to tyranny. In fact, weak democracies have been breeding grounds for four totalitarian states, "the February Revolution in Russia, the Weimar and Italian republics, and Chiang Kai-shek's China."[67] Other weaknesses of democracy include its tendency to produce politicians who pander to instead of leading the masses, its feebleness in dealing with the violence of terrorists and criminals, its difficulty in raising people above mass culture, and its inability "to check unrestrained profiteering at the expense of public morality."[68]

Despite his criticism of democracy, Solzhenitsyn admires that form of government. He claims to be a critic only of democracy's weaknesses, and he applauds "good democracies." He goes so far as to encourage autocratic and totalitarian states to adopt some of the positive aspects of representative government. He calls for the separation of powers, complete freedom of speech and press, government powers made responsible to public opinion, and a decision-making process that promotes compromise and, above all, deliberation. Solzhenitsyn's suggestions lead one to believe that whatever the ultimate source of sovereignty within a nation, be it the people or some ruling class, it ought to be checked by institutions, laws, and moral restraints—and preferably all three.[69]

Solzhenitsyn's reluctance to present an ideal state does not keep him from showing his preference for small, inward-looking communities where relations between citizens rest on mutual friendship and respect. While he recognizes that the requirements of the modern age, and especially the challenges of foreign affairs, make the ideal of the small community impractical, he still wonders whether decentralization may not be an antidote for the impersonality and crassness that are so much a part of contemporary life. He restates Tocqueville's argument in favor of a society drawn together by patriotism and dedication to the common good, and of a government as committed to the inculcation of duties as to the protection of rights.[70]

Because he places such importance on the common good, he questions the need for political parties. They represent, he says, the particular rather than the general interest and reflect material rather than spiritual concerns. He asks—without providing a conclusive answer—if there are no "non-party paths to national development."[71]

Those schooled in the virtues of representative government, find it difficult to answer that question in the affirmative. After all, parties have existed in one form or another almost since the dawn of political life. As James Madison explains, to rid society of the "spirit of faction" it would be necessary to do away with liberty or to force everyone to hold the same opinions. Because freedom of thought must exist, a "non-party path" seems impossible, and parties will remain an integral aspect of political life.[72]

It is important to note that Solzhenitsyn poses his exploration of a nonparty state as a question. It is likely that he explores the possibility this way because he is aware of the problems with such an approach. In fact, the real question is not whether parties should be abolished but whether the spokespersons of those parties can rise above their own parochial and material interests?

The answer to that query depends, to a large extent, on whether a moral revival actually is plausible. Solzhenitsyn's optimistic remark that such a transformation of Western culture is in the offing may be wishful thinking. His analysis of modernity makes one wonder whether a change of this sort is even conceivable. Indeed, he has come to doubt whether people actually can learn from experience. Does this mean that the West is destined to reenact the errors of the East because of its bondage to all-consuming materialism?[73]

Whether a moral revival is likely or not, Solzhenitsyn's grim account the degeneration of the high hopes of the Enlightenment into Marxist totalitarianism makes us believe that Western culture is confronted with a great challenge. While it is true that Communism has been discredited, the goals of Marx's teaching remain attractive in the West. Moreover, for many in the developing world, Marxism seems to provide a ready-made solution to the poverty and inequity of their social situation. It continues to inspire revolutionary fervor, for it promises equality, community, and liberation.

In the advanced nations of the West, only a small minority of the intellectuals embrace Marxism. Yet a wider group of the educated class, while rejecting the harsh political realities of revolutionary ideology, avows an affinity for the goals of Marxism: full social, economic, and political equality; communitarianism; and a liberation from all socially enforced moral dictates. Such people are opinion leaders, and their views always come to play an important role in the making of public policy.

Indeed, the effect of progressive intellectual opinion has given rise to the most onerous predicament facing the West, relativism. Relativism, now widely accepted in popular culture, poses great risks to the health and stability of the Western way of life. It is premised on the belief that there are no commonly shared moral standards, or, as it plays out in daily life, no one has a right to judge another's values. As Solzhenitsyn argues, the loss of a higher moral purpose makes it difficult for people to defend a particular way of life. They come to accept that all opinions and lifestyles are of equal merit. Without a moral bulwark to keep base passions in check, many come to seek gratification in the most convenient manner possible; crime and drug use are on the rise. Without a commitment to spiritual principles, the goals of human life become little more than the pursuit of physical well-being. People who accept such a doctrine fall easy prey to a political system that, though more beneficent than past dictatorships, claims all power unto itself in order to meet the material needs of all its citizens equally. Such people are tempted to follow a political doctrine that offers what religion once provided—the hope of perfection. A regime based on such principles might be less fearsome than a Marxist totalitarian state, yet it would be dispiriting nonetheless. It would hinder the full development of character and the pursuit of human excellence.

Solzhenitsyn's work, more than the writings of any other of his generation, reminds us of the bitter truth revealed by Tocqueville more than a century ago: The scientific, rationalist, technological, and democratic era in which we live has confronted us with a choice between spiritual freedom and materialist tyranny.[74] Solzhenitsyn's terrifying account of that tyranny made us cherish freedom and dignity all the more. Working alone, using only his pen, Aleksandr Solzhenitsyn lifted the human race upward on the currents of the spirit so that it would not sink beneath the crushing burden of matter.

Notes

1. *Gulag III*, 350. As is the case with many of Solzhenitsyn's estimates, the numbers cited here are far higher than those usually given. He claims that the higher figures are more accurate since the true extent of Soviet brutality has never before been revealed. For an example of Solzhenitsyn's association of the spirited with the spiritual, see Aleksandr Solzhenitsyn, *A Lenten Letter to Pimen, Patriarch of All Russia*, trans. Keith Armes (Minneapolis: Burgess, 1972), and "Live Not by Lies." Scammell reports that Solzhenitsyn regards himself as "a sword" in the "Hand of the Highest" (Scammell, *Solzhenitsyn*, 769).

2. *Gulag I*, 3; see also *Gulag III*, 49.

3. *Gulag I*, 49, 462.

4. Ibid., 564; *Gulag III*, 260, 263, 265, 320-23.

5. *Gulag III*, 119, 125-91, 210-17. Scammell, *Solzhenitsyn*, 291.

6. "Live Not by Lies," A26.

7. *East*, 61.

8. Ibid., 61-63.

9. Carter, *Politics of Solzhenitsyn*, 137.

10. *Warning*, 42.

11. Ibid., 41-44; *Gulag III*, xi; *Oak*, 197.

12. Aleksandr Solzhenitsyn, "Speech before the AFL-CIO," 30 June 1975, quoted in Dunlop, "Exile," 152-53. See also *Warning*, 41-42.

13. There is some evidence that Solzhenitsyn places himself in this group. He explains that prison "nourished his soul." *Gulag II*, 616-17. See also Scammell, *Solzhenitsyn*, 291.

14. Ibid., 310, 372-74.

15. A student of Socrates, Nerzhin, loves ideas, but not as a means of changing the world. He is dedicated to contemplation. *First Circle*, 31.

16. *Gulag I*, 590-92.

17. Ibid., 591.

18. *Gulag II*, 619. Central to all Solzhenitsyn's novels is an ordeal of conscience. He portrays people—whether in their hospital bed, on the battlefield, or in the camps—at a spiritual juncture. It is as if, for the first time, the distractions and cares of everyday life are suspended and the more serious questions of life's meaning are thrust upon them. See, for example, *First Circle*, 275, 340; *Cancer Ward*, 93-105.

19. *East*, 83.

20. *Gulag I*, 175-77; *Gulag II*, 273; see also *Gulag III*, 436.

21. *Gulag I*, 225.

22. Ibid., 224, 484, 516, 560; *Gulag II*, 522-23; *First Circle*, 38-39, 95-96, 229, 340.

23. *Gulag II*, 489-91n.

24. Actually he is quoting Shamalov in *Gulag II*, 623. See also Carter, *Politics of Solzhenitsyn*, 46.

25. *Rubble*, 137.

26. Fernand Braudel, *Les Structures du Quotidien: Le Possible et L'Impossible* (Paris: Librairie Armand Colin, 1979), 23-333.

27. *Rubble*, 106-7, 123.

28. Ibid., 106-7, 136-42; *East*, 176-77; *Warning*, 79, 133.

29. As Solzhenitsyn notes in *Rubble*, 106.

30. Winthrop, "Solzhenitsyn: Emerging," 14.

31. Barker asserts, however, that a small technology would codify existing social and economic inequalities. Barker's prediction may be true enough, but that does not necessarily condemn Solzhenitsyn's proposal. Barker judges political societies on the basis of how egalitarian they are. But if people could lead a satisfying life in which neither scarcity nor pollution threatened them, what need would they have of social equality? Furthermore, since nature has not given us comparable abilities, there can never be equality in the most important sense. Barker, *Solzhenitsyn*, 61-62.

Yet there is a deeper sense in which Solzhenitsyn's desire for a small technology might be criticized. In order to limit technology there would have to be a respite from the international arms race. If competition exists to build ever-more modern armaments, then necessity compels nations to (1) discover new technologies, (2) sustain scientific investigations, and (3) maintain an industrial base capable of supporting arms production. Will not the new inventions of technology and the new discoveries of science be used to establish a consumer society in which those who produce by using economies of scale have an advantage? Given that human beings normally choose the goods produced by the most cost-effective means, large industries seem inevitable.

32. *East*, 95-101.

33. *Rubble*, 107-11.

34. Ibid., 128.
35. Ibid., 120, 127.
36. Ibid., 115, 129, 133; Winthrop, "Solzhenitsyn: Emerging," 15.
37. *Rubble*, 142.
38. Ibid., 120, 127, 137.
39. Ibid., 137.
40. Ibid., 113,128-32.
41. Ibid., 104.
42. Aleksandr Solzhenitsyn, "Letter from Solzhenitsyn to Three Students," in Leopold Labedz, *Solzhenitsyn: A Documentary Record* (London: Penguin Press, 1970), 101. Perhaps morality is not so easily derived from simple feelings of conscience. Human hearts are sometimes troubled by irregular rhythms and eventually stop altogether. Nonetheless, the analogy may have been sufficient to satisfy the three students to whom it was addressed.
43. *Rubble*, 105.
44. Sidney Hook writes that Solzhenitsyn's "profoundest error" is his insistence that "moral responsibility derive[s] from belief in a Supreme Being, and that erosion of religious faith spells the end of moral decency." Hook reasons that "morality is logically independent of religion, as Augustine, Kierkegaard and the authors of *The Book of Job* well knew." Sidney Hook, "Solzhenitsyn and Secular Humanism: A Response," *Humanist* 38 (November/ December 1978): 5.
Morality may be independent of religion, but what Solzhenitsyn recognizes and Hook fails to consider is the mechanism by which morality is inculcated. How many people will take morality seriously if it rests on a mere supposition concerning the nature of existence? While some people may create morality for themselves, others can choose to disregard it. The human race needs firmer ground as a basis for counteracting the evil tendencies within it. Although organized religion has been at times the worst offender of its own principles, at the very least it has taught that there are proper limits to human actions. For generations those limits, though often breached in practice, served as a bulwark against our baser instincts. Has rationalistic humanism had any greater success? Its age has been the twentieth century, when—Hook's assertions to the contrary notwithstanding—its ideals have been applied to society. The result has been to undermine the belief that humanity needs limits.
45. "A Journey along the Oka," in *Stories*, 214-15; *Gulag II*, 613-15; Clement, *Spirit of Solzhenitsyn*, 217-28.
46. Solzhenitsyn writes about religious people in the camps, but he never places himself among them. *Gulag II*, 612. 47 Both Winthrop and Charles Kesler make strong and often convincing arguments that Solzhenitsyn's ideas show a marked similarity to many in the basic texts of classical philosophy. Winthrop, "Solzhenitsyn: Emerging." Charles Kesler, "Up from Modernity," in Berman, *Solzhenitsyn at Harvard*. There is some evidence to the contrary, however. First, Solzhenitsyn claims that only a fool would wish to go backwards. By this I gather he means that the Enlightenment let the genie of scientific knowledge out of the bottle. Humanity has been enriched—at least in part—by its passage through the modern era. As if to attest to this enrichment, Solzhenitsyn accepts what the ancients rejected: technology. Compare Aristotle, *Politics*, 1253b 20-23. To develop even a small technology, people need to be open to scientific discovery. It also requires circulation of the kinds of information that may have cost an ancient philosopher his life. Aristophanes, *Clouds*, trans. Thomas G. West and Stacy Starry West (Ithaca, N.Y.: Cornell University Press, 1984).

Solzhenitsyn's acceptance of technology may be dismissed as a minor, if necessary, concession to contemporary life. There are, however, deeper problems raised by an unqualified alignment of Solzhenitsyn with the camp of classical philosophy. He is, of course, an artist, not a philosopher. "Through art," he writes, "we occasionally receive—indistinctly, briefly—revelations the likes of which cannot be achieved by rational thought." *East*, 6.

Finally, he makes no claim that life is purposive and he provides no account of the whole, no cosmological argument, except that which presupposes a "Supreme Complete Entity," which he unashamedly refers to elsewhere as God.

Winthrop's claim that philosophic pursuits and artistic creativity give meaning to Solzhenitsyn's life, if not to life in general, is difficult to dismiss. Winthrop "Solzhenitsyn: Emerging" 23; Winthrop, "Solzhenitsyn Reconsidered II," 14. See also *Gulag I*, 145, 181, 193, 225, 271, 444, 595; *Gulag II*, 597, 606-7, 611; *Gulag III*, 66, 104; *First Circle*, 31, 33, 39-43, 47, 78-79, 157, 449; *Oak*, 146; *Cancer Ward*, 427-28.

Yet sometimes Solzhenitsyn admits to praying, and he uses his artistic skills to create poems about, and even to, God. *Gulag III*, 104; *Gulag II*, 65; Aleksandr Solzhenitsyn, "Prayer," *Time*, 3 April 1972, 31.

Nielson suggests that Solzhenitsyn is not a Christian but a theist. Niels C. Nielson, Jr., *Solzhenitsyn's Religion* (Nashville: Thomas Nelson, 1975), 25-26, 40-41. See also Roy H. Donald, "Solzhenitsyn's Religious Teaching," *Faith and Reason* 7, no. 4 (1981): 305-19.

Scammell reports that Solzhenitsyn did not attend Orthodox services regularly, even though the rest of his family did. Scammell, *Solzhenitsyn*, 991-92; also 769). Alexander Schmemann calls Solzhenitsyn "a Christian writer" Although he allows that Solzhenitsyn may be a "non-believer." Schmemann "humbly asserts" that the "official declarations" of an author are not "a trustworthy test to qualify his work as essentially Christian." Schmemann, "On Solzhenitsyn," in Dunlop, *Critical Essays*, 39, 44.

In his response to Schmemann's essay, Solzhenitsyn stated that the article "was very valuable to me. It explained me to myself. . . . It also formulated important traits of Christianity which I could not have otherwise formulated myself." Solzhenitsyn quoted in Dunlop, *Critical Essays*, 44. This from a person who does everything "according to plan." *Oak*, 180.

At one point Solzhenitsyn writes: "Justice has been the common patrimony of humanity throughout the ages. . . . Obviously it is a concept inherent in man, since it cannot be traced to any other source. . . . The love of justice seems to me to be a different sentiment from the love of people (or at least the two coincide only partially)." Solzhenitsyn quoted in Labedz, *Solzhenitsyn*, 110. Which is of greater worth, love of people or of justice? Compare Matt. 5:2.1-2.6; Matt. 22.:38-4o; Mark 12: 31-41: Luke 11: 24-37; John 13:31-35; John 3:29; John 5: 7-21; John 1:5-6.

Solzhenitsyn was asked in an interview to clear up the whole matter. He was asked directly: "Are you a Christian?" Alluding to his earlier statement that he was not a socialist, but, while in the Soviet Union, "had to be careful and express" himself "as indirectly as possible," he chose to respond. "I think that question is even clearer from my books than the one asked here about a socialist world view." "Solzhenitsyn Speaks Out," 609.

Indeed, he may be like Silin. *Gulag III*, 107-9. But also see his argument, in the middle of the central volume of his major work on Marxism, concerning the way in which Christianity can be used as a weapon against Communism. *Gulag II*, 370-74. See also *East*, 180; *A Lenten Letter to Pimen, Patriarch of All Russia*, 6.

48. Kesler, "Up from Modernity," in Berman, *Solzhenitsyn at Harvard*, 55.

49. *Warning*, 45.

50. *Gulag I*, 226; *Gulag II*, 611; *First Circle*, 42, 340, 370; *Rubble*, 22, 109; *Mortal*, 61.

51. *East*, 4. Evidently, Solzhenitsyn objects to Nietzsche's philosophy as well as to Marx's, although perhaps not as strongly. It seems he rejects Nietzsche's attempt to create a wholly human ground for nobility. For Solzhenitsyn, human life has purpose only if that purpose is beyond mere survival. Nietzsche's endeavor to raise man above himself has not always borne the intended fruit.

52. *Gulag I*, 145, 595; *Gulag II*, 597, 607; *Gulag III*, 66, 104; *Oak*, 494; *First Circle*, 104.

53. *August 1914*, 472.

54. Ibid., 474-75. Carter notes that this is an attack on Rousseau. Carter, *Politics of Solzhenitsyn*, 7. But Hegel and Tolstoy are mentioned in the chapter. Solzhenitsyn seems intent on formulating a notion of history somewhere between the two extremes of complete wisdom (Hegel) and utter ignorance (Tolstoy). See Raymond J. Wilson III, "Solzhenitsyn's *August 1914* and *Lenin in Zurich*: A Question of Historical Determinism," *CLIO* 14 (Fall 1984): 15-36.

55. This is why he claims that Communism attempted to destroy the heart of national cultures.

56. *August 1914*, 473 -74. See also *Gulag III*, 477.

57. For instance, Solzhenitsyn makes a great deal of the wisdom contained in Russian folk proverbs. *Mortal*, 11-12.

58. In sum, he objects to the historicism implicit in attempting to base a community solely on the traditions of the past. Compare, for example, Solzhenitsyn's position with that of the English philosopher Edmund Burke, *Reflections on the Revolution in France*. Critics of Solzhenitsyn were surprised to discover that he "was not in the tradition of Milton, Paine, Mill, Jefferson, and 'not even' of Edmund Burke." Scammell, *Solzhenitsyn*, 917.

59. *Mortal*, 61-62; *Rubble*, 274.

60. *Gulag I*, 226; *Gulag II*, 611; *First Circle*, 42, 340, 370.

61. *August 1914*, 473.

62. *Mortal* 64.

63. Although Communists tried, oppressing the church was more difficult in places such as Poland, where it was very powerful.

64. *Rubble*, 22.

65. Ibid.

66. Ibid., 23; *East*, 123-24; "Solzhenitsyn Speaks Out," 608.

67. *Mortal*, 60.

68. Ibid., *Rubble*, 20-21 *East*, 130-34. Those who accept democracy as the political standard find these objections particularly difficult to comprehend. Because Solzhenitsyn is guided by a higher standard than any in political life, he is able to criticize every type of existing government.

69. *East*, 23, 135; *Oak*, 460; *Gulag III*, 81, 92-93; "Live Not by Lies"; *Mortal*, 62.

70. "Matryona's House," in *Stories*, 1-42. In Russia he called for abandonment of Marxism, retention of an authoritarian nationalist state, development of Siberia instead of the support of client states; and husbanding of Russia's natural resources. He favored the establishment of government ruled by law with separation of powers and protection of civil and religious liberties. *East*, 75-142, 181; *Rubble*, 21, 135-41; *Mortal*, 55-62; *Warning*, 107. Scammell, *Solzhenitsyn*, 883-84.

71. *Warning*, 17.

72. Alexander Hamilton, John Jay, and James Madison, *The Federalist Papers No. 10* (New York: Modern Library, n.d.), 56.

73. Ibid., 101.

74. Tocqueville, *Democracy in America*, 680.

SELECTED BIBLIOGRAPHY

BOOKS AND COLLECTIONS OF ESSAYS BY SOLZHENITSYN

Solzhenitsyn, Alexander. *August 1914*, translated by Michael Glenny. New York: Batam, 1974.

_____. *August 1914: The Red Wheel*, translated by H. T. Willets. New York: Noonday Press, 1989.

_____. *Candle in the Wind*, translated by Keith Armes. New York: Bantam, 1974.

_____. *Cancer Ward*, translated by Nicholas Bethell and David Burg. New York: Bantam, 1969.

_____. *Detente: Prospects for Democracy and Dictatorship*. New Brunswick, N.J.: Transactions, Inc., 1976.

_____. *East and West*, translated by Alexis Klimoff and Hillary Sternberg. New York: Harper & Row, 1980.

_____. *Invisible Allies*, translated by Alexis Klimoff and Michael Nicholson. Washington, D.C.: Counterpoint, 1995.

_____. *The First Circle*, translated by Thomas P. Whitney. New York: Bantam, 1968.

_____. *The Gulag Archipelago*, translated by Thomas P. Whitney. New York: Harper & Row, 1973.

_____. *The Gulag Archipelago* II, translated by Thomas P. Whitney. New York: Harper & Row, 1975.

_____. *The Gulag Archipelago* III, translated by Harry Willetts. New York: Harper & Row, 1978.

_____. *Lenin in Zurich*, translated by Harry Willetts. New York: Farrar, Straus & Giroux, 1976.

_____. *Lenten Letter to Pimen, Patriarch of All Russia*, translated by Keith Armes. Minneapolis: Burgess, 1972.

_____. *The Love Girl and the Innocent*, translated by Nicholas Bethell and David Burg. New York: Farrar, Straus & Giroux, 1969.

_____. *The Mortal Danger*, translated by Michael Nicholson and Alexis Klimoff. New York: Harper & Row, 1980.

_____. *The Oak and the Calf*, translated by Harry Willetts. New York: Harper & Row, 1979.

_____. *One Day in the Life of Ivan Denisovich*, translated by Max Hayward and Ronald Hingley. New York: Bantam, 1963.

_____. *Prussian Nights*, translated by Robert Conquest. New York: Farrar, Straus & Giroux, 1977.

_____. *Stories and Prose Poems*, translated by Michael Glenny. New York: Bantam, 1971.

_____. *Warning to the West*, translated by Harris Coulter, Nataly Martin, and Alexis Klimoff. New York: Farrar, Straus & Giroux, 1976.

_____. *We Never Make Mistakes*, translated by Paul W. Blackstone. New York: W. W. Norton, 1963.

_____. Mikhail Agursky, A. B., Evgeny Barabanov, Vadim Borisov, F. Korsakov, and Igor Shafarevich, *From under the Rubble*, translated by A.M. Brock, Milada Haigh, Marita Sapiets, Hilary Sternberg, and Harry Willetts under the direction of Michael Scammell. Boston: Little, Brown, 1975.

ARTICLES AND INTERVIEWS BY SOLZHENITSYN

Solzhenitsyn, Alexander. "The Artist as Witness," translated by Michael Glenny. *Times Literary Supplement*, 23 May 1975, 561-62.

_____. "Brezhnev Cannot Look a Priest in the Eye." *Christianity Today* 24 (6 June 1980): 113.

_____. "Communism at the End of the Brezhnev Era," translated by Alexis Klimoff. *National Review*, 21 January 1983, 28-34.

_____. "Live Not by Lies." *Washington Post*, 18 February 1974, A26.

_____. "Our Pluralists." *Survey* 29:2 (Summer 1985): 1-28.

_____. "Prayer." *Time*, 3 April 1972, 311.

_____. "Schlesinger and Kissinger," translated by Raymond H. Anderson. *New York Times*, 1 December 1975, 31.

_____. "Solzhenitsyn on Communism," translated by Alexis Klimoff. *Time*, 18 February 1980, 48-49.

_____. "Solzhenitsyn Speaks Out," translated by Albert and Tayna Schmidt. *National Review*, 27 (6 June 1975): 603-9.

_____. "Solzhenitsyn Speaks Out on Poland." *Cleveland Plain Dealer*, 24 January 1982, 2AA, 7AA.

_____. "The Third World War Has Ended." *National Review* 27 (20 June 1975): 652.

_____. "Those Who Would Disarm." *Washington Post*, 28 June 1983, A15.

_____. "Three Key Moments in Modern Japanese History," translated by Michael Nicholson and Alexis Klimoff. *National Review* 81 (9 December 1983): 1536-46.

BOOKS AND COMMENTARY ABOUT SOLZHENITSYN

Allaback, Stephen. *Aleksandr Solzhenitsyn*. New York: Taplinger Publishing, 1978.

Barker, Francis. *Solzhenitsyn: Politics and Form*. London: Macmillan, 1971.

Beglov, S., et al. *The Last Circle*. Moscow: Novosti, 1971.

Berman, Ronald, ed. *Solzhenitsyn at Harvard*. Washington, D.C.: Ethics and Public Policy Center, 1980.

Bjorkegren, Hans. *Aleksandr Solzhenitsyn: A Biography*, translated by Kaarina Eneberg. New York: Joseph Okpalu, 1972.

Burg, David, and George Feifer. *Solzhenitsyn*. New York: Stein & Day, 1972.

Carlisle, Olga. *Solzhenitsyn and the Secret Circle*. New York: Holt, Rinehart, & Winston, 1978.

Carpovich, Vera V. *Solzhenitsyn's Peculiar Vocabulary: Russian-English Dictionary*. New York: Technical Dictionary Co., 1976.

Carter, Stephen. *The Politics of Solzhenitsyn*. New York: Holmes & Meier, 1977.

Clardy, Jesse V. *The Superfluous Man of Russian Letters*. Washington, D.C.: University Press of America, 1980.

Clement, Oliver. *The Spirit of Solzhenitsyn*, translated by Sarah Fawcett and Paul Burns. London: Search Press Ltd., 1976.

Curtis, James M. *Solzhenitsyn's Traditional Imagination*. Athens: University of Georgia Press, 1984.

Dunlop, John, Richard Haugh, and Alexis Klimoff, eds. *Aleksandr Solzhenitsyn: Critical Essays and Documentary Materials*. Belmont, Mass.: Nordland, 1975.

Dunlop, John,, Richard Haugh, and Michael Nicholson, eds. *Solzhenitsyn in Exile: Critical Essays and Documentary Materials*. Stanford, Calif.: Hoover Institution Press, 1985.

Ericson, Edward E., Jr. *Solzhenitsyn: The Moral Vision*. Grand Rapids, Mich.: William B. Eerdmans, 1980.

Feuer, Kathryn, ed. *Solzhenitsyn: A Collection of Critical Essays*. Englewood Cliffs, N.J.: Prentice Hall, 1976.

Freeborn, Richard, Georgette Donchin, and N.J. Anning. *Russian Literary Attitudes from Pushkin to Solzhenitsyn*. New York: Barnes & Noble, 1976.

Galler, Meyer. *Soviet Prison Camp Speech: A Survivor's Glossary*. Madison: University of Wisconsin Press, 1972.

Grazzini, Giovanni. *Solzhenitsyn*, translated by Eric Mosbacher. London: Michael Joseph, 1973.

Kelley, Donald R. *The Solzhenitsyn-Sakharov Dialogue*. Westport, Conn.: Greenwood Press, 1982.

Kodjak, Andrej. *Aleksandr Solzhenitsyn*. Boston: G. K. Hall, 1978.

Kovaly Pavel. *Rehumanization or Dehumanization?* Boston: Branden Press, 1974.

Krasnov, Vladislav. *Solzhenitsyn and Dostoevsky: A Study of the Polyphonic Novel*. Athens: University of Georgia Press, 1980.

Labedz, Leopold, ed. *Solzhenitsyn: A Documentary Record*. London: Penguin Press, 1970.

Lukàcs, Georg. *Solzhenitsyn*, translated by William D. Graf. London: Merlin Press, 1969.

Mahoney, Daniel J. *Aleksandr Solzhenitsyn: The Ascent from Ideology*. Lanham, Md.: Rowman & Littlefield, 2001.

Medvedev, Zhores A. *Ten Years after Ivan Denisovich*, translated by Hilary Sternberg. New York: Random House, 1974.

Nielson, Niels C., Jr. *Solzhenitsyn's Religion*. Nashville: Thomas Nelson, 1975.

Panachas, George, ed. *The Politics of Twentieth-Century Novelists*. New York: T. Y. Crowell, 1974.

Pomorska, Krystyna, ed. *Fifty Years of Russian Prose: From Pasternak to Solzhenitsyn*. Cambridge: MIT, 1971.

Reshetovskaya, Natalya A. *Sanya: My Life with Aleksandr Solzhenitsyn*, translated by Elena Ivanoff. Indianapolis: Bobbs-Merrill, 1975.

Rothberg, Abraham. *Aleksandr Solzhenitsyn: The Major Novels*. Ithaca, N.Y.: Cornell University Press, 1971.

Rzhevsky, Leonid. *Solzhenitsyn: Creator of Heroic Deeds*. University: University of Alabama Press, 1978.

Scammell, Michael. *Solzhenitsyn: A Biography*. New York: W. W. Norton, 1984.

Ulam, Adam B. *Ideologies and Illusions: Revolutionary Thought from Herzen to Solzhenitsyn*. Cambridge, Mass.: Harvard University Press, 1976.

Weerakoon, R. *Aleksandr Solzhenitsyn: Soldier, Prisoner, Writer*. Colombo, Ceylon: Gunaratne & Co., 1972.

Yakovlev, N. *Solzhenitsyn's Archipelago of Lies*. Moscow: Novosti, 1974.

ARTICLES AND COMMENTARY ABOUT SOLZHENITSYN

Allen, James. "Solzhenitsyn's Vision of the Reconstruction of East and West." B.A. honors thesis, Kenyon College, 1982.

Aron, Raymond. "Aleksandr Solzhenitsyn and European 'Leftism.'" *Survey* 22:3/4 (Summer/Autumn 1976): 233-41.

Aurich, P. "Solzhenitsyn's Political Philosophy." *Nation* 219 (October 1974): 273-74.

Buckley, William F., Jr. "Continuing Presence of Solzhenitsyn." *National Review* 28 (15 October 1976): 1140-41.

_____. "Estrangement of Solzhenitsyn." *National Review* 30 (21 July 1978): 913.

_____. "Solzhenitsyn v. Kissinger." *National Review* 28 (23 October 1976): 53.

Burnham, James. "The Logic of Détente." *National Review* 27 (15 August 1975): 873.

Casillo, Robert. "Techne and Logos in Solzhenitsyn." *Soundings* 70:3/4 (Fall-Winter 1987): 519-37.

Clardy, Jesse V., and Betty Clardy. "Solzhenitsyn's Ideas of the Ultimate Reality." *Ultimate Reality and Meaning* 1 (1978): 202-22.

Diakin, Nadia Odette. "Solzhenitsyn's *First Circle*." *Explicator* 42 (Fall 1983): 59-61.

Donald, Roy H. "Solzhenitsyn's Religious Teaching." *Faith and Reason* 7 (Winter 1981): 305-19.

Dunlop, John. "Solzhenitsyn in Exile." *Survey* 21 (Summer 1975): 133-53.

_____. "The Almost Rehabilitation and Re-anathematization of Aleksandr Solzhenitsyn." Working paper, Hoover Institution, Stanford University, February 1989.

Fairlie, Henry. "Mother Russia's Prodigal Son." *New Republic*, 29 July 1978, 18-20.

Feifer, George. "The Dark Side of Solzhenitsyn." *Harpers* 260 (May 1980): 48-51.

Gleason, Abbott. "Solzhenitsyn and the Slavophiles." *Yale Review* 65 (Autumn 1975): 61-70.

Grey, Paul. "Russia's Prophet in Exile." *Time*, 24 July 1989, 56-60.

Hallet, Richard. "Beneath the Closed Visor: Dimitry Panin and the Two Faces of Sologdin in Solzhenitsyn's *First Circle*." *Modern Language Review* 78 (April 1983): 365-74.

Halperin, David M. "Solzhenitsyn, Epicures, and the Ethics of Stalinism." *Critical Inquiry* 7 (Spring 1981): 475-97.

Heller, Michael. "*The Gulag Archipelago* and Its Inhabitants." *Survey* 20 (Summer 1974): 211-27.

_____. "*The Gulag Archipelago* vol. 2: Life and Death in the Camps." *Survey* 20 (Autumn 1974): 152-66.

_____. "Lenin, Parvus, and Solzhenitsyn." *Survey* 21 (Autumn 1975): 188-94.

_____. "Survivors from Utopia." *Survey* 23 (Autumn 1977): 155-65.

_____. "Yesterday and Today in Solzhenitsyn's *The Red Wheel*." *Survey* 29 (Summer 1985): 29-45.

Hook, Sidney. "Solzhenitsyn and Secular Humanism: A Response." *Humanist* 38 (November/December 1978): 4-6.

Howe, Irving. "Open Letter to Solzhenitsyn." *New Republic* 182 (3 May 1980): 18-19.

Hunter, Holland. "The Economic Cost of the Gulag Archipelago." *Slavic Review* 39 (December 1980): 588-92.

Jatras, James George. "Solzhenitsyn and the Liberals." *Modern Age* 2.8 (Spring 1985): 143-52.

Jones, Jack. "Solzhenitsyn's Warning: A Secular Reinterpretation." *Chicago Review* 32 (Winter 1981): 141-64.

Johnson, Paul. "Solzhenitsyn: Hero of Our Time." *Washington Post Book World*, 2 September 1984, 1, 11.

Kennan, George. "Between Heaven and Hell." *New York Review of Books*, 21 March 1974, 3-7.

Kerns, Gary. "Solzhenitsyn's Portrait of Stalin." *Slavic Review* 33 (Autumn 1974): 1-22.

Kraft, Joseph. "Solzhenitsyn's Message." *Washington Post*, 3 July 1975, A23.

Kramer, Hilton. "Solzhenitsyn in Vermont." *New York Times Review of Books*, 11 May 1980, 3, 30-32.

Krasnov, Vladislav. "The Social Vision of Aleksandr Solzhenitsyn." *Modern Age* 28 (Spring-Summer 1984): 215-21.

―――. "Wrestling with Lev Tolstoi: War, Peace, and Revolution in Aleksandr Solzhenitsyn's New *Avgust Chetyrnadtsatovo*." *Slavic Review* 45 (Winter 1986): 707-19.

Kuhn, Harold. "Solzhenitsyn and Some Spiritual Implications." *Christianity Today* 23 (3 November 1978): 55-56.

Laber, Jeri. "The Real Solzhenitsyn." *Commentary* 37 (May 1974): 32-35.

Lukacs, John. "What Solzhenitsyn Means." *Commonweal* 102 (1 August 1975): 269-300.

Medvedev, Roy. "Solzhenitsyn's *Gulag Archipelago II*," translated by Georg Saunders. *Dissent* 23-24 (Summer 1974): 155-63.

Mills, Richard, and Judith Mills. "Solzhenitsyn's Cry to the Soviet Leaders." *Commonweal* 100 (August 1974): 433-36.

Morganthau, Hans. "What Solzhenitsyn Doesn't Understand." *New Leader* 61 (3 July 1978): 12-13.

Morris, Roger. "Solzhenitsyn with a Grain of Salt." *New Republic* 173 (16 August 1975): 310-12.

Mudrich, Marvin. "Solzhenitsyn versus the Last Revolutionary." *The Hudson Review* 3 (Summer 1981): 195-217.

Muggeridge, John. Review of *Solzhenitsyn: A Biography* by Michael Scammell. *American Spectator*, 8 August 1985, 31.

Niemeyer, Gerhardt. "The Eternal Meaning of Solzhenitsyn." *National Review* 25 (19 January 1973): 83-86.

Oja, Matt F. "Shamalov, Solzhenitsyn, and the Mission of Memory." *Survey* 29 (Summer 1985): 62-69.

Perlinski, Jerome. "Solzhenitsyn's Spirituality." *Christian Century* 95 (27 September 1978): 901-2.

Podhoretz, Norman. "The Terrible Question of Aleksandr Solzhenitsyn." *Commentary* (February 1985): 17-24.

Purcell, Brendan. "Solzhenitsyn's Struggle for Personal, Social, and Historical Anamnesis." *Philosophic Studies* 28 (n.d.): 62-82.

Rancour-Laferriere, Daniel. "The Deranged Birthday Boy: Solzhenitsyn's Portrait of Stalin." *Mosaic* 18 (Summer 1985): 61-72.

Remnick, David. "Ivan Denisovich' Returns." *Washington Post*, 21 November 1989, D1.

―――. "Deep in the Woods." *The New Yorker*, 6 August 2001, 32-40.

―――. "Solzhenitsyn—A New Day in the Life." *Washington Post*, January 1990, B3.

―――. "Solzhenitsyn Denies Talking with Soviets." *Washington Post*, 28 June 1988, A10.

―――. "Soviet Journal to Publish Solzhenitsyn." *Washington Post*, 21 April 1989, C1, C9.

―――. "The Exile Returns." *The New Yorker*, 14 February 1994, 64-83.

―――. "Witness to the Gulag." *Washington Post*, 9 July 1989, B7.

Rosefielde, Steven. "The First 'Great Leap Forward' Reconsidered: Lessons of *The*

Gulag Archipelago." *Slavic Review* (December 1980): 559-87.

Shin, Un-chol. "Conscience, Lie, and Suffering in Solzhenitsyn's *The First Circle.*" *Modern Age* 29 (Fall 5985): 344-52.

Siegal, Paul N. "Solzhenitsyn's Portrait of Lenin." *CLIO* 14 (Fall 1984): 1-13.

Trueheart, Charles. "Solzhenitsyn and His Message of Silence." *Washington Post*, 24 November 1987, D1, D4.

Uzzell, Lawrence A. "Solzhenitsyn the Centrist." *National Review*, 28 May 1990, 29.

Wilson, Raymond J., III. "Solzhenitsyn's *August 1914* and *Lenin in Zurich*: A Question of Historical Determinism." *CLIO* 14:1(Fall 1984): 55-36.

Winthrop, Delba. "Solzhenitsyn: Emerging from under the Rubble." Paper presented at the annual meeting of the American Political Science Association, New York, August 1978.

_____. "Solzhenitsyn: Emerging from under the Rubble." *Independent Journal of Philosophy* 4 (1983): 91-101.

_____. "Solzhenitsyn Reconsidered II." *American Spectator* 13 (December 1980): 14-16.

Wood, Alan. "Solzhenitsyn on the Tsarist Exile System: A Historical Comment." *Journal of Russian Studies* 41 (1981): 39-43.

Yarup, Robert L. "Solzhenitsyn's *One Day in the Life of Ivan Denisovich.*" *Explicator* 40 (Spring 1981): 61-63.

GENERAL BIBLIOGRAPHY

Allen, James. *No Citation*. London: Angus & Robertson, 1955.

Alliluyeva, Svetlana. *Twenty Letters to a Friend*. New York: Harper & Row, 1967.

Amalrik, Andrei. *Notes of a Revolutionary*, translated by Guy Daniels. New York: Alfred Knopf, 1982.

_____. *Will the Soviet Union Survive until 1984?* translated by Peter Reddaway. London: Pelican Books, 1970.

Andies, Helmut. *Rule of Terror*, translated by A. Lieven. New York: Holt, Rinehart & Winston, 1969.

Arendt, Hannah. *The Origins of Totalitarianism*. New York: Harcourt, Brace & World, 1968.

Aristophanes. *Clouds*, translated by Thomas G. West and Stacy Starry West. Ithaca, N.Y.: Cornell University Press, 1984.

Aristotle. *Nichmachean Ethics*, translated by J. A. K. Thompson. Middlesex, England: Penguin Books, 1955.

_____. *Politics*, translated by Carnes Lord. Chicago: University of Chicago Press, 1984.

Aron, Raymond. *Marxism and the Existentialists*, translated by Helen Weaver, Robert Addis, and John Weightman. New York: Simon & Schuster, 1970.

Avineri, Shlomo. *The Social and Political Thought of Karl Marx*. Cambridge: Cambridge University Press, 1968.

Balabanoff, Angelica. *Impressions of Lenin*. Ann Arbor: University of Michigan Press, 1968.

Beck, R., and W. Godin. *Russian Purge*. London: Hurst & Balckett, 1951.

Berdyaev, Nicholas. *The Origins of Russian Communism*. Ann Arbor: University of Michigan Press, 1972.

Billingsley, Kenneth Lloyd, "Hollywood's Missing Movies: Why American Films Have Ignored Life under Communism," *Reason* 32 (June 2000), 20-28.

Billington, James. *The Icon and the Axe*. New York: Vintage Books, 1970.

Braudel, Fernand. *Les Structures du Quotidien: Le Possible et l'impossible*. Paris: Librairie Armand Colin, 1979.

Brown, Edward. *Russian Literature since the Revolution*. New York: Collier Books, 1969.

Brzezinski, Zbigniew. *The Permanent Purge*. Cambridge, Mass.: Harvard University Press, 1956.

Bukovsky, Vladimir. *To Build a Castle*, translated by Michael Scammell. New York: Viking Press, 1978.

Burke, Edmund. *Reflections on the Revolution in France*. New Rochelle, N.Y.: Arlington House, 1966.

Cart, Edward H. *The Bolshevik Revolution: 1917-1923*. New York: Macmillan, 1951.

Ceaser, James W. *Presidential Selection: Theory and Development*. Princeton, N.J.: Princeton University Press, 1979.

Chemiavsky, Michael. *Tsar and People: Studies in Russian Myth*. New York: Random House, 1969.

Conquest, Robert. *The Great Terror*. New York: Macmillan, 1968.

_____. Kolyma: *The Arctic Death*. New York: Viking Press, 1976.

_____. *Power and Policy in the U.S.S.R*. New York: Harper & Row, 1967.

Cracraft, James, ed. *The Soviet Union Today*. Chicago: University of Chicago Press, 1987.

Cropsey, Joseph. *Political Philosophy and the Issues of Politics*. Chicago: University of Chicago Press, 1977.

Dallin, Alexander, and W. Breslauer. *Political Terror in Communist Systems*. Stanford, Calif.: Stanford University Press, 1970.

Dallin, Alexander, and Alan Westin. *Politics in the Soviet Union*. New York: Harcourt, Brace & World, 1966.

Dante. *The Divine Comedy*, translated by Dorothy Sayers, New York: Penguin, 1949.

Deutscher, Isaac. *The Unfinished Revolution: Russia, 1917-1967*. Oxford: Oxford University Press, 1975.

Dostoevsky, Fydor. *The Devils*, translated by David Magarshack. New York: Penguin, 1953.

_____.*The House of the Dead*, translated by Constance Garnett. New York: Dell, 1959.

Easton, Lloyd, and Kurt Guddat, eds. *Writings of the Young Marx on Philosophy and History*. Garden City, N.Y.: Doubleday, 1976.

Etkind, Efim. *Notes of a Non-conspirator*, translated by Peter France. Oxford: Oxford University Press, 1978.

Fainsod, Merle. *Smolensk under Soviet Rule*. New York: Vintage Books, 1958.

Fanon Frantz. *Wretched of the Earth*, translated by Constance Farrington. New York: Grove Press, 1968.

Fleron, Frederick, ed. *Communist Studies and the Social Sciences*. Chicago: Rand McNally, 1969.

Fremantle, Anne, ed. *Mao Tse-tung: An Anthology of His Writings*. New York: New American Library, 1961.

Friedrich, Carl, and Zbigniew Brzezinski. *Totalitarian Dictatorship and Autocracy*. Cambridge: Harvard University Press, 1956.

Fromm, Erich. *Marx's Concept of Man*. New York: Ungar, 1961.

Germino, Dante. *Beyond Ideology*. Chicago: University of Chicago Press, 1976.

_____. *Machiavelli to Marx*. Chicago: University of Chicago Press, 1979.

Ginzburg, Euginia. *Journey into the Whirlwind*. New York: Harcourt, Brace & World, 1967.

Goldman, Marshall. *Gorbachev's Challenge*. New York: W. W. Norton, 1987.

Gorbachev, Michail S. *Perestroika: New Thinking for Our Country and the World*. New York: Harper & Row, 1987.

Hamilton, Alexander, John Jay, and James Madison. *The Federalist Papers*. New York: Modern Library, n.d.

Hamison, Leopold. *The Russian Marxists and the Origin of Bolshevism*. Boston: Beacon Press, 1955.

Hayward, Max, ed. *On Trial*. New York: Harper & Row, 1967.

Heller, Mikhail, and Aleksandr Nekrich. *Utopia in Power: The History of the Soviet Union from 1917 to the Present*. New York: Summit, 1987.

Hitchens Christopher. "So Long, Fellow Travelers," *Washington Post*, 20 October 2002, B1, B3.

Hobbes, Thomas. *Leviathan*. Cleveland: Meridian Books, 1963.

Hough, Jerry. *Russia and the West: Gorbachev and the Politics of Reform*. New York: Simon & Schuster, 1988.

_____. *Soviet Leadership in Transition*. Washington, D.C.: Brookings, 1980.

Hyde, Montgomery. *Stalin*. London: Rupert, Hart & Davis, 1971.

Inkles, Alex, and Raymond Bauer. *The Soviet Citizen*. New York: Atheneum, 1968.

Johnson, Chalmers. *Change in Communist Systems*. Stanford, Calif.: Stanford University Press, 1970.

_____. *Revolutionary Change*. Boston: Little, Brown, 1966.

Kant, Immanuel. *Critique of Pure Reason*, translated by F. Max Mueller. New York: Macmillan, 1957.

_____. *Fundamental Principles of the Metaphysics of Morals*, translated by Thomas K. Abbott. New York: Liberal Arts Press, 1940.

Karklins, Rasma. "Perestroika and Ethnopolitics in the USSR." *PS: Political Science and Politics* 21 (June 1989): 208-14.

Kissinger, Henry. *The White House Years*. Boston: Little, Brown, 1979.

_____. *Years of Upheaval*. Boston: Little, Brown, 1981.

Koestler, Arthur. *Darkness at Noon*, translated by Daphne Hardy. New York: Bantam, 1966.

Kuznetsov, Edward. *Prison Diaries*, translated by Howard Spier. New York: Stein & Day, 1975.

Lapenna, Ivo. *Soviet Penal Policy*. London: Bodley Head, 1968.

Laue, Theodore H. Von. *Why Lenin? Why Stalin? A Reappraisal of the Russian Revolution, 1900-1930*. New York: J. B. Lippincott, 1971.

Lenin, Vladimir 1. *Collected Works*. 45 vols. London: Lawrence & Wisehart, 1960.

Lincoln, Bruce W. *Passage through Armageddon: The Russians in War, 1914-1918*. New York: Simon & Schuster, 1987.

Linden, Carl A. *Khrushchev and the Soviet Leadership*. Baltimore: Johns Hopkins University Press, 1966.

Machiavelli, Niccolò. *The Prince and the Discourses*. New York: Random House, 1950.

Mandeistam, Nadezhda. *Hope against Hope*, translated by Max Hayward. New York: Atheneum, 1983.

Marchenko, *Anatoly. My Testimony*, translated by Michael Scammell. New York: E. P. Dutton, 1969.

Marcuse, Herbert. *Eros and Civilization*. New York: Vintage Books, 1962.

_____. *Reason and Revolution*. Boston: Beacon Press, 1969.

Marx, Karl. *Capital*. New York: Modern Library, n.d.

_____. *Capital III*. Moscow: Progress Press, 1976.

———. *Collected Works*. 25 vols. to date. New York: International Publishers, 1975.

———. *Critique of Political Economy*. Moscow: Progress Press, 1976.

———. *The German Ideology*, edited by R. Pascal. New York: International Publishers, 1933.

———. *The Poverty of Philosophy*. Moscow: International Publishers, n.d.

Medvedev, Roy. *Let History Judge*, translated by Colleen Taylor. London: Macmillan, 1971.

Mendel, Arthur, ed. *Essential Works of Marxism*. New York: Bantam, 1965.

Merleau-Ponty, Maurice. *Humanism and Terror*, translated by John O'Neill. Boston: Beacon Press, 1969.

Mickiewicz, Ellen. "Mobilization and Reform: Communication Policy under Gorbachev." *PS: Political Science and Politics* 21 (June 1989): 199-207.

Milosz, Czeslaw. *The Captive Mind*, translated by Jane Zielonko. New York: Vintage Books, 1953.

Moore, Barrington, Jr. *Social Origins of Dictatorship and Democracy*. Boston: Beacon Press, 1966.

Nobokov, Vladimir. *The Provisional Government*. New York: John Wiley, 1970.

Oliva, Jay L. *Russia and the West from Peter the Great to Khrushchev*. Boston: D. C. Heath, 1965.

Pasternak, Boris. *Doctor Zhivago*, translated by Max Haywood. New York: Pantheon Books, 1958.

Payne, R. *The Life and Death of Lenin*. New York: Pan, 1964.

Pipes, Richard. *Russia under the Old Regime*. New York: Charles Scribner's Sons, 1974.

———. *The Russian Intelligentsia*. New York: Columbia University Press, 1961.

Plato. *Republic*, translated by Allan Bloom. New York: Basic Books, 1968.

Podhoretz, Norman. "Why Can't You Call a Communist a Communist?" *Washington Post*, 16 March 1986, D8.

Remnick, David. "Corrupt Soviet Uzbekistan Learns about 'Our Rotten History.'" *Washington Post*, October 1988, A1, A27.

———. "Lenin's Errors Aired in Pages of Pravda." *Washington Post*, 30 December 1989, A12.

Riasanovsky, Nicholas. *A History of Russia*. London: Oxford University Press, 1969.

Rigby, T. H., ed. *The Stalin Dictatorship*. Sydney: Sydney University Press, 1960.

Rubenstein, Joshua. *Soviet Dissidents*. Boston: Beacon Press, 1980.

Sakharov, Andrei. *Progress, Coexistence, and Intellectual Freedom*, translated by *The New York Times*. New York: W. W. Norton, 1968.

Santoli, Al. "Why the Viet Cong Flee." *Washington Post*, Parade section, 11 July 1982, 1-6.

Schapiro, Leonard. *The Communist Party of the Soviet Union*. New York: Vintage Books, 1960.

Seton-Watson, Hugh. *The Decline of Imperial Russia: 1855-1914*. New York: Praeger, 1962.

Shalamov, Varlam. *Kolyma Tales*, translated by John Glad. New York: W. W. Norton, 1980.

Simms, James Y. "The Crisis in Russian Agriculture at the End of the Nineteenth Century: A Different View," *Slavic Review* 36:3 (September 1977): 377-93.

Stalin, Joseph. *Leninism*, translated by Eden Paul and Geden Paul. New York: International Publishers, 1933.

Stevenson, Adlai. *Friends and Enemies*. New York: Harper & Brothers, 1959.

Strauss, Leo. *On Tyranny*. Ithaca, N.Y.: Cornell University Press, 1968.

_____, and Joseph Cropsey, eds. *History of Political Philosophy*. New York: Rand McNally, 1972.

Talbott, Strobe, ed. *Khrushchev Remembers*. Boston: Little, Brown, 1975.

Tatu, Michel. *Power in the Kremlin: From Khrushchev to Kosygin*, translated by Helen Katel. New York: Viking Press, 1972.

Tocqueville, Alexis de. *Democracy in America*, translated by George Lawrence. Garden City, N.Y.: Doubleday, 1969.

Tolstoy, Leo. *War and Peace*, translated by Louise and Aylmer Maude. New York: W. W. Norton, 1964.

_____. *What Men Live By*, translated by Louise and Aylmer Maude. New York: Pantheon Books, n.d.

Tucker, Robert C., ed. *The Marx-Engels Reader*. New York: W. W. Norton, 1978.

_____. *The Marxian Revolutionary Idea*. New York: W. W. Norton, 1970.

_____. "Stalin, the Last Bolshevik." *New York Times*, 21 December 1979, 35.

_____, and S. Cohen, eds. *The Great Purge Trials*. New York: Grosset & Dunlap, 1965.

Ulam, Adam. *A History of Soviet Russia*. New York: Praeger, 1976.

_____. *The Bolsheviks*. New York: Collier Books, 1965.

_____. *Lenin and the Bolsheviks*. New York: Fontana, 1966.

Valladares, Armando. *Against All Hope*. New York: Alfred Knopf, 1985.

Voegelin, Eric. *From Enlightenment to Revolution*. Durham: University of North Carolina Press, 1975.

Weisskopf, Michael. "Spring in Peking Is Birdless, Shrubless." *Washington Post*, 26 April 1982, A24.

Witten, Thaddeus. *Commissar: The Life and Death of Beria*. New York: Macmillan, 1972.

Wolfe, B. *Three Who Made a Revolution*. New York: Pelican, 1966.

Yanov, Alexander. *The Russian Challenge and the Year 2000*, translated by Iden Rosenthal. Oxford: Basil Blackwell, 1987.

INDEX

ABOUT THE AUTHOR

James F. Pontuso is William W. Elliott Professor in the Department of Political Science at Hampden-Sydney College in Virginia. He is author of *Václav Havel: Civic Responsibility in the Postmodern Age* (Rowman & Littlefield, 2004), and coauthor with Roger Barrus, et al. of *The Deconstitutionalization of America: The Forgotten Frailties of Democratic Rule* (Lexington Books, 2004). He is editor of *Political Philosophy Comes to Rick's: **Casablanca** and American Civic Culture* (Lexington Books, forthcoming).

LaVergne, TN USA
18 February 2010
173515LV00001B/210/P